REBORN

ALSO BY Katie Price

Non-Fiction
Being Jordan
Jordan: A Whole New World
Jordan: Pushed to the Limit
Standing Out
You Only Live Once
Love, Lipstick and Lies

Fiction
Angel
Angel Uncovered
Crystal
He's the One
In the Name of Love
Santa Baby
Sapphire
The Comeback Girl
Paradise
Make My Wish Come True

KATIE PRICE

Reborn

CENTURY

1 3 5 7 9 10 8 6 4 2

Century
20 Vauxhall Bridge Road
London SW1V 2SA

Century is part of the Penguin Random House group of companies
whose addresses can be found at global.penguinrandomhouse.com.

First published in 2016 by Century

www.penguin.co.uk

A CIP catalogue record for this book is available from the British Library.

HB ISBN 9781780893464
TPB ISBN 9781780894867

Typeset in 11.5/17 pt Melior LT Std by Jouve (UK), Milton Keynes
Printed and bound in Great Britain by Clays Ltd, St Ives plc

Penguin Random House is committed to a sustainable future for
our business, our readers and our planet. This book is made from
Forest Stewardship Council® certified paper.

I dedicate my book to my amazing family and friends, and my gorgeous children Harvey, Junior, Princess, Jett and Bunny, who give me my strength.

CONTENTS

ACKNOWLEDGEMENTS

Many people have helped me with this book, and it hasn't been easy to write because so much of it was painful to remember. Special thanks to Helena Drakakis, who worked so hard with me, and also to the team at my publishers, Century. Of course a very special thank you goes to my friends, family and my amazing children, who have helped me all along and brought me to a new beginning in my life.

PHOTOGRAPHIC ACKNOWLEDGEMENTS

In order of appearance:

Third Plate Section

- Full-page image: © James Shaw/REX/Shutterstock
- Inset Image: © Karwai Tang/Getty Images

All other photographs are author's own.

Every reasonable effort has been made to contact all copyright holders, but if there are any errors or omissions, we will insert the appropriate acknowledgement in subsequent printings of the book.

INTRODUCTION

I sat upright in my hospital bed. I was in absolute agony and feeling really groggy. Everything around me seemed blurry. As I forced my eyes to focus, I could see Bunny in the nurse's arms and Kieran standing beside me, dressed in a theatre gown with a surgical mask covering his face.

I was handed Bunny what seemed like immediately, and held her so tight to my chest. 'Wow, you're here,' I whispered, stroking her soft cheek.

It was when I was finally wheeled into the recovery room that things started to go badly wrong.

Bunny had been cleaned and wrapped in a white towel. I cupped her face but I could hear her breathing wasn't right. It was rapid and shallow and, when I looked down, her cheeks didn't have the reddish glow of a newborn.

'There's something not right,' I kept saying, as I watched her turn pale and then go a purplish-blue. 'She's changing colour. She's just not right.'

The nurse reached for her and laid her on the sheet.

'Come on then, sweetie,' she was repeating, her fingers gently squeezing and patting the baby's cheeks. 'She'll be fine. She'll be okay in a minute,' she reassured us. But the room fell silent and then the nurse said the words I'd never wanted to hear. 'I'm taking her to ICU immediately.'

My whole body tensed with panic and my stomach knotted up. 'Shit. Is she all right?' I was terrified. She's going to stop breathing. She's going to die, I thought. 'Please, please, do something to help her *right now*,' I kept pleading.

Kieran and I looked at each other. He was desperately trying to be strong but I could see the fear in his eyes. Somewhere at the back of my mind I knew our baby was in the best place and with the best people looking after her, but she was six weeks premature, delivered by emergency C-section, and she looked so tiny and helpless.

After the horrendous year I had had since my fairytale wedding to Kieran at the beginning of 2013, I'd wanted a safe birth for our baby girl more than anything in the world. Deep down, she was my only hope – a way through what had been one of the worst periods of my life. At times I'd hit rock-bottom, but she was the one thing that had stopped me from falling into the abyss. I couldn't contemplate losing her.

Suddenly waves of nausea hit me. Had the stress of finding out that Kieran, the man of my dreams, had been having an affair with two of my closest friends, Jane Pountney and Chrissy Thomas, harmed my baby? Had the anxiety of being told my pregnancy would not go full-term scared me so much that her health had been affected?

I'd piled the pressure on Kieran, telling him before Bunny's birth that if anything happened to our baby I would lay the blame firmly at his, Jane's and Chrissy's door. They'd put me through so much. Despite everything, I'd been so careful about following doctor's orders and had rested and tried to stay calm, knowing that in all of this heartbreak, our baby remained my number one priority.

Although I had been warned that initial breathing difficulties are common in premature babies – their underdeveloped lungs can't make the transition from the womb to the outside world as easily as full-term babies – in the chaos of that moment I felt an over-whelming need to protect her.

'Mummy loves you so much,' I whispered as I watched the nurse leave the room with our daughter in her arms. Kieran followed her and looked on as Bunny was rushed upstairs and hooked up to a feeding tube and an oxygen support machine. All I could do was sit there, alone . . . and wait.

Kieran and I now had two children together: Jett, almost a year old and born in even more traumatic circumstances in France, and now this little one, fighting for her life in an incubator. And, all the time, the same confused questions were going round and round in my head. Did I have a future with Kieran? Did we have a future as a family? We'd come so far since he'd shattered my world only four months before. But was it far enough?

I desperately wanted this to work, for the sake of Harvey, Junior and Princess, for our son Jett and now for the sake of our precious baby girl. My children and my family are my life. Everything I do, I do for them, and I want more than anything to give them a happy secure life.

They say some of the most stressful events in life are marriages, births, moving house and divorce, don't they? Well, I'd done all of them a few times and here I was again, teetering on the verge of a third divorce – and all in the two years since my last book, *Love, Lipstick and Lies*, had appeared!

People say to me all the time, 'Kate, I can't believe you're not on anti-depressants or that you haven't hit the booze big time.' But I haven't. I'm still here, I'm still me, I'm still trying to be strong, I'm still trying to be the best mum in the world, and I'm still working through it.

Whatever anyone else thinks they know about me and Kieran, they know nothing. However people judge the decisions I've made, they haven't a clue why I've made them.

I always said my last book was my most sensational yet and that after it I was looking forward to settling down to a life with less of my usual drama with a capital D. I think I spoke too soon! Back then, I had no idea what was waiting for me just around the corner . . .

CHAPTER 1

WHAT IF?

I've always said my life would make a brilliant movie, action-packed with adventure, drama, love, heartbreak and loss, but before I met my husband Kieran Hayler, it was definitely a case of *Sliding Doors*.

I love that film starring John Hannah and Gwyneth Paltrow. The whole story hangs on whether Gwyneth's character Helen catches a train or not, and in each of the film's parallel plots there's a different outcome. In one scenario she meets James and they fall in love. In the other, their paths never cross.

It's always got me wondering, what would've happened if I hadn't met Peter André when we both took part in *I'm a Celebrity . . . Get Me Out of Here!* back in 2004? Would I have fallen for my second husband Alex Reid if Pete and I hadn't split five years later, when

I was still reeling from a miscarriage and completely devastated? Could I have chosen someone other than Kieran Hayler, for better or for worse, third time around?

Of course, there are many things about my life that I wouldn't change for the world. That includes my family – my mum Amy, stepdad Paul, my brother Danny and his family, my little sister Sophie, and my five amazing children.

I learn from my son Harvey, born in 2002 with severe disabilities, every single day. Princess and Junior, my children with Pete, light up my life. My mischievous little Jett and my baby Bunny, born in the two years since my marriage to Kieran, both saved me from losing my mind after I discovered that their father had cheated on me. All of my kids are beautiful. I love them just as they are and I wouldn't want them any other way.

But the men in my life? That's a whole different story. I'm the kind of person who 100 per cent needs to be in a relationship. I've got so much love to give, and only being with someone strong and protective makes me feel complete. I crave commitment and security. In truth, that's all I've ever wanted.

I know there are men out there who would treat me like a princess, worship me, love me, and be faithful to me, but somehow I don't end up with them. I'd love it if some rich man whisked me away and bought me diamonds and designer clothes, but it's always been the other way around. I joke that my life also mirrors the film *Pretty Woman*. The problem is, I'm always Richard

Gere in the relationship, when I'd *really* like to be Julia Roberts!

Before I met Kieran there were several roads I could have taken. It's funny to think that right now I could be in a different place, with a different person, leading a different life, but I chose Kieran – my knight in shining armour. And the rest, as they say, is history. But what would have happened if, like Helen in *Sliding Doors*, I never got on that train, I never started seeing Kieran and we never fell in love?

If I'm brutally honest, had I not fallen pregnant with Jett before my Caribbean wedding to Kieran in January 2013, and then had our daughter Bunny less than a year after I gave birth to her brother, I don't think I'd be here today with Kieran by my side. I'm aware that sounds harsh, but it's true.

I already had two children, Junior and Princess, who split their time between me and their father Pete. Adjusting to having them part-time was painful for me. I still miss them so badly when they're away; it hurts. Very reluctantly, I've had to get used to that. The last thing we as a family needed was another estranged man who saw his kids every other week.

That said, I could never imagine saying to Kieran: 'Let's be together for the sake of the children.' I can't think of anything worse than staying in an unhappy marriage surrounded by a constant atmosphere. I want my home to be a happy place, and the bottom line is that no matter what Kieran has put me through, we get on brilliantly. I haven't yet been able to flick the switch that announces 'I don't love you any more'.

When Pete and I split in 2009 I changed the locks at our house immediately and boarded a flight to the Maldives. I'd asked him to come with me so we could be on our own, away from the press. But Pete didn't come. Even though I wanted us to work things out, I knew in my heart there was no going back.

When I had final proof of Kieran's infidelity, the circumstances were completely different. We were at the start of a two-week holiday in Cape Verde, unable to get a flight home. Although my gut instinct was to escape to another universe and lick my wounds, away from the agonising intensity of the situation, I had to stay. Kieran and I were forced to face each other and start the painful process of repairing my heart and our marriage.

But writing about this now makes me want to turn the clock back to before I met him. I was then newly single, out having fun but always on the look-out for Mr Right. I needed a man who loved me, a man I could feel comfortable around; someone who didn't want me for the perfect home and the perfect celebrity lifestyle I brought with me but who accepted me for *me*.

I thought I had found Mr Right in my second husband Alex Reid even though my family and friends disliked him from the start. They had warned me that he had a thirst for celebrity. He was a failed actor, a failed model, by then making a career as a cage-fighter . . . but who would be sad enough to view marriage to me as a pathway to fame? Clearly him! I now bitterly regret that relationship.

Before I married Alex I had known that he had a secret. Initially, I'd been attracted to him because he was rugged and manly, but I soon discovered that in private he liked to dress as a woman. I was intrigued rather than shocked by the revelation. I was in love and accepted him for who he was. To those closest to me and even the press, I defended him. But the more I encouraged Alex to dress up as his alter-ego Roxanne, the more I realised she fuelled a dark and disturbing sexual side to him.

His transformation behind closed doors evolved from a harmless bit of role-play in the bedroom into a process that frightened me, and left me feeling vulnerable. Slowly, Roxanne started taking over our sex life and our marriage and I found myself being sucked into Alex's sick and sordid world.

When I finally said enough's enough, it was as if a black cloud had lifted. What a relief when Alex moved out of our home! I hadn't realised how much he and Roxanne had destroyed me, and it took me a long time to rebuild my self-confidence.

Looking back, I'm sure that's why I became engaged to the Argentinian model Leandro Penna soon after what turned out to be a long, drawn-out divorce from Alex. Although my head was telling me to wait, be single for a while and not run blindly into another relationship, my heart won out. What can I say? I'm an all-or-nothing person. I always have been and I think I always will be. The truth is I never loved Leo, but after everything I'd been through, I suppose I wanted to believe we had a future together.

Like me, Leo was a real outdoorsy type. A mutual passion for horse-riding drew us together. Some of the best days we spent together were while trekking high in the mountains around Córdoba – the breathtaking region of Argentina 700 kilometres north-west of Buenos Aires that Leo called home. There I felt free, surrounded by the most stunning scenery and with a man I was quickly falling for.

At first, Leo seemed to have all the right ingredients for the perfect boyfriend and being with him felt like a welcome breath of alpine air compared to the suffocating stench of Alex. But, in the end, horse-riding became the only thing we had in common. It didn't take long for the real Leandro Penna to step forward.

Leo wasn't the equal I'd first imagined he was. When he eventually moved in with me, he wasn't getting any modelling work in the UK, which meant he had no money. He was a man – or should I say boy? – with a taste for luxury, but only when I paid for it! See what I mean about Richard Gere? Even Leo's broken accent, which sounded so exotic at first, ended up grating on me. In fact, everything about Leo ended up grating on me.

When we split, I felt no regrets whatsoever. Deep

down I knew it wasn't to be and I'm not sure what possessed me to give him a second chance when he reappeared in my life a few months later armed with an engagement ring.

My friends kept telling me he'd changed, and for a while I believed he had too. But not only did Leo turn out to be just the same as ever but he began to display a jealous, angry streak that was an unnerving part of his character. No wonder I felt that I could never commit to him.

I wrote at length about our final break-up in my last book, but it was after we split the first time around that my life could have gone in any number of directions. There was one relationship that I've never spoken about openly before and I guess I want to talk about it now because there's a large part of me that needs to understand why, one year later, I ended up choosing to marry Kieran Hayler.

And perhaps it will act as a cautionary tale to all married women out there. After everything that's gone on between me and Kieran over the past couple of years, I've got a very different opinion of men and what they are capable of doing behind their partners' backs.

*   *   *

At the end of 2011 I flew to LA for a round of business meetings with managers and film executives. At home, I usually get into a regular fitness routine but when I'm abroad with a hectic schedule to manage it often falls by the wayside. This time I was determined to stay in shape and so I asked my then PA, Catherine, to hook me up with a Stateside trainer.

When she told me who she'd found, I promise you, I nearly died! Mark Smith, AKA Rhino in the ITV series *Gladiators*, was a real blast from the past. Not only had I been an avid watcher of the early 1990s show where incredibly fit and muscular men and women battled it out with members of the public in front of a live studio audience, but I'd appeared with Mark in a panto production of *Robinson Crusoe* in Worthing in 1997. Let's just say acting wasn't my forte, but I think everyone agreed I had stage presence!

It was great catching up with Mark after all that time. He's a lovely guy and, several hardcore training sessions later, I certainly felt fitter. During our final workout, the day before I was due to fly home, Mark tweeted a picture of us together in the gym. Not long after that one of his high-profile friends texted Mark, saying he'd seen the snap and was dying to meet me.

'He's fancied you for years, Kate, but he's never been able to contact you,' Mark said. To be honest, I didn't know much about the guy, other than that he was a media personality, and asked Mark to bring his picture up on Google so I could see him again.

I recoiled immediately. 'Ooh,' I confirmed, 'he's definitely not my type!' He wasn't exactly the dark, tanned sort I usually fall head over heels for. Still . . . he could be a laugh, and he's interested in me, I thought.

And, remember, I was at a painfully low ebb after splitting from Leo.

I don't think I realised how much of a child Leo was until he got on a plane back to Argentina. After the way he'd ponced off me, I was on the look-out for someone who didn't want me for my money. This guy had his own money and his own success. Was he single? I asked. 'Yes,' Mark confirmed. 'Perfect! Give him my number,' I agreed. Well, there's no harm in texting . . .

That's another decision I came to regret, but I can't deny that his intense interest in me was very flattering. Talk about the floodgates opening! He was on my case from day one. Right up until the time the crew were shutting the aircraft door on my return flight from LA we were messaging each other, so much so that I found myself hopelessly swept up in the moment.

By now you're probably wondering why I haven't given this man a name. The truth is, I've decided not to. Let's call him Mr X. After everything that happened later on, he deserves to be exposed. But I'm not a kiss-and-tell person and there's a family involved. After my own experience of being cheated on I know how devastating it is to discover your partner has been unfaithful, but if this man has any balls he'll admit the affair.

One thing I did notice was that he was very direct, which I like in a man. *We've got to meet, we've got to meet,* he kept texting, and no sooner had one message arrived than it felt like another had landed in my inbox.

Somehow, I found myself agreeing to meet him only hours after I was due to land back in the UK. I do remember thinking it was strange, but he insisted on coming to my house. He's keen! I thought. And sure enough, as I was slapping on the concealer around my jet-lagged eyes, his sports car was pulling up in the driveway.

In the flesh I instinctively knew I wasn't deeply attracted to Mr X but there was something intriguing about him. And I'm a sucker for a fit pair of legs and a muscular chest, and he had those in spades! Even so, I did catch myself thinking, *Kate, what the hell are you doing letting this man through your front door and into your life so quickly?*

Leo had not long gone, and I'd also had a very brief and disastrous fling with the rugby player Danny Cipriani, who'd turned out to be a liar and womaniser and who'd also left me a broken woman. I needed someone to want me again, but even though this guy had pursued me from the start, there was a part of me that was determined not to let my barriers down.

I stuck to the age-old tradition of treating them mean, keeping them keen, resisting the urge to sleep with him on that first meeting. Instead we talked and ended up kissing on my silver sofa. I was positive he wanted to take things further because, although he was a smooth-talker, I could sense his underlying impatience. On that occasion he left disappointed, but those texts kept on coming . . . He said everything to make me think he was really into me. His, low, soft voice was hypnotic, and he knew exactly how to make me feel special. But our first kiss? Hmmm ... the sparks weren't exactly flying. I couldn't put my finger on it, but there was something clinical about it. Perhaps he's a dark horse, I decided.

Sadly, I was soon to discover that he wasn't hiding anything. That same emotional detachment continued when we eventually ended up falling into bed together. Put it this way: if I'd needed a shelving unit erected, he would have been the perfect man. Instead of handling me gently and passionately like most women want to be handled, he was like a cordless drill on a multi-speed setting! In fact he reminded me of a red Bosch that I have in my garage. Bang ... bang ... bang, bang, bang. At one point I panicked, thinking, Shit, if he doesn't stop soon, I'm going to be permanently attached to the bed!

My heart sank. Mr X wasn't having sex *with* me, he was having sex *at* me. What about my pleasure? I questioned silently, as proceedings came to an abrupt end. We cuddled briefly but I felt totally confused. After all that build up, didn't he fancy me? Didn't he want to make me happy? Or did he want the sex to be over and done with as quickly as possible?

Almost straight away, I discovered why he was so ... how can I describe it? ... efficient. He couldn't stay. He had a wife he claimed to be divorcing but they had three kids together. Inside I was squirming. *Oh, fucking hell, Kate, what have you got yourself into?* I could have kicked myself, and Mark for that matter, for playing up Mr X's 'single' status.

'Ah ... so you've got a wife. This isn't for me,' I said, backing off, but he was very convincing. He was adamant that he and his wife were splitting soon, and the way he described their marriage it certainly didn't sound like they were getting on. Unsure whether to believe him or not, I ended up giving him the benefit of the doubt – strangely, my instinct was that he was telling the truth.

In fact, that instinct turned out to be bang on. Mr X *was* in the throes of a divorce, but there was a large part of me that was convinced he would have played away even if he'd been in the perfect relationship. During the four months or so that we saw each other he was friendly and we had fun together, but in the bedroom he was nothing more than businesslike. Unnervingly, he seemed able to separate the physical from the emotional in a single heartbeat.

Still, in between our meetings, his texts to me continued. He would text me from home; before work; after work; but he never stayed overnight at mine. In fact, the only time we ever spent the night together was if we booked into the same hotel in central London. Maybe he'll loosen up when his divorce comes through and we can see each other more openly, I hoped.

Despite the spontaneity of our meetings, it didn't take long for them to become predictable. We'd meet; I'd listen patiently while Mr X moaned about his marriage;

we'd have detached sex, and then he'd come up with some bullshit excuse that usually involved his family: 'Oh, baby, you know I don't want to, but I've got to go.' After a shower and a change of clothes, he'd be off faster than I could say the words 'love cheat'.

In the beginning, I stupidly excused his disappearing acts as an admirable sign that he was taking responsibility for his children. I know exactly the demands they place on a parent's time. I can't pretend that I wasn't excited by the moments we snatched together, even if they were lacking in the satisfaction department.

Of course, there's a part of me now that thinks, Why the hell did I accept that crap? I'm so much better than that! In my own defence, I think Alex followed by Leo and the horrendous Danny Cipriani had messed with my head more than I'd realised. I was scared of tumbling into another relationship with someone I *really* didn't love, but my self-esteem had also been shattered so I found it hard to end the affair there and then.

Mr X's game was becoming clearer to me, though. Hang on, I began to realise. I'm basically your fucking agony aunt, helping you through your marriage break-up, giving you all the love and attention you need . . . and what do I get? Screwed! Literally.

It's probably why, when Leo reappeared in the UK, I took him up on his offer to meet again. Initially I'd been resistant to the idea but, like I said before, he had seemed like a changed man. His English had come on in leaps and bounds and he'd clearly been working out loads.

And his money problem appeared to have mysteriously resolved itself.

Just before Christmas that year he came to my house armed with piles of presents bought from Harrods for the kids and Dolce and Gabbana designer clothes for me. And . . . the engagement ring. The last thing I wanted was to get engaged to Leo but my head was spinning. On the one hand, he was proposing. On the other, Mr X was still bombarding me with texts yet acting uber-cool when we were together.

I was caught between two men. A boost for any girl's ego, sure. But it also turned out to be one big pain in the arse. I didn't want to commit to Leo because of how he'd behaved before. But I didn't want to commit to Mr X either. Not only was he still legally married but we'd started seeing each other as a casual fling and I was determined to keep it that way until I felt myself to be on a steadier footing with him. I decided I wouldn't be hurting anyone if I carried on dating them both, to see what happened.

In the weeks that followed Leo and I started getting closer and spending more time with each other. I fancied him again and liked the way that he seemed more grown-up and independent. Then Mr X did something to make me realise how little he cared about me.

Up until that point, I'd taken him at face value. I'd sat and listened to the epic tale of his divorce and perhaps there was always a part of me that thought we could make a go of it once he'd finally split from his wife.

But one night we stayed with each other at a London hotel. Not long after we'd had breakfast the next morning and said goodbye, I received a text from my manager who was having a meeting in a Mayfair hotel. *You're not going to like this, but guess who I've seen walking in?* he wrote. It was Mr X, but it turned out he wasn't there on his own. He'd pulled up in a Limo and sauntered in draped around another woman.

You two-timing bastard, I thought. I was so furious I dialled his number immediately. 'Oh, yeah,' I said to him calmly, even though I felt anything but. 'What are you doing in a hotel with another woman?'

'What? What? No, I'm not!' he shot back, but when I described the girl and exactly what she was wearing he knew he'd been caught red-handed.

Suddenly, all of the trust I'd put in Mr X melted away. If he can do that to me, I thought, maybe he isn't divorcing his wife. Maybe he is just a player. Sex to him seemed like a drug, something he couldn't get enough of regardless of who he was with. He just loved the chase.

That was the end of me and Mr X, but soon I had another crazy situation on my hands. By then Leo had his suspicions that I'd been seeing someone in his absence but he had no idea who it was or that I'd continued to see Mr X for a short time after Leo returned to the UK. Unfortunately, it all came out one evening in early 2012 when I was preparing for a skiing holiday with my friend Derrick and my now ex-friend Jane Pountney.

Leo was planning on coming too, and we'd realised at the last minute that we were missing loads of ski gear. As we headed into town, I left Jane at home looking at pictures of our accommodation on my computer. (Oh, how I trusted Jane back then!) That evening, Leo asked to see our chalet too. 'Sure,' I replied casually. 'There's pictures on the laptop in the other room. Bring it through and I'll find them.'

I was lying in bed when suddenly Leo stormed through the door. 'Who's this?' he was spitting in his broken accent, waving my computer in the air. 'What the fuck's he got?'

I panicked. Leo was so worked up, the veins in his neck were pulsating, but I had no idea what he'd seen . . .

'Oh, shit!' It suddenly hit me that Jane hadn't logged out of my email. There were messages there from Mr X and pictures of us together. Leo must have trawled through the whole lot and now he was pacing around like a wild animal. 'Stop! Stop!' I screamed as he ripped open my drawers and cupboards, presumably looking for evidence. Before I could stop him, he'd pulled out a couple of men's shirts that Mr X had left the times he'd come to my house!

Leo turned and flew downstairs. In the kitchen, he yanked open the door to my wood burner which was roaring hot and threw them in. As the flames licked around the material, Leo was snapping away on his mobile like a man possessed. He must have found Mr X's number from somewhere because later I learned that he sent those pictures to him with a message threatening to break his knees and his neck. *Oh, please!*

Straight away, I realised I needed help. Leo was kicking off big time and I had no idea how far he was going to go. He was consumed by jealousy and it wasn't pretty. In the confusion, I ended up ringing my manager who warned Leo that he was calling the police if he didn't leave my house immediately.

Eventually, Leo did calm down. I explained to him that the relationship with Mr X had fizzled out and that we were no longer seeing each other. However, when we all ended up in Paris together a couple of months later it was a full-time job keeping a lid on Leo's uncontrollable temper. Paris is supposed to be the city of love, but quite frankly, by the end of that trip, I would have loved it if Leo and Mr X had both stayed there – together!

* * *

I was supposed to be travelling for a mutual friend's birthday in May but she'd had to cancel last-minute. As the hotels and Eurostar had been booked months before, I decided to take a bunch of friends anyway. Mr X had already reserved his travel and hotel before we'd stopped seeing each other, and I was booked on the same train and in the same hotel as him.

Now, though, I was starting to get worried. Since the Mayfair hotel incident, we were barely on speaking terms and since Leo was back in my life, he naturally wanted to come to Paris too. But Leo had no idea Mr X would be there and, judging by Leo's past performance, who knew what he'd be capable of if they met?

I ended up booking a separate journey for Leo alongside my friend Derrick. Not that travelling first-class stopped Leo from whinging. 'Why can't I go with you?' he moaned. 'Because it's full, that's why!' I snapped, but the reality was I had no idea if the carriage was full or not. There was just no way I was being stuck in an enclosed space with him and Leo, waiting for it all to kick off. No way, José.

As it turned out, Mr X boarded the train with a friend, but before we set off he did invite me for a drink at the lounge bar. He was acting all blasé, as if nothing had happened between us. I responded politely, but underneath I still felt angry with him. When we arrived in Paris and finally met up with Derrick and Leo at the hotel, that feeling got even worse.

Leo and I were about to head for a swim when my mobile rang. It was my friend Melodie, who had travelled in my party and was waiting for me by the pool.

'OMG, who do you think I've seen around the corner?' she whispered.

'Who?' I asked, but I already had that sinking feeling it was Mr X.

Sure enough, when Leo and I continued downstairs and got settled on the pool loungers, Mr X strolled past, six-pack out, dressed in nothing but a tight pair of Speedos. Right in front of Leo, he slowly lowered himself into the water. It was so obvious he was parading himself on purpose and it had the desired effect. 'That's him,' Leo hissed through gritted teeth.

'Where?' I replied, peering over the top of my sunglasses, totally playing it down. 'No, it's not!'

Leo threw his arms in the air and marched inside. He must have googled Mr X to double check because later that day he told me, 'It *was* him at the pool. I knew it!'

'For fuck's sake, Leo,' I shouted, 'I'm here with *you*! I'm sharing a room with *you*! And I'm paying for *you*! What more do you want?'

A couple of nights later Mr X was in the same restaurant as Leo and me. I wasn't sure if Leo had spotted him, but by then Leo was so obsessed with any man I spoke to it was a case of take your pick.

One highlight of the evening was being invited by a guy I'd been talking to at the bar to join his table. I wasn't going to be rude and refuse, even though I could see Leo getting jealous. When it was time to say goodbye, I gave this generous gent a peck on the cheek – nothing more, nothing less – but in front of everyone, Leo grabbed me by the neck and slapped me. I was gobsmacked by his aggression. I know Mr X saw the whole drama unfold, too, even though he didn't rush to help me.

That was the beginning of the end for me and Leo too but I was surprised that when Leo started to sell stories about me to the press some months later, my relationship with Mr X was never exposed. I can only imagine it was because Leo had found out about it by trawling through my computer and so couldn't use any of his 'evidence'.

The day after the restaurant incident we were due to travel home, but I wasn't even sure I'd make the train. I'd had far too much to drink that night and I was ridiculously hungover. But I was also still so shaken by Leo's behaviour that I felt dangerously close to a full-blown panic attack. I did make it, by a whisker, and Mr X and I ended up sitting next to each other. I'd like to say the conversation was scintillating, but I was so jittery that I was barely able to speak.

Then, before we arrived back in London, Mr X leaned over and said something that completely floored me. 'I liked you, but I didn't like you *that* much,' he whispered in my ear. I felt so insulted and I wasn't even sure what he meant: that he didn't like me enough to defend me in the restaurant? Or he didn't like me that much because I was with Leo now and his precious ego had been bruised? I said nothing but, seriously, I had to bite my lip. You cocky fucker! I thought. You were quite happy to tell me how much you liked me before you fucked me. How dare you make me feel so shit about myself!

I quietly raged in the queue through Customs and as soon as I got in the taxi with my friends I fired off an angry text to him. *You arrogant twat*, I called him. Not only had he never bought me anything when we were together, but I also reminded him that he hadn't made me come once in all the times we'd slept together. And, by the way, did he know I'd shagged one of his mates?

To my shame, I can't remember too much about that one. Admittedly, it wasn't my finest moment. Mr X and I were seeing each other but it was very early days and Leo hadn't yet reappeared in my life. One weekend when my kids were away I'd thrown a party and he turned up with a few mates. An hour or so into the evening he had a call from his wife. Apparently one of his kids was sick and he needed to go home immediately. His mates decided to party on and, to be blunt, it got to the point where I was too shit-faced to care where Mr X had got to. Besides, in a certain light one of his friends looked quite fanciable . . . A friend of mine remembers us being wrapped around each other although I don't remember much at all.

As I dragged myself out of bed the next morning this guy was nowhere to be seen, but I did find his necklace in my spare room. I had to go back through my security cameras to work out the finer details of the night and when I rewound to the part where we were naked in the kitchen, the grim reality came flooding back.

Finding out about his friend must have been the final straw for Mr X. Aha, so there's one rule for you and one rule for everyone else, I figured. The journey back from Paris was the last I ever heard from him, and I had absolutely no interest in contacting him either.

When I heard he'd finally divorced and remarried, I thought 'good luck' but I couldn't help feeling sorry for his new wife. Not long after, his ex-wife got in touch with me and asked if we'd been seeing each other. I held my hands up. I felt horribly like 'the other woman', even though, like his wife, I'd been taken in by Mr X. We actually ended up texting, like some first wives' club, but unlike her, I thanked my lucky stars I could close the door on Mr X without any deep emotional or family ties.

The whole episode made me want to find someone I truly trusted. I definitely knew that wasn't Leo; after his behaviour in Paris the writing was on the wall. I felt ready for a relationship with a person I could fall head-over-heels in love with and who felt exactly the same about me.

CHAPTER 2

FOOL IN LOVE

Even though my relationship with Mr X had been casual, I'd felt hurt and messed around the moment I'd heard he'd been seen going into a hotel with another woman – even if it might have been perfectly innocent. Then, there was the insult he had thrown at me on the journey back from Paris. I couldn't believe someone could stoop so low.

By September 2012 I was convinced Leo had to go too. I'd been patient with him, given him time to get a job and earn some money, but none of that ever happened. The final straw came when he denied selling a story to an Argentinian magazine revealing he had walked out on me. *He* walked out on me? If only! My manager alerted me to the piece. Not only was it absolute crap, but it was obvious that Leo was behind it. Even so, he stood there lying, lying, lying, and continued to play the innocent after my manager emailed me the entire article and I waved it in front of Leo's face.

As soon as his bags were packed, I couldn't wait for Leo to make a sharp exit. At last I could move on! I've never been one to let bad experiences stop me from picking myself up and getting on with life, but I admit I felt pretty battered. Over the last months with Leo I had felt myself sinking and, for the first time in three years, I went back on anti-depressants if only for a few months. I was so scared my mood would spiral like it did when I'd suffered post-natal depression after Junior's birth. There was no way that I wanted to be in that dark place again.

In the weeks that followed, I did start to feel stronger. I always think the measure of true love is how long it takes to miss a person after they've gone and I didn't miss Leo one bit. Maybe it was the medication kicking in but there were even days when I felt ready to get right back on the horse that threw me.

It was around this time that my friend Phil told me about this guy he'd known for three years. According to Phil, he was really nice and had been pestering Phil for my number. Of course, that guy turned out to be Kieran, and boy, was he persistent! I think now that if I'd known what Kieran was really like, I would have run a mile, shouting, 'Keep that man away from me!' But at the time I reckoned, why not? I've got nothing to lose.

I'd been receiving some flirtatious texts from other

guys, and that didn't stop, but I guess Kieran gradually started taking over. I'd given Phil my BBM pin and allowed Kieran to contact me on that – it's great because on BBM you never have to reveal your phone number so you can delete someone if you decide you've had enough of them. At one point I *did* delete Kieran. He was messaging me so much it was like, *Stop! Please! Take a breath!* I liked the attention but he was so full on.

He must have got my number from somewhere because as soon as I pressed delete I got a phone call from him asking me why I'd done that. How the hell can I get rid of this guy? I wondered, but we started chatting and immediately I liked the sound of him. He was quietly spoken and funny – not what I expected at all. After we met for the first time I was in even more of a dilemma. I'd invited him over to watch a marathon thriller session in my cinema room. He certainly made an impression, not least because he was tall and broad-chested and I felt protected by him. That night we didn't kiss but we did cuddle and I also noticed that he was so shy he was shaking. I could really see myself with this man. Crisis!

However, my experience with Leo and Mr X had left me very weary. I kept thinking, what if Kieran is the same kind of player? What if he just wants me for a meaningless fling and has no intention of committing? I'd kept my guard up with Mr X, which turned out to be a wise move, but I couldn't help thinking there was more to Kieran, and this was a man I could fall head over heels in love with.

That was it. The more Kieran and I saw of each other, the more I didn't want to miss out on the opportunity of being with him – he seemed so kind and gentle. Physically, he was just my type, and I noticed that he had a playful side to him too. It was great to connect with someone with my sense of humour. We ended up laughing so much. 'Pick your tongue up off the floor, Kate,' I kept reminding myself. And God! He turned out to be such a good kisser. This doesn't sound very appealing, I know, but the only way I can describe our first kiss is like Andrex toilet tissue – soft, strong and very long!

There was one other happy coincidence that tipped the balance in Kieran's favour too, although it wasn't the deal-breaker that the tabloids reported when they got hold of the story. After my relationship with Mr X ended I had a clairvoyant come to my house. God, how I'd like to ring her now and ask for my money back!

Having gazed into her crystal ball she promised that I would find my happy ever after in a man whose first initial was 'K'. 'Ooh, I think his name's Kevin,' she said, winking at me. I'm not being funny, I couldn't see myself with a 'Kevin', but apparently if we met, we'd fall in love in an instant and spend a lifetime together. Kevin – Kieran: it wasn't too much of a leap. After Kieran and I got married I named our new puppy Kevin. He's a beautiful fox-red Labrador that I bought Kieran for his birthday. The funny thing is that dog's turned out to be the most loyal and trustworthy companion of the lot, so maybe she wasn't so wrong after all.

* * *

Knowing now exactly what Kieran ended up doing with two of my best friends, it's hard to turn the clock back and think about how naive I was when I met him. The truth is, he didn't seem like all the other men I'd met.

Unlike Alex, I never got the impression Kieran was after fame. He'd been a full-time plasterer by day and a personal trainer in a local gym in the evening. Then, by the time we finally met, he'd gone into stripping for a living, doing the circuit of hen nights and ladies' nights at weekends. If he wanted attention, he had it after every curtain up, taking his kit off to reveal his super-ripped, waxed body in front of hundreds of screaming women.

Back in 2012 he'd also taken on the role of a male stripper in *EastEnders* before the wedding of gay couple Christian and Syed. That same year, he appeared as an extra on the panel show *Argumental*, hosted by the comedian Sean Lock. Kieran strode out on set in a crisp white sailor's uniform and left with nothing but a sailor hat covering his dick! It was enough to float my boat, but if Kieran's aim was to gain recognition, he didn't need me. He was doing fine by himself.

Admittedly, I was in two minds about him being a stripper. I know what strippers are like, I kept reminding myself. They'll shag anything with a pulse. But Kieran even managed to allay those fears. Now, I realise what a clever manipulator he was, and perhaps there was a hint of his split personality the first time I saw his show. Normally, he was so nervous and quiet, but I can't pretend I wasn't taken aback by his ultra-confident act, strutting around the stage like he owned it. I secretly liked it. Fucking hell! Is that Kieran? I thought. So you do have a bit of oomph in you!

Thankfully, offstage he wasn't arrogant or full of himself at all. From early on, he went out of his way to buy me things. He had a bit of money saved up. He wasn't loaded, but it didn't stop him sending me flowers, Louboutin shoes or my favourite Bijan perfume. Finally, I got to be Julia Roberts! When he asked me to marry him only weeks into our whirlwind romance, he even promised me a gorgeous ring. Okay, he jokingly placed a Haribo ring on my finger until the real one turned up. Like any girl, I love a bargain, but not that much of a bargain! Eventually, he did present me with a square-cut diamond set within a glittering diamond band. I felt like the luckiest woman in the world.

The real test of a man for me, though, is how they hit it off with my kids. I certainly don't let everyone meet them. Mr X didn't, which probably reveals a lot about my intuition. I'm sure, though, if my relationship with Mr X had gone further he would have done. I guess it wasn't meant to be. I held off introducing Kieran too, but both of us realised early on that this wasn't a casual fling or a rebound relationship and, when the time was right, I felt completely comfortable welcoming him into my family. It felt like it did when I first met Pete, as if we were always meant to be together: a complete, all-encompassing, passionate romance.

When Kieran did meet my brood, he was so patient and calm with them and I noticed he responded brilliantly to Harvey, which is always the biggest test for anyone. It was as if everything had clicked into place. I'd got this perfect guy, he was gorgeous-looking, bought me presents, we loved spending time with each other and he didn't take any crap off me either. What's not to like?

Suddenly all my other flings paled into insignificance. Kieran felt like my reward for having put up with them! Well, a girl has to kiss a lot of frogs before she finds her prince, doesn't she? The thought of Mr X's fly-by-night visits and the dire sex now made my skin crawl. However, when Kieran's true colours were finally revealed I couldn't help wondering where I'd be now if I'd pursued other men. All my friends had told me, 'Kate, you deserve a man who really loves you.' That may be so, but by the time Kieran and I got married I didn't question whether he was genuine.

I was convinced I'd made the right decision. And by now I was so in love with him that no one could tell me otherwise.

CHAPTER 3

THE 'F' WORD

I've always loved spending quality time with my friends. There are some I'm still in touch with from when I first started out as a glamour model. I trust them wholeheartedly, but with some others I've realised too late how opportunistic they really are.

I probably learned the true value of friendship back in 2009 when Pete and I split. My business relationship with CAN Associates, headed by Claire Powell, and my PA Nicola Partridge, came to an abrupt end, and behind the scenes I not only lost my husband, I lost four of my closest friends too.

Claire had been my manager since 2004 and, over the years, she'd become part of our family. She was the driving force behind the reality TV series starring Pete and me, and although in the end I'd found the constant filming of our lives overwhelming and had wanted a change to the way we worked, I had hoped that our friendship would last the distance. Unfortunately, that wasn't meant to be.

Nicola knew everything about me too. She'd even filmed Princess's birth for us – not for use on our reality show, but as a private memento. And I also lost the friendship of Jamelah Asmar and Michelle Clack. Michelle, one of my oldest friends, even sold a story blaming me for the break-up of our marriage. Jamelah Asmar attempted to follow suit, although the *News of the World* did not publish it.

To have let those people into the most precious occasions in my life only to lose those friendships was not only incredibly disappointing, it was very painful too. Publicly, the press were churning out a constant diet of negative stories about me. Personally, it felt like part of my family had died – the only way I can describe it is that it was like experiencing a deep physical pain, like actual grief.

I can't ever forget the people who supported me, though. There were a handful of close girlfriends, and my friends Gary and Phil. My old friend Neil, who I'd known since my clubbing days in Brighton, even came back into my life. It was like he'd never been away. Neil used to be an instructor at the gym my mum went to in Brighton. When I started going I really fancied him but he's turned out to be one of those friends who I've shared countless beds with over the years but never, ever slept with. A lot of friends and previous boyfriends have found our relationship hard to fathom. 'He's great-looking, fit and you get on. You're so going to end up together,' they'd say, but we've always been in other relationships and I guess it's never happened. During my marriage to Pete, I didn't see much of Neil except for the occasional text.

Then there's Derrick. Again, I knew him from my clubbing days, and he is good friends with Neil. After my marriage split, we all went to Ibiza together to shoot my calendar. Predictably, the press had a field day. I'd taken a film crew and in between shooting pieces of footage I'd wanted to shake off the past and hit the clubs. Of course, the newspapers portrayed me as a complete slapper, off my face on drink and drugs. They seemed hell-bent on bringing back bad-girl Jordan, but the picture they painted couldn't have been more wrong. First of all, I don't take drugs and, I promise you, I was tucked up with my pals Julie and Melodie by 2 a.m. if we went out at all!

I cannot tell you how brilliant all those friends were at a time when I really needed them, but by the time my marriage to Pete was over in 2009 my life had changed immeasurably. Unlike during the old days in Brighton, I wasn't getting into the wild scrapes I used to. I was a single mother of three and, although I loved to let my hair down – I still do! – I needed to be responsible too. Derrick and his wife Jane were the only people around me with kids. Their two children, George and Ruby, were exactly the same age as Junior and Princess and we naturally gravitated towards each other.

I'd first met Jane years before. It must have been when I was about sixteen. Derrick is a good fifteen years older than me and Jane's only a bit younger than Derrick, although if you ever went on a night out with them you would never guess. Back in the day they were such a fun couple, and even when they'd settled down and had kids they didn't stop being total party animals. Whenever we went away on holiday together they were the ones who would want to stay up dancing all night while we were begging to go home. Respect is due!

When she and Derrick first started seeing each other, Jane worked for an airline and was always flying off to exotic places. Over the years she would drop in and out of my life but we never became close in the way Derrick and I were. The funny thing about Jane was she wasn't glam in the slightest. In fact, she dressed in a very mumsy way, but she was so full of beans and I loved that she was so warm and bubbly – the sort of person you could take anywhere and not have to worry about whether she'd make friends or not.

Knowing now what I know about Jane and how she's ended up destroying my life, it's very hard to talk about the past objectively. I torture myself with it, but I now wonder whether any of Jane's openness towards me was ever real. I'd like to think it was an honest friendship but I can't stop myself constantly going over the last few years in my head. Was she waiting for the right moment to stab me in the back? If Jane was playing a game, it was a bloody good one. She certainly had me fooled.

Along with my family, Jane became my rock during my divorce from Pete. I'd started seeing my therapist Gaylin and there were times when I didn't think I could go on. Jane listened if I needed a sympathetic ear and she also helped me out practically. For example, if I needed an outfit for a court appearance she would help me choose it or sometimes she'd go into town and get something for me.

Gradually, Jane became involved in all the events in my life, happy and sad. She had come to my wedding to Pete as Derrick's guest; when I married Alex I chose her as one of my bridesmaids. That's how close I felt to her! Dressed in a baby-blue chiffon outfit, Jane sat next to me on the top table and even cried when Alex made a speech calling me his 'precious pearl'. In my speech, I said that I'd known most of my bridesmaids since I was fifteen and that I'd chosen them because they meant something very special to me. It was a comment that came from the bottom of my heart.

Later that year, when it was clear my marriage to Alex was on the rocks, she and Derrick clocked up so many brownie points that I lost count. They lived in Hove at the time, which was around forty-five minutes' drive from my Surrey home, yet Jane would travel up with her children at weekends and be there at the drop of a hat if some drama was going on. She knew how scary Alex was becoming when he dressed up as Roxanne because those times were usually fuelled by booze. I'd find him in this trance-like state, speaking in his creepy, quiet Roxanne voice. Even to me, his wife, he'd become totally unreachable.

There was one occasion when I was at a book signing and couldn't get hold of him by phone. I had that awful feeling he wasn't picking up because he was at home playing out his private fantasies. Frightened and unsure what to do, I called Jane and Derrick and asked them to accompany me home. Without hesitation, Jane agreed. There was no way I could have gone there alone and I felt very reassured by their presence. When I entered the house to find that my bedroom had been transformed into a sex dungeon, with Alex at the centre of it dressed in stockings, suspenders, make-up and heels and doing something with a dildo best left to the imagination, I was doubly relieved I had my good friends around me.

When Jane's and Kieran's affair hit the tabloids it was claimed Jane had testified for me in court when I finally divorced Alex. That wasn't true, but the fact that I let her into my life in times of such personal turmoil shows she was someone I truly trusted.

We became even closer when I started seeing Leo. By then I'd sold my Surrey home and was in the process of converting my last home – a farmhouse near Horsham in West Sussex. While the renovations were underway and a huge log cabin was being built in the grounds to house us temporarily, Leo and I stayed at Jane's in Hove for a month. As Derrick was travelling most of the time with his work, she was generous enough to offer us her bed while she slept with her daughter Ruby. I remember feeling touched by her kindness but now I can only question whether the real reason Jane offered us her room was because she was in awe of me. Was plain, dumpy, mumsy Jane desperate to have a taste of my life – getting involved in all the highs and lows of my dramas and being overly generous while nursing some ulterior motive? I guess I'll never know.

Back then, I always repaid Jane's kindness. I'm not the sort of person to give a shit how much money I spend on my friends. I'm not into any of that mystical bollocks but I am a true believer in karma. By my reckoning, what goes around comes around, and if I was planning a holiday and I wanted Jane, Derrick and their kids to come along then I'd rent a villa with a pool and not dream of asking them to contribute. We all went to Marbella for a month while my house was being refurbished. Other than Leo behaving like a spoiled brat while we were out there, it was fantastic to watch the kids splashing around in the pool and we had a real laugh hanging out together.

After that, whenever we went away, I'd always tried to include Jane and her family. And when eventually the work on the house was completed and Leo moved in, Jane became a shoulder for me to cry on when our relationship started turning ugly. There were many nights when she witnessed Leo's uncontrollable anger and stayed with me after the histrionics had died down.

My mum even reminded me recently that Jane became the go-between in all of my arguments with him. I can't say I thought about it at the time, but looking back it was weird.

When I met Kieran, Jane was one of the first people I confided in. By then, she and Derrick had moved from Hove to Storrington, five minutes down the road from me. I can't help thinking now that was weird too! It was Jane's choice to up sticks and be nearer to me, and Derrick went along with it. At first I thought, Great! The kids get on brilliantly and they can be closer together. Every second weekend Jane would bring them over, and George, Ruby, Junior and Princess would play upstairs or outside while we'd catch up on all the girlie gossip over a cuppa.

But there was one occasion when the kids created such a mess, and it struck me that Jane didn't insist her kids help clear up. I didn't want to mention anything to her about it. I'm far too polite in those situations and in the grand scheme of things it was no big deal. But I know that if the boot were on the other foot, I'd be shouting, 'Junior! Princess! Make sure you leave someone else's house the way you found it!' Come Monday, I felt awful for my nanny Lizzie and housekeeper Lucy. I couldn't stop apologising. They were the ones faced with clearing up the bomb-site of clothes and make-up and toys scattered everywhere.

Apart from that niggle, I always made Jane and her family welcome. I was happy that the kids could play at weekends and it was fun for me to have a female friend around. I'd make such a big thing of it. They'd always stay on a Saturday night and I'd order in pizza or an Indian takeaway and we'd curl up on the sofa in our trackies and watch *X Factor* or *I'm a Celebrity . . .*

'Oh my God, Kate, he sounds really nice,' Jane said when I first told her about Kieran. In fact, all my friends said the same, although I'm sure they were thinking, Yeah, Kate, we've heard it all before. But so what if they had? Kieran fitted perfectly into my life. From very early on, being with him felt 100 per cent right, and if a man gets on with your mates, I reckon that's an even bigger bonus. The great thing was, Kieran really did!

We'd kept our wedding plans to ourselves because I knew people were bound to say it was too soon and we were rushing into things. Okay, looking back, maybe they had a point. We got married five weeks after we'd met. I know, I know! I charge headlong into relationships without waiting. I can't help it. I'm an all or nothing person and I don't see why I should apologise to anyone for wearing my heart on my sleeve.

But the great thing was, Kieran felt exactly the same about me as I did about him and secretly we both wanted to tie the knot as soon as possible. When we announced our engagement before Christmas 2012 we'd already made plans to marry in January. Typically, the world and his wife had their say. Apparently Ladbrokes had 4–7 odds that our engagement would be called off before January 2014. Ha! Well, we proved them wrong. And some columnists even started calling me 'Bridezilla', which I actually thought was hilarious. I'm really not the sort of woman who goes into a relationship because I want a wedding. I was truly in love with Kieran and, unlike my other weddings, both of us talked about a quiet affair with only close family and a very select group of friends present. I was all for wearing a big white dress for the blessing later in the year, but for the actual ceremony we settled on small and simple. The irony is that I didn't think twice about asking Jane to be my maid of honour again. After all the heartbreak I'd been through, I wanted people around me I loved and trusted. She said 'yes' without even blinking.

When we chose to marry in the Bahamas, Kieran and I flew out a little earlier to set up the venue – the Sandals Royal Bahamian Resort. Don't even get me started again on what a disaster that place turned out to be. It would make me too furious! I know all that glitters isn't gold but nothing about that place glittered: not our suite, not our wedding, not the sand and not even the sunshine. And, if I'm brutally honest, it wasn't too long after that the shine came off the groom too!

I can't forget my feeling of sheer excitement, though. Not only was I about to marry my Prince Charming but the night before Jane, Derrick, my mum, Kieran's mum, and my friend Tania all arrived in Nassau, I'd discovered I was pregnant. When I told Kieran he was as over the moon as I was. 'Let's tell everyone over dinner. It'll be the perfect end to the day,' we agreed. And everyone was thrilled when we broke the news. My pregnancy meant I didn't drink at our wedding meal but I didn't care. I was Mrs Hayler and that was all that mattered. On the other hand, perhaps it was because I was stone-cold sober that I noticed Jane really knocking the champagne back. Like I mentioned before, she and Derrick can be proper party animals but there was a difference in Jane then and I wasn't the only one to clock it.

If you'd asked me what Jane wore back in England, I wouldn't have been able to tell you. Her taste was normally so nondescript. 'Molly', I call it: leggings and big, baggy jumpers . . . really 'Molly'. Out in the Bahamas I'd paid for everyone to have their hair and make-up done. I've treated my bridesmaids at all of my weddings. Afterwards everyone commented on how gorgeous Jane looked. The fact that she'd lost a bit of weight didn't go unnoticed either and she had on a beautiful cerise pink Grecian-style dress. As soon as she'd tried it on we all exclaimed, 'Jesus, you look completely different!' 'Really? Me?' she laughed. Wow, I thought, it's great that a makeover has boosted Jane's confidence so much!

But halfway through our wedding dinner, all of a sudden Jane got up on her chair, then climbed barefoot on to the table and started dancing. I have no idea what the song playing was because, let me tell you, all eyes were on Jane. I was gobsmacked. Why are you doing this, Jane? I was thinking to myself. I laughed it off as just her being pissed, but she didn't only dance for one song, she stayed up there, wiggling her bum in the air, showing off her cleavage to the world and floating around with her arms outstretched. It was pure cringe – a forty-nine-year-old woman flaunting herself on a tabletop at someone else's wedding! I looked directly at my mum, who was glaring back at me with a 'WTF is Jane doing?' look on her face. I had no answer.

Paranoia started to get the better of me. Derrick and Kieran were the only men at the table, and so naturally I was thinking: Who the hell is Jane doing this for? Although she and Derrick were still together, I knew they didn't have the happiest marriage in the world. She'd told me they'd stopped having sex aeons ago. It's impossible to know what goes on inside someone else's marriage, but if she wasn't dancing and being all flirtatious for Derrick's benefit, then the only other man there was Kieran . . .

I sat watching her intently and I even saw her throw Kieran this prolonged, sultry look. Ugh! It was like some alter-ego had taken Jane over and she was saying, 'Look at me! I'm the sexy one. I might be older but I'm the one you want.' Snap out of it, Kate, it's your hormones, I thought. I'm pregnant, I'm needy, and I know exactly how that plays tricks on the mind. I held my breath until Jane's 'performance' was over and decided on the spot not to make a big deal of it. It's a sign of how secure I felt with Kieran. I dismissed the incident. I know Kieran loves me and it's nice she's enjoying herself.

My mum, on the other hand, has known Jane for years and she approached me in private afterwards. 'Don't you think Jane's starting to look like you?' she pointed out.

'Mum, I have noticed, but it's nice Jane's starting to take care of herself, don't you think? Please don't say anything to her,' I begged.

My mum raised her eyebrows with an 'If I were you, I wouldn't let it lie' look. Trust me, if looks could kill, my mum would be serving several life sentences!

*   *   *

Back in the UK, it was down to business as usual. Kieran made the decision to return to work after we were married – up at six in the morning for his plastering job and stripping or off to the gym in the evenings and weekends. Phew! A man who actually wanted to work and contribute to the relationship. That made a change. 'I'm so lucky to have you,' I kept telling him. And I really did feel blessed to be married to Kieran. From my perspective, there was no game playing between us and no reason to believe that he would ever cheat on me.

Kieran even asked me if I wanted him to give up stripping now we were having a family. I didn't! I'd seen his show and it seemed obvious to me that that Kieran had one persona in front of an audience and was a different guy at home. It was an act and I could see that he enjoyed it. Why would I ever ask him to give it up? I even thought it was a great boost for his ego to be looked at by countless women every weekend. 'As long as they look and don't touch!' I joked, but I much preferred that way of Kieran feeling great about himself than thinking he had to pull some stranger in a club behind my back. It makes me feel sick when I think about what has happened since, but that's how I felt at the time.

I respected Kieran for wanting to make his own way career-wise, and I was glad too. As soon as we got back from honeymoon I was starting to feel exhausted from my pregnancy, more than I can remember with any of my others. Pregnancy hadn't slowed me down in the past. I kept saying, 'Don't worry about me. I'm not ill, I'm only pregnant!' but underneath I did feel different – definitely not my bubbly self. Not only did I have the worst morning sickness on the planet but my obstetrician Dr Gibb discovered I was anaemic too. I was put on a course of iron tablets, which not only made me feel hideously nauseous but left me constipated. A nice touch! 'God, I must seem so unattractive to Kieran!' I kept saying.

Dr Gibb was also concerned about my low blood pressure and low platelet count. Platelets are cells in your blood that help it to clot, but because of my low reading I was going to have to be monitored very carefully. If the count got too low I might need a transfusion, and that could mean I wouldn't be able to have a C-section or an epidural.

Dr Gibb delivered Junior and Princess and he'd always made me feel reassured. I was happy to leave things in his hands but I was getting larger and larger with this pregnancy and anxiety overwhelmed me at times.

I think part of the problem was I didn't want to be seen out. Usually, the paps can't wait to get shots of me looking ridiculous. Most of the time, at my book or perfume launches, I ask to dress outrageously. I've been a pink pantomime horse, a sexy Mrs Christmas complete with reindeer and elves, a space alien princess, an inflatable pair of red lips – you name it. I enjoy the spectacle and I always want to give the tabloids something to talk about. But this was different. I've NEVER wanted to dress up as a beached whale, but that's exactly what I felt like. There wasn't a scarf big enough to cover my huge belly and sagging arse. Even though I'd been playing badminton and tennis with Kieran, I was piling on the pounds without really understanding why. I felt absolutely gross! There were times when I would pray: Please let this baby come early so that Kieran doesn't have to see me like this any longer. How crazy is that? He said he didn't care what I looked like but, seriously, there are limits!

Initially I put it down to me feeling all over the place, but Kieran didn't seem too interested in the development of our baby. Whenever I asked him he said he was excited, and he dutifully came to all the scans, but I felt I had to keep prodding him: 'It's your first child and you could be a bit more enthusiastic!'

When it came to babies, I guess the only person I could compare him to was Pete. Whatever's gone on between me and Pete in the past, I will never say a bad word about him as a father. From the moment I was pregnant with Junior he was 100 per cent there for me and he took an active interest in every stage of my pregnancy. Okay, he might not have been as obsessed I was! But I think that's just men, full stop. I'd lie in bed with my laptop on my knees googling every detail and imagining our baby as small as a grape and then with tiny fingers and toes, yawning and stretching. Even after five children, I never cease to be amazed by all the stages women's bodies go through during pregnancy and I love checking up on everything that's happening week by week.

As Junior was born after Harvey, I remember Pete being worried that if anything went wrong with this baby too, he wouldn't be able to cope. I reassured him that he'd handle it fine. After the first scans confirmed that our baby was healthy we would sit for hours and dream about his or her arrival and what he or she was going to look like or what their first words were going to be. It was so refreshing to be with someone who cared after having gone through my pregnancy with Harvey alone. Harvey's father, Dwight Yorke, took no interest whatsoever in his birth and has taken even less interest in his life since, but more of that later.

Perhaps it's unfair of me to keep comparing Kieran to Pete, because everybody handles first-time fatherhood differently. Even so, I couldn't help feeling disappointed that Kieran wasn't visibly excited when I talked about the baby or if I ever asked him to place his hand on my bump. He asked me very few questions too. I can't put my finger on it, but he was distant. Each time I broached the subject he didn't react. And whenever that happened I felt as if my bright pink helium balloon of excitement had suddenly been popped. His reaction was totally deflating.

Kieran appeared a little more animated when it came to plans for our Willy Wonka-themed wedding blessing in March 2013. I had been feeling so out of sorts that I think I overcompensated by putting a lot of energy into making it the happiest occasion ever, especially after the frustration of our Bahamas fiasco. It was all a bit last minute because I'd not been well. But cancelling was out of the question. There was no way I was getting married looking even bigger than I already did! When we eventually settled on Rookery Manor in Western-super-Mare for the venue, the wedding planners had a week and a half to get everything decorated. No one could ever accuse me of doing things by halves!

And, you know what? Whatever's happened since, I do look back on that day and remember how much fun it was. I had brightly coloured drapes put in the main hall. There were giant toadstools, giant cupcakes, stripy candy sticks, giant lollipops, slabs of chocolate, giant tubes of love hearts, sherbet fountains and table decorations filled with sweets. The venue looked exactly like it had in my imagination and, I promise you, that's a pretty wild place!

Again, I chose bridesmaids who were very special to me. I had twelve in total including Jane. Princess and

Jane's daughter Ruby both looked beautiful as flower girls and, alongside Junior, Jane's son George made a fantastic page boy. Can you believe that Jane even made a speech at my wedding? I remember welling up with tears listening to it. Her words were very emotional. She said how much our friendship meant to her and how happy she was for Kieran and me on our special day.

It's horrible to think about now, but I can't help analysing everything Jane said or did in the run-up to our wedding. For example, the night before, Kieran and I had kept to the tradition of the bride and groom not seeing each other before the big day and stayed in separate hotel rooms. Kieran took Junior and I took Harvey and Princess. If Harvey's with me, it's great to have my mum on hand. Other than me, she's the only person who really understands how to handle Harvey, especially if something disturbs him in a strange place, like a loud noise or a banging door. Jane knew this and yet she insisted on taking the room opposite me on the top floor. 'We'll be next to each other for our hair and make-up in the morning,' she said forcefully, even though I'd already mentioned I wanted my mum to take that room. At the same time, I didn't want to upset Jane. If it means that much to you, have it, I thought. I'll put Mum downstairs. And that's what ended up happening.

On the morning of my wedding I had arranged for the make-up artists to do the bridesmaids' make-up and my mum's and Kieran's mum's. It was a weird feeling because I was so happy, but the morning sickness gremlin wouldn't leave me alone either. I kept having to run to the loo to be sick, and so I ended up letting everyone have their make-up done before me. Again, Jane was adamant she was going to be first in the queue. She had a hair-piece attached to make her hair look like mine and friends have told me since that, among themselves, they'd talked about the way that Jane seemed intent on cloning my appearance. No one said a word to me, although I'm not sure I would have listened if they had. Jane's changing look did cross my mind, but I took it as a compliment and didn't dwell on it too seriously. Good on you, Jane, I thought. You can look sexy, but I know my man will never be interested in you. I'm madly in love with Kieran and he feels exactly the same about me.

At the time Kieran really made me feel that secure.

CHAPTER 4

CALAMITY JANE

'Kieran's absolutely besotted with you,' my friends Gary and Phil said to me on the day of our wedding blessing.

'Do you really think so?' I asked, still feeling like I needed reassurance. Even though Kieran made me feel safe, experience has told me never to count my chickens. But for the first time in a long while I felt utterly contented.

Once the celebrations were over, Kieran fitted in well with family life. I watched him play with the kids and spend time with them. His strong family values attracted me to him, as well as his love of the outdoors. As a little boy he'd been very close to his granddad, who'd been a pig farmer. His granddad knew everything there was to know about the countryside and would take Kieran out on nature trails and teach him all about pigs and goats and bugs and birds and butterflies. Kieran did exactly the same with Princess and Junior. They'd come back from exploring in the fields or feeding the hens, their heads filled with everything they'd learned. Kieran kept all the stamps he'd collected with his granddad too, and the little storybooks his granddad wrote and would read to him. In fact, he kept everything that was special to him in a tin box. 'For a male stripper, you're very sensitive and sentimental,' I would tease him, but Kieran knew I was kidding. I loved him that way.

According to his mum, Kieran had been badly bullied at school, so much so that on one occasion she'd gone to pick him up and found him in the playground surrounded by classmates pelting him with stones. After that she was forced to place him in another school. There are also some other horrific things that have happened in Kieran's past that I don't want to go into. They're not an excuse for what he's done but, let's just say, he's been through an experience that no child should have to go through and it might have influenced some of his subsequent behaviour.

Despite those childhood traumas, the great thing about Kieran was that he was open with me from the start about never feeling like he fitted in. Although he's tall and manly, I loved that vulnerable side to him. He wasn't afraid to show it and I kept thinking, He's more of a man than any of the others put together! Not only do we get on, we don't hide anything from each other either. Kieran even confessed that he was such a nervous kid that he wet the bed between the ages of 11 to 16. Bloody hell! For a bloke that's a big thing to reveal — especially to a girl he's just met and is trying to seduce!

Honestly, the first time Kieran showed me a picture of himself as a boy, I hardly recognised him. Instead of the gorgeous, chiselled man I'd fallen in love with he was this geeky kid with terrible acne and glasses — a real-life Adrian Mole. Talk about an ugly duckling blossoming into a swan! No girls ever fancied him at school, he admitted. To get them to date him he'd steal his mum's jewellery and give it to them as presents so they'd say 'yes', but they never did.

'Awww, well, you don't have to steal jewellery now,' I'd told him. 'You've got a job so you can just buy me diamonds!'

His track record with girls was one of the main reasons Kieran joined an indie band when he was at secondary school, and why he got seriously into bodybuilding. At college he studied sports science, and going to the gym and working out was another way of trying to be popular. The more groomed and muscular he looked, the more the girls took an interest in him. He told me that when he'd started working as a personal trainer he'd shag loads of his female clients. He had threesomes — the lot! And the worst thing was he didn't even need to be drunk to do it. Kieran, I was thinking when I heard this, I didn't know you had it in you! When a girlfriend suggested he try stripping for a living, he found himself striding out on stage in a club one evening and has never forgotten how amazing it felt to have the whole audience at his feet.

Now, you might be wondering why the alarm bells weren't ringing when Kieran told me all of this, but in fairness he could have said exactly the same about me. I'm not exactly a shrinking violet in the bedroom and I've had my fair share of adventures: I started out as a glamour model and my second husband was a transvestite, for God's sake! But it doesn't mean I can't settle down and be faithful to one person. And sure, Kieran loves the fact that I can glam up and be sexy, but he also knows that I'm a home-lover underneath. I reckoned that once he had made a commitment to me he'd think and act the same way.

Not once did I suspect there was anything between him and Jane. Not at first anyway. But after our March wedding I did notice that Jane wasn't just changing, she was under-going a major transformation. Months before, at the end of my relationship with Leo, she'd had her teeth done. I could tell she was self-conscious about her smile because she had these big gappy teeth at the front. You could have driven a bus between them! 'Have them polished and straightened like mine,' I persuaded her because she was always commenting on how she loved my teeth, and even she agreed she looked amazing afterwards.

And I took her to beautician Nilam Patel's spa in Milton Keynes so she could have HD brows. I'd done an eyebrow-shaping course with Nilam in 2012. I love

So in love! Our beautiful Willy Wonka wedding before Kieran broke my heart.

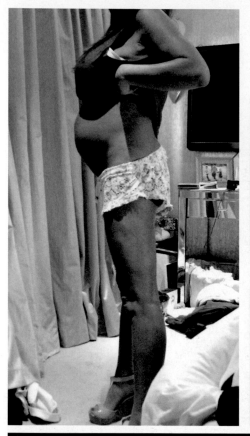

My pregnancy with Jett was so different from all the others.

Poultry in motion: Kieran's birthday bash with his latest bird.

Princess and Junior welcome a prickly new visitor to our home.

Right: Me and old friends Phil and Gary. I was soon to learn the true meaning of friendship.

At first Kieran was the perfect gentleman, but I was yet to discover his Jekyll and Hyde character.

All glammed up at the Grand Prix Ball with Kieran and my mates Neil and Becky.

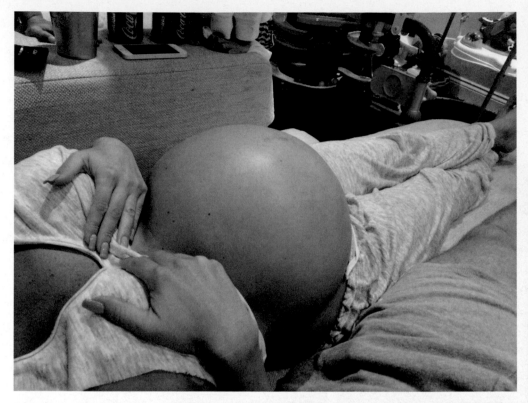

Almost ready to pop…
but first I had our
disastrous holiday in
France to get through.

Always time for
giggles with my
gorgeous Junior.

Harvey and Jett are the best of friends, but only when Jett doesn't annoy the man of the house!

The happy couple, or the calm before the storm?

Hubble bubble... Princess and Junior loved Jett from the minute they met.

New Bentley, new me! But even a spot of retail therapy couldn't make up for how Kieran devastated our family.

Princess cuddles one of our gorgeous lambs. So cute!

Love, love, love everything about my oldest horse Wallis.

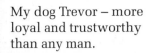
My dog Trevor – more loyal and trustworthy than any man.

Our animals are our family – and we love them so much!

Country air and riding were the best therapy in the aftermath of Kieran's affairs.

Jett snuggles into the best pillow in the house.

learning new skills, and to get the high definition look you have to perfect a combination of waxing, threading and tinting which, believe me, looks a lot easier to do than it is. I was so chuffed to read later that Nilam said I was one of her best, most attentive students. Words I never thought I'd hear. Two gold stars for Katie Price!

I even suggested to Jane that she try playing around with her hair and paid for her to have extensions put in a couple of times. I encouraged her: 'Go on, have it done like I do, it'll look so glam.' That wasn't because I actually wanted Jane to look like me, but I loved that she was enjoying feeling good about herself. That's what friends are for, isn't it?

When Derrick's fiftieth birthday rolled around I persuaded Jane to put on two sets of false eyelashes for that extra-sexy look and gave her one of my tight dresses to wear. It was a gorgeous white sparkly bandage dress. I kid you not, she looked like a different person. 'You're looking well good, Jane!' I encouraged her.

'Do I *really*?' She got all embarrassed as if she didn't truly believe it, which only made me want to dress her up more.

Let's be honest about it, I'd rather step out with someone who looks hot than with a frump. Some women don't want their friends to look good, but I'm not like that. I can always see how people can improve themselves, but in a supportive way. I would never have pushed Jane to change her appearance if she hadn't been into it herself.

What surprised me were the friends at Derrick's party who weren't pleased at all. Apparently when Jane arrived everyone thought she was me. 'Fucking hell, Kate, she's totally cloned into you,' one friend took me aside and whispered. Had I not been the person behind Jane's new look I might have been pissed off, but to me it resembled girlie dressing up, like I used to do with my friend Claire when we were at school. It wasn't as if Jane was doing all this behind my back. I was the one saying, 'Let's shock everyone, let's turn up at the party looking alike.' It was a laugh!

I think people thought Jane was changing so much because we spent loads of time together but that wasn't the case either. During the week I wouldn't speak to or see Jane at all, even though she'd moved to live close by. But whenever we were arranging a weekend with the kids I'd text her with a plan, usually on a Thursday. Several times I pointed out to Kieran that Jane never invited us to her house, and I did think that was strange. At first I put it down to her being a crap cook. She was renowned for it. Even Derrick joked that the only time he ever got fed properly was at mine when I'd cook up a Sunday roast. During the week he even resorted to eating at the local Harvester before he went home from work. I remember one Christmas buying her the book *Mary Berry Cooks*. Jane unwrapped the present but never took it home and I ended up using it, but I never understood why she couldn't have invited us round and ordered a takeaway.

Then Jane's son George let the cat out of the bag, which did make me curious. One weekend he stepped into my living room and asked, 'Mum, isn't the rug you've bought exactly like Kate's?' Another time he came right out with, 'Kate, Mum's done her curtains like yours . . .'

'NO! No, I haven't, don't be silly, George,' Jane instantly hushed him up. But on the very rare occasions I did see the inside of her house it was almost *identical* to mine: the same cream, taupe and silver tones, and similar light fittings only in a much cheaper version. Instead of having real Swarovski crystal chandeliers, hers were obviously fake. You can tell because the crystals don't sparkle.

It wasn't a huge issue for me that Jane stayed at my house, but when she started skipping down my stairs in the morning in tight shorts and make-up, I thought, What the fuck's going on? Before this we'd always slobbed out in T-shirts and trackie bottoms. I was quietly registering a real difference in her, and there was a pattern to it. One day I'd be moaning that I was getting fat and how badly I wanted to look nice for Kieran. I complained that I couldn't wait to give birth and be able to wear tight leggings and sexy shorts again . . . and surprise, surprise, the next week she'd arrive wearing exactly what we'd discussed. She'd become really flirtatious around Kieran too, lots of batting her eyelashes and giggling. One Sunday evening after we'd all said goodbye I brought it up with him, to see if he'd noticed.

'Don't you think Jane's lost a lot of weight?' I said casually. Kieran grunted. Typical! I was going to have to dig around some more.

'She's changed and I'm sure it's around you. I think she fancies you,' I went on. I was watching intently for Kieran's reaction but he raised his eyebrows and gave me that look that said, What are you like! I mentioned Jane a couple more times that evening but he brushed it aside and said, 'Get lost, Kate! She's old enough to be my mother!'

Hmmm ... so my man's head wasn't turned that easily. I should have given Kieran more credit, I decided. As usual, it was me being pregnant and paranoid.

*   *   *

By the beginning of the summer I was feeling like this was my worst pregnancy ever. I even went on *Daybreak* and was interviewed by Lorraine wearing a brightly coloured scarf draped around me because I couldn't bear the size I'd become. I wasn't used to putting on a whole four stone, let alone in the space of six months. If I could have gone out wearing a bag over my head, I would have been happy. Two bags would have been even better!

Halfway through June my ninth novel, *He's the One,* came out. I usually love doing publicity for my books but this time I had to haul myself to The Worx in Fulham for the photo-call. I reckoned it would be a great idea to dress Kieran as the Frog Prince and me as a pantomime princess head to toe in pink. I had this huge bustle attached to me, which neatly disguised my enormous bump. I can't deny dressing up was fun but now I can hardly bear to look at those pictures, remembering how fat and depressed I was at the time.

I was in a real panic too. Pete wanted to take Junior and Princess to Australia at the start of August for the whole month. That left me June to arrange a family holiday with them in July. By then we wouldn't be able to go anywhere we had to fly to because it would be too close to my due date, and with my low platelet count my pregnancy had become problematic. Instead, I was searching through brochures trying to book a last-minute break in France. I'd mentioned taking Derrick, Jane and their kids too, but the closer we got to going away the more I seemed to be having second thoughts.

Not long after my book launch we had a barbecue at the house and Jane turned up in the tiniest, tightest dress. She'd had her hair and make-up done and it looked like she'd lost even more weight. All of Kieran's mates, who are half her age, were hollering, 'Phoaar, look at you, Jane!' I don't know, maybe it's because I'm so open, but I was happily running with it, joining in and bigging Jane up.

'I know! Check Jane! Doesn't she look amazing for fifty?' I exclaimed.

But Jane didn't react as coyly as she normally did. She was flicking her hair and smiling. 'Do you think so? I don't even work out at the gym!' she told them.

Who are you trying to kid, Jane? I thought. I've known you for donkey's years. You've never had a six-pack like that before. There's no way it's just miraculously appeared.

'And I don't even have Botox,' she continued. *Yes, you fucking do, Jane!* I was yelling inside. *I've had Botox with you!*

Underneath, I felt furious, but I would never have embarrassed her in front of our guests by saying anything. I'm not like that. Besides, I was taken aback because I'd never had Jane down as someone who'd lie about cosmetic treatments. It really annoys me when people do that. All those Hollywood A-listers who've obviously had work done but claim it's all natural. It's ridiculous! But I stupidly let Jane thrive on the fact that she looked good.

She'd never mentioned a personal trainer to me but her abs were more toned than ever, and she'd even started to show her tummy. Suddenly Jane was turning up in crop tops. When I asked her about it, she told me she was on a diet of bubble gum and coffee.

'You know how you wear your hair in a ponytail?' she asked me one day when we were messing around. 'How do you get that boompf effect in the front? I'd love to do that with my hair.'

'I don't know, maybe it goes like that because I'm naturally curly. I guess I'm lucky I've got thick hair,' I replied through gritted teeth. What I really wanted to say was: 'Jane, you're far too old for a ponytail and it wouldn't even suit you. What the fuck are you on?' And then I loaned her my tongs for a whole week because she wanted to curl her ends like mine. I even showed her how to do it!

I wasn't jealous of Jane but I was starting to resent her. I hated that feeling because it's so unlike me. There I was, piling on the weight, and she was flouncing around flaunting her fit body. Whether it was to piss me off or not, I don't know, but every time I saw her it was as if she was announcing: 'I'm the one with the abs now, and you're the fat fucker!' I kept going back to Kieran and saying, 'She fancies you. It's as obvious as a fart in a car. Look how she is around you. Don't you sense it at all?'

'*No, I don't!*' he'd shoot back. One time I got him to admit that he thought Jane was fit for her age. I was watching his eyes to see if he looked guilty but he didn't flinch. He genuinely didn't seem bothered by her at all.

The worst thing was that usually Kieran and I never argued and Jane being around was starting to drive a wedge between us. Maybe I'm blowing everything out of proportion, I kept telling myself. Although I had this nagging doubt, it wasn't fair to keep whinging on to Kieran about Jane. It also crossed my mind that maybe she was having an affair behind Derrick's back and would tell me about it sooner or later. If ever we were out and I was texting someone, she'd always ask me if I was messaging guys behind Kieran's back. I could never work out why she was so obsessed with it, but maybe she was trying to tell me something. What a complete dick I felt when everything came out! I despise Jane for making me feel that shit.

As hard as it was, I kept my feelings to myself. Then, a week later, Kieran had an accident on the quad bike. I was heavily pregnant and on my way back from a publicity trip in Ireland where I'd been promoting my new perfume, Kissable. I wasn't in the best of moods as the launch hadn't been well co-ordinated and I like things done professionally. Just before I got on the plane I debated, Shall I turn my phone on? Surely nothing else bad can happen today!

It could. Kieran had texted saying he was in an ambulance and on his way to Worthing Hospital with a busted shoulder. Apparently, he'd taken Princess and Junior out on the quad bike and although he'd only been travelling at 5 m.p.h. they'd hit a tractor rut in the field at the back of our house. As the quad bike started to flip over, Kieran had enough time to get Princess on his back and protect her from the fall. Thankfully, Junior scrambled out and landed on his bum. But the weight of Princess and the quad bike on top of Kieran's shoulder had badly ripped the tendons. With his collarbone popped out and the adrenalin still pumping, he carried Princess all the way back to the house, calling the paramedics as he walked. That day he truly was my hero! And it turned out to be a serious injury, which eventually needed an operation to fix it. He'll have a three-inch scar for life and there's still a metal pin in his shoulder holding it together.

By the time we were due to leave for France I could hardly move either. I looked like such a frump and I was carrying so heavily in front that I had shooting pains up my back, which the doctor said were a symptom of sciatica. At first I thought that if we packed up my pink horse box then Jane might offer to drive or a least share the driving to France with me . . . but no. Apparently she'd hurt her arm too and Kieran was obviously in pain and out of action. 'Fuck it, I'll drive,' I told them, although I wasn't sure I'd be able to. The villa I'd booked was in Aix-en-Provence, not far from Marseille on the French Riviera. The journey this side of the Channel didn't bother me too much. It was the twelve-hour long-haul on the French side that I was dreading. Fortunately, Derrick offered to do a stint behind the wheel. Even so, driving my horse box is a far cry from manoeuvring a car – you've really got to give it some welly!

As usual, I kept my anxiety to myself but the night before, while I was loading up the trailer barely able to bend over, I could feel the anger welling up inside me. There were moments when Kieran and Jane were nowhere to be seen. Hang on! I was thinking. Since when is it okay to leave a pregnant woman shifting cases and bags into a horse box? Fuck the lot of you!

The next morning I was even more taken aback when Jane insisted on lounging on the leather sofas in the back of the trailer where Kieran was resting. When

Derrick arrived, he kindly offered to sit up in the front with me. This is bonkers, I thought as we pulled out of the driveway. All the time, I could hear Jane and Kieran giggling in the back. I shoved the trailer hard into gear. *God*, this was going to be a long trip.

One big plus was that when we finally did arrive at the villa it was just what I had wanted. If I'm honest I prefer ultra-modern apartments and this was one of those olde-worlde French gîtes but it was the right size and the pool looked stunning in the morning sunshine. After leaving the UK feeling so uptight I'd made a conscious decision that I was going to relax, no matter what, and recharge my batteries before baby number four came along. If only . . .

On the morning after we arrived I was making tea when I watched Jane prance out of her room in full make-up and wearing a pair of the skimpiest Hello Kitty shorts with a matching vest top. My jaw almost hit the floor. 'Jane! Look at you in your Hello Kitty shorts, all done up . . .' I exclaimed, but underneath I was livid. *WTF? You so fancy Kieran. It's so fucking obvious.*

Later, I learned that Derrick also suspected that something was going on between them. Apparently she'd shown him flirty texts from Kieran, no doubt in an effort to cover her own back. The sad thing was that no one had thought to tell me. I felt like I was going mad. All these scenarios were running through my head and I had no proof of anything. It was like the worst form of torture.

Because Jane's interest in Kieran was becoming so blatant I couldn't get into the swing of the holiday at all. My antennae were up constantly, looking for signals that something was going on – a knowing glance or a secret touch. As if it couldn't get any worse, that same day Jane brought out a glittery bikini and began sashaying around the poolside in it. Trust me, I've been away with her on enough occasions and she normally needs peeling from her sunlounger by the end of the day. But there she was, strutting her stuff. The worst thing was that the bikini didn't even suit her. It was the sort of thing I would wear. Mmmm . . . you've thought out your outfits for this trip, haven't you, Jane? I realised.

By day two I was feeling like an out and out gooseberry. Derrick was off doing his own thing. My own husband was frolicking around in the water with Jane and the kids while I was stuck poolside barely able to see over my baby bump. 'Don't mind me, guys. I'm only Kieran's wife and the person paying for your holiday!' I was tempted to call out sarcastically.

'I'm not going away with Jane again,' I told Kieran once we were on our own. 'She fucking fancies you.' Again, he gave me a look as if to say, 'Don't start, Kate!'

'I don't fancy her at all,' he kept promising me, but somehow I didn't believe him.

That evening, I showered Kieran. He couldn't do it himself because of his shoulder, but just as I'd finished drying him I felt a wetness around my shorts. 'I'm leaking water,' I exclaimed, but everybody said it was from being in the swimming pool. After I put the kids to bed, the water began running down my legs and immediately I suspected something wasn't right. 'Your waters have definitely broken,' Jane said. But it was far too early! After phoning Dr Gibb, my obstetrician in England, we decided it was better to be safe than sorry. I would admit myself to hospital in France.

Because we had Harvey with us, Kieran had already worked out where the hospital was from his trips into town with Derrick to buy food. With Harvey we never know if we might need emergency medical help, but I hadn't ever considered that the help might be for me! Derrick drove Kieran and me there at around midnight. The place was like something out of a horror film. As the glass doors slid open all I could see were bright striplights and empty white corridors. Nobody in sight for yards and then from nowhere two doctors appeared, saying, 'Can we help you?'

Once I was hooked up to monitors, the hospital called Dr Gibb again. Fortunately his wife is French and she was able to translate. They were keeping me in overnight, she told me. Kieran stayed with me that night in a room with two single beds. No one came in to check on us and in the morning I was handed a tray with a bowl of hot water to drink. Kieran was offered nothing. Then I was scanned and moved to another room where I really started to panic.

I hate enclosed spaces and I was stuck in this box-room in a French hospital in the middle of a strange town, with a single bed, no WiFi, and a small TV. The worst part was that no one spoke to me at all, or if they did it was in French. Other than being given food occasionally, I was mostly left on my own. I couldn't even ask to be talked through the procedure because I wouldn't understand the answer. Waves of fear kept washing over me. If I were to give birth now, would my baby survive? He would be two months premature, and I was so confused about Kieran that I wasn't even sure if the father would give a shit. What a disaster!

On arrival, I'd been given antenatal steroids to delay my contractions. I was being monitored, and after the first dose the doctor had pointed at the bed, then at me, and wagged his finger from side to side. I worked out that this meant I wasn't allowed to walk around or to get out of bed because Jane had been right: my waters were breaking.

After a very disturbed second night's sleep on my own in my box-like room, I woke praying Kieran would be by my side. Unsurprisingly, he was nowhere to be seen. Perhaps he doesn't understand how genuinely petrified I am, I thought. But this is his baby too! Why this lack of interest? Why hasn't he visited? Eventually, when he did turn up, he was super-moody, which put my back up no end. 'What's wrong with you?' I asked. He complained that his shoulder wasn't improving but had become infected and so I sat there in bed, ringing the doctor's back in England to book him an appointment to have it checked out. And I arranged for him to have it seen in the French hospital as well. Maybe I was being unfair, he was clearly in pain. Was I expecting too much from him? But he could still make it to the hospital to check on me and our baby, surely?

As the days went by Kieran's no-shows became more frequent. I was permanently on tenterhooks looking out for him, hoping he'd appear with the kids, but it didn't happen. I kept texting him, his mum, my manager, and my mum, saying, *I'm okay, but Kieran's not here. Why hasn't he come?* If he did turn up, it was in the evening alongside Derrick or Jane. Her outfits were getting more ridiculous by the day. Honestly, she looked like a hooker! They would bring Harvey, Princess, Junior, George and Ruby with them, but it was getting to the point where I didn't want Jane or her family anywhere near me.

I longed to spend time alone with Kieran and the kids so it was a relief when the doctor finally agreed to discharge me even if it was only for an hour or so at a time. I say a relief, but when I got back to the villa it felt like Jane had taken over. One time I went back and I was sunbathing by the pool and Jane and all the kids were playing at the other end. Kieran was splashing about with them. The noise of them laughing and shouting to one another made me feel demented. Miraculously, Kieran's shoulder didn't look like it was causing him too many problems either! Something was going on, but what? I'm here for one hour, I thought. Why the fuck isn't Kieran up this end of the pool with me? Why isn't Jane talking to me? Have I done something wrong here?

I'm paying for everyone to stay in this villa. I'm pregnant. I've had a major health scare and I could give birth at any moment. Kieran's not behaving like my husband or the father of this child. He's behaving like a mate who's bagged a free holiday!

Like any expectant mum, I was quietly shitting myself. I might have already given birth to three children but nothing prepares you for the anxiety of not carrying a baby full-term. In between feeling isolated and alone I kept rubbing my belly saying, 'Please, please, hang in there, little one. I'm doing my best.'

It's weird, but in France I couldn't stop imagining what the experience would have been like if Pete had been there. He wouldn't have left my side. He would constantly have been there, checking to see if I was okay or if I needed anything. Kieran didn't even ask! What confused me the most was that he seemed so different from the person I'd married. Only a few months before he couldn't do enough for me. He was tripping over himself to buy me presents and make me happy then.

Now, it was looking increasingly likely that we were going to have to stay in France. I was under strict instructions not to travel or put any stress on my body. The problem was, Princess and Junior needed to be back in the UK to fly to Oz with Pete. Being abroad with Harvey was becoming stressful for me too. I was in hospital much of the time and when I was discharged I had none of the energy necessary to keep him happy and entertained.

With time running out on our villa rental too, I arranged another property for us only five minutes from the hospital. Lizzie, Harvey's nanny, flew out to take care of him and I also arranged for my brother Danny to fly to Marseille to pick up Princess and Junior and take them home. I deliberately arranged for the villa to be close by so there'd be no excuse for Kieran not to visit me. I even sorted out a hire-car so Lizzie could bring him there. Not that Kieran was replying to any of my texts.

Grudgingly, I was forced into texting Jane to ask whether he wanted to come to the ward with a DVD and a takeaway. Anything to relieve the boredom! I didn't know at the time but I do now that Jane never passed any of those messages on. According to Kieran, she was also secretly telling him that I wanted to be on my own and that I'd even told her Kieran needed to save his strength for when the baby arrived. What utter bullshit! I couldn't have wanted him there more.

Even my manager was texting Kieran, pleading with him to see me, *She's asking for you, Kieran. Please get in touch with Kate. She needs you.* And both our mums were on his case. But he was lying even to them, claiming to be down and depressed because of his shoulder. I wasn't so sure about that. In desperation, I was texting girlfriends to ask their advice on whether something was going on with Kieran and Jane. *Kate, you're hormonal*, they answered. *He's so into you!* Eventually, when Kieran did surface, I arranged for another bed to be put next to mine.

'You can stay here,' I told him. 'If you want pillows, I'll get you pillows. I need you here. I'm your wife.' Again, Kieran said nothing. 'This is crazy. This is our child and I'm doing this on my own. What the fuck is wrong with you?' I went on, but it had no effect whatsoever. He seemed far away in another world.

What I also couldn't understand was why Jane was choosing to stay on in France. Junior and Princess had gone and Harvey, Lizzie and Kieran were at the villa. There was no reason for her to be there with George and Ruby and it wasn't as if there was much space in the new place, so she had to share a room with her kids. Derrick was about to return to work in the UK.

'I suppose I'm leaving my wife here with your husband to play Happy Families,' he whispered to me before he left.

'I know what you mean, Derrick,' I replied.

'Seems like we've opened a whole can of worms here!' he snorted.

No sooner had we started talking than Kieran walked over. 'What are you two whispering about?' he asked, cockily.

'Nothing,' I quickly lied, but I knew Derrick was on to something.

CHAPTER 5

HELLO JETT

The fun of our French holiday had really worn off for me. During our stay I'd seen more of the inside of a French hospital than of our villa or the pool and I longed to be back in the UK. Although the hospital was bursting with bright, shiny equipment I was kept in the dark about everything. Language barrier, my arse! I'm sure half the time the doctors were talking in French deliberately so that they didn't have to pay any attention to me. I was desperate for information about the delivery of my baby.

Work was completely on hold too. I'd already had to cancel a scheduled trip to Australia to launch my shoe range which I was really pissed off about, and even more so because I was stuck in this tiny box room, feeling like I couldn't escape. And I was hooked up to a drip and a heart monitor with my legs permanently raised, so even if I'd wanted to leave, I couldn't. One morning, after a barrage of texts from me, Kieran made it in, but he spent more time playing around on his mobile phone than he did chatting. 'What shall we do? Shall we watch a film?' I suggested, feigning enthusiasm to make him feel better.

'Come on, sit on the bed with me,' I gestured, but there was a battle raging inside me. It felt so wrong that I was having to grovel just to get him to acknowledge me. I really wanted him to stay. In fact, I dreaded him being back at the villa with Jane, but I was also asking myself why I was having to entertain my own husband? I was the one in hospital!

He was eerily quiet and moody. 'Why have you changed?' I asked. 'Why aren't you here for me?' Tears rolled down my face. Kieran sat with his head in his hands. I could see that he was crying too but he couldn't even look at me. It sounds odd but, at that moment, I felt like such a burden to him. It was as if me being in hospital, having his baby, was an imposition, though I had no idea why that should be.

In the end, he said that he preferred to be back at the villa. My heart sank. Here we go again, I thought. I'm going to be bringing up another child on my own. But only minutes after Kieran had left a very strict-looking nurse marched into my room. 'You have five minutes. You shower. Then we do emergency C-section,' she announced.

WTF? My heart almost leaped out of my chest. I wasn't

expecting that at all! I furiously texted Kieran: *You've got to come back. They're going to deliver the baby!*

His behaviour towards me had been so dismissive that by now I was terrified he wouldn't reappear, but he did and I couldn't have been happier to see him. The thought of having our child alone filled me with horror. I remember how scared I'd been when Harvey arrived. He'd been ten days late and I'd given up any hope of Dwight being there at the birth so my family and birthing partner Sally stayed with me instead; then I'd left it too late for an epidural and relied entirely on gas and air. Fucking hell, it hurt! The idea of doing that again makes me shudder but I'm happy that I managed a natural birth with Harvey. What would have made a real difference was if someone had held my hand, told me how strong I was and how proud they were of me for having their baby. It just didn't happen then, and it didn't happen this time either.

As soon as I caught sight of Kieran the nurses began wheeling me up the corridor and into the operating theatre. 'You're having the baby now?' He looked surprised and continued to play around on his mobile as he spoke to me.

'Yes!' I barked at him. 'And you are too!'

But by now the doctor was signalling that Kieran would not be allowed in the room. He pointed straight at him.

'You, no!' he said sharply. Charming guy, our doctor . . .

'Why not?' I shouted. 'He's my husband!' No one would give me a straight answer. They worked around me as if I wasn't there. I wanted to click my fingers in front of the doctor's face and say, 'Excuse me. I'm the woman having the baby!' They made me feel so powerless.

The worst thing was that Kieran didn't even cuddle me before I was taken away. He stood there like a useless lump, then bent down to give me a quick kiss. I'm not sure what I was expecting but something . . . anything . . . would have been nice. 'I love you and you're having our baby.' That would have been a good start, but no . . . absolutely nothing.

Tears streamed down my face. As the doors started to close, I was looking back at him. 'I love you, Kieran! I love you!' I was screaming. Any passers-by must have wondered if they'd been transported to the Planet Lunatic, but I didn't give a shit.

Once I was laid out on the operating table I could hear conversation around me, none of which I understood. 'I'm needle-phobic,' I was crying. 'I really need my husband here!' But again, I was completely ignored. Panic rose in me. I could barely breathe. My whole body started flinching at the thought of them sticking a needle into me, but the theatre staff positioned me sitting upright and bent me forwards. The anaesthetist carried on regardless even though I was bawling my eyes out.

I can still feel every millimetre of that injection. 'Don't move!' one of the nurses barked as I began to writhe with discomfort. When I looked up, the anaesthetist had begun chatting on his phone and I knew that I was about to be cut. I was tipped back and a cloth screen placed across my chest to stop me from looking down. Although an epidural had been administered, I knew it hadn't taken effect.

'Please, please, don't do anything yet. I'm not numb enough!' I kept crying and jiggling my legs up and down so it was obvious I wasn't. 'Shhhhh, shhhhh!' A nurse told me off like I was in a library disturbing other readers, not in a hospital having a baby!

As soon as the knife started to cut me, I felt this immense pressure in my lower body. My hands and shoulders started shaking uncontrollably. At first I could sense this slight burning sensation in the pit of my belly but rapidly it crept through me as if I was on fire. I can barely think about it now, it makes me so upset. There was worse to come. I felt every movement as that doctor sought around inside me before finally bringing out Jett.

'We stitch. Then you rest,' a nurse told me, without even asking if I was okay.

'But where's my baby?' I was screaming. 'I really need to see my baby!'

'What about the baby?' I appealed to the doctor, but he glanced over with a slightly confused expression on his face. Jett had been held to my face briefly then immediately taken from the operating theatre to God knows where. 'Where's my husband? I need to see my husband!' I carried on, but no one went to fetch Kieran either.

He eventually appeared after I was taken to the recovery room, but I was there for hours, alone and waiting for him. For someone whose first child had just been born, the atmosphere between us couldn't have been more awkward. 'Did you see him?' Kieran asked calmly, showing me a picture of Jett that he'd taken on his phone. That's all you can say? I thought. There was no, 'Well done . . . I love you . . . You're so brave.' One fat zilch.

Kieran has since told me that meeting Jett for the first time had felt like being on a supermarket conveyor belt. Jett was wheeled out on a trolley to a room filled with other expectant dads. 'This is yours,' Kieran was told, like he was at the deli-counter. He'd followed the doctors upstairs with Jett to the special-care baby unit but had felt very removed from and disorientated by the experience, not least because he'd been in a completely separate room from me when Jett was born. But I had no idea about how he felt at the time.

Instead, I was frantically questioning in my head, Is this a dream? Am I actually in the worst nightmare ever? What have I done wrong? Do I look *that* awful? All the post-labour hormones were coursing through my body and I was in complete agony too. 'Please, please, can I have more painkillers?' I begged the doctor, but apparently I'd already had my quota. 'Please, please, can I see my baby?' I begged again. 'No. Not allowed. French rules,' he replied.

All I wanted to do was shake him and shout, 'Fuck you and your French rules,' but instead I burst out crying and begged him even more. I tried to explain that I had suffered from post-natal depression with my second child and it was important for me to see the baby straight away and acknowledge that I'd actually given birth. For me, those initial moments of bonding are the most precious time a mother can spend with her newborn and I'd been denied them.

For more than three hours I waited in my room without Kieran or Jett. The stress building up inside me had reached fever pitch. By now, I didn't give a fuck what the staff thought of me. 'Hello! Can anyone take me to see my baby?' I was calling out sarcastically at the top of my voice.

'Tomorrow,' a nurse replied.

'Tomorrow! No way,' I yelled back. 'I need to see him RIGHT NOW.'

After some discussion the doctor agreed that Jett could be brought down for me to hold briefly. 'Thank you!' I said, feeling totally exasperated. My first proper meeting with my son turned out to be for thirty seconds tops. He was a tiny 5lb 2oz .The nurse placed him in my arms.

'Hello, Jett,' I said softly, but as I went to kiss him she was already lifting him and taking him back to the incubator upstairs.

'I'm going to the villa,' Kieran announced not long afterwards. Great timing! I thought. My baby's back upstairs,

I can't even touch him, and now my husband's about to fuck off too. I pleaded with him to stay but it was clear his mind was made up.

Physically I felt a complete wreck and mentally could feel myself retreating into my shell. It wasn't only the strangeness of a French hospital or the rudeness of the medical staff that was distressing me. The whole experience felt so different from any other birth I'd gone through. I couldn't understand how this had happened. When I'd met Kieran, and during the first few months of our marriage, he'd been so into me. Now he was cold, unfeeling and unreachable – a real-life Jekyll and Hyde. I just wanted to slap him and say, 'Why the hell are you doing this?'

The minute Kieran left I texted my hairdresser Mikey. He was already on a flight from London. Because I'd only expected to be in France for the duration of our holiday, I'd taken my hair extensions out beforehand, to let my hair rest for a week. Now, bizarrely, other than Jett, the next most important thing to me was that I looked good so Mikey was bringing a set over. When I think about it now, I think, How fucked up is that? I've just given birth and I'm worried about what my hair looks like. *Please!*

I hadn't told Mikey over the phone that I'd had Jett, but when he came to the hospital first thing the next morning I was in a terrible state. The doctors hadn't let me go upstairs to see Jett again. I'd had no update on how he was and there was no sign of Kieran either. I'd had a catheter fitted after Jett's birth so I could wee properly and it still hadn't been taken out. It felt so uncomfortable and the burning sensation in my belly was still there. I looked gross, but I felt worse for not having anyone close around me.

Stressing about my hair wasn't normal but I couldn't help myself. Every time I thought about where Kieran was I kept picturing Jane at my villa in her glittery bikini in the pool, and my husband playing Happy Families with her kids, and all that fear and insecurity gripped me again.

As Mikey got to work putting in my extensions, my stomach felt more and more knotted up. Anyone looking on would have thought we were crazy. Less than twenty-four hours after going into labour I was perched on the end of my hospital bed while Mikey carefully braided each extension into my hair. 'I just want Kieran to fancy me again. Is that crazy?' I kept asking him. The only reason I could think of for my husband losing interest in me was that pregnancy had made me unattractive. I'd even begged him to tell me if that was the problem. I asked if that was why he fancied Jane. 'Kate, you're creating shit for nothing,' had been his response.

Although we'd discussed names for the baby in the hospital, in the end I left Kieran to name Jett. I believed my husband didn't love me any more but I was still desperately trying everything I could to make him bond with me and his newly born son. I thought that if he had the responsibility of naming our baby it would make him feel closer to us. Now the most difficult thing for me to understand about all this is how I could have put my faith in someone who turned out to be so devious and calculating.

Eventually, Mikey was the person to wheel me into the lift and upstairs to see Jett. As we approached my heart melted at the sight of my baby, who was hooked up to several machines through a series of tubes. He looked so tiny. I could only place my fingers on the glass and imagine holding him. It was so hard. All I wanted to do was cuddle him. 'I love you, Jett,' I told him, while inside I felt this unbearable sadness. Your dad should be here with me, I kept thinking. Apparently Kieran had been to see Jett and had spent time with him that morning, but no one had bothered to tell me and he didn't come to see me until that evening.

In the meantime, doctors said they were observing Jett closely. He was breathing with the help of a ventilator, but it would be another forty-eight hours before his lungs were strong enough for him to try and breathe on his own.

Not only that: as soon as he came off the ventilator we learned he was suffering from sleep apnoea, which was completely terrifying. If the condition didn't improve we wouldn't be able to leave the hospital. Basically it meant that for ten to twenty seconds at a time while Jett was asleep, he'd stop breathing. There'd be total silence. Then suddenly he'd gulp in air. Listening to the machine beeping every time it happened was absolutely awful.

I imagined his tiny lungs fighting for oxygen. Apparently, during this interruption in a baby's breathing pattern, their heart rate drops to a dangerously low level.

The French hospital staff had been appalling in their treatment of me, but I could see they were absolutely brilliant with babies. To give them their due, Jett was being very well taken care of. In fact, every single baby in the neonatal ward had the full attention of all the staff. Even so, there's nothing like being in your own country, with your own doctor, for that extra reassurance that everything is going to be okay.

What ramped up my anxiety even more was that not long after Jett was born we discovered that some idiot had set up a fake Twitter account in his name. I didn't read what was written, but Kieran did and had asked me not to look at it. Apparently, some of the messages were disgusting. He knew I'd be devastated by them, especially as Jett wasn't yet out of the woods and I was with him 24/7 making sure he was looked after. The troll had even attacked Harvey too. You have to wonder what kind of sick people there are out there. In the past, trolls have even set up websites dedicated to Harvey and posted horrific material on them, about me and his disability. I've always said, 'Think what you like about me. I'm big and ugly enough to deal with it.' But a defenceless child and my disabled son? *Get a life!* Fortunately, Kieran managed to have the account suspended.

Finally, a week after Jett was born I was discharged

back to the villa. Although I was still spending much of the day and evening at the hospital, it felt like heaven to be out of that prison. The day before, Jane had announced she was going to go home and I thought, Thank God! I still couldn't understand why she was hanging around. In fact I'd asked Kieran to tell her to piss off but he'd refused. 'I can't! She's your friend, not mine!' he argued. With her gone, though, at least Kieran could give his full attention to me and the baby.

When I think about it now, it does my head in, but Jane left for the airport wearing the tiniest see-through dress. She might as well not have worn anything. 'You have to laugh, but who goes to an airport dressed like that?' I commented to Kieran. She'd even had the nerve to visit me every day since Jett's birth. She brought me Marmite sandwiches, when I was the one paying for the food!

I remember the first time she came to the hospital clearly. Jett was still upstairs in the incubator, and I was with him when she arrived. I was polite, but felt confused about her coming to see me then. She was still my friend but I was all over the place, thinking our relationship had changed. She arrived with George and Ruby but I really didn't want her kids there either. As it turned out they saw Jett before his own brothers and sister and that still preys on my mind. It's not how I wanted things to be. I watched Jane as she placed her hand on the glass.

'Oh, he's gorgeous, Kate,' she told me, and the tears

started to roll down her cheeks. For a moment, I felt close to her. I genuinely thought she was pleased for me and touched by the sight of Jett, tiny and helpless and hooked up to all those tubes. Despite everything being touch and go, he'd been delivered safely. I wanted her to be happy for me and Kieran. Wouldn't a true friend be happy for us? Now I reckon those weren't tears of happiness. They were 'What the fuck have I done?' tears. One hundred per cent, tears of guilt.

*   *   *

After Jane and her kids left, Kieran was coming in to help bathe Jett and we did alternate feeds. The hospital's routine was to feed the babies every few hours. Once Kieran had gone, I was doing Jett's 11 p.m. feed and staying with him until around 1 a.m. Then the nurses took over and fed him throughout the night while I went home and caught up on some sleep.

Although it was nice to have Kieran finally showing some attention, I was still puzzled when I watched him with our son. Kieran is naturally a very quiet guy but most new fathers would have said something like, 'Look, Kate, it's our baby!' or had that glint in their eye that says, 'We did this together.' Something was missing. Here was our little family. We needed Kieran, but although he was there for Jett it didn't feel like we were a strong unit at all. It felt like we were breaking up. Everything inside me wanted to stop that happening but I simply couldn't change it.

'When we get home, I don't want Jane coming up to the house. In fact, I don't care if I don't see her again,' I told Kieran.

I didn't really want to see anyone. Part of the reason my post-natal depression was so bad with Junior was because in the first few weeks of being home with him, Pete's parents ended up moving into our house. It was too much, too soon. Not only did I feel obliged to entertain them, but I also found the sight of other people picking up Junior and cuddling him difficult. I knew I wasn't coping and having them there felt like a constant reminder of how badly I was failing. I know I sound like a real misery guts. Normally it's lovely to have people around you who love you and your baby, but with depression you're not thinking rationally at all.

When Princess came along, the one thing I did differently was to insist that it was just us as a close family unit for the first few weeks, so I could bond with her and feel more secure in our relationship before anyone else stepped in. In the end, I don't remember doing much work-wise either for quite a few months. I'm such a workaholic that it felt very weird, but I have some great memories of that time. How blessed I was to be able to say, 'That's it. I'm not working for a few months. I'm just going to spend time with my baby.' I know so many women don't have that option.

* * *

It took six exhausting weeks of doctors monitoring Jett's sleep apnoea before we could finally bring him home. During that time we bought his carrycot and buggy in France and had to have his birth registered and passport issued. Although we were doing it together, all the time Kieran seemed really offhand. His reserved behaviour made me feel so unattractive, I went clothes shopping just to try and feel normal again. In the end, we had to travel home by private jet with a doctor on board because Jett couldn't be transported on a domestic flight.

After all we'd been through, I just wanted to get back into the swing of things. To be fair, I'd spent quality time with Jett in France even though he'd been in the neonatal unit for much of it. But at the beginning of September we could be a family again in our own home. I had a housekeeper to help me keep on top of things there. I felt it was important for Kieran to keep working too, because that's what he wanted, but for the first few weeks anyway we did share Jett's night-time feeds. By one month after his birth he had doubled in size to ten pounds, which was brilliant. He was waking twice in the night and Kieran offered to do the first feed while I took care of the second. I'm not sure whether it was down to his poor breathing as a newborn, but OMG, that baby could snore! At first I thought it was Kieran. It sounded like a proper man's snore. But whenever I woke the noise led me next to the bed where Jett's Moses basket stood. Bloody hell!

Within weeks of arriving back in England it felt like my relationship with Kieran was improving. It sounds harsh, but I'd totally put my foot down about not seeing Jane and sensed that Kieran seemed more connected to me and Jett as a result. The children were fantastic with the new arrival too.

I'd been disappointed that when Junior and Princess returned from Australia we were still in France. I'd been nervous too about how they were going to react to having another baby in the house. Typical me! Stressing out for nothing. As soon as they got back from school Junior burst through the front door and was all over Jett. Princess, who I'd been the most worried about because she was my last-born, loved her new brother from day one. If Jett cried she copied me and picked him up and jiggled him over her shoulder to pacify him. So sweet! She was actually very gentle with him, not in any way jealous or moody – a huge weight off my mind.

Another was that my insurance company were brilliant about covering all hospital bills for our extended stay in France. I still had to fork out for the villa but hospital bills can seriously rack up if you're a foreigner and a few pounds spent on proper insurance can really make all the difference. I read a case recently where a British couple had their son eleven weeks early while on holiday in Manhattan. The hospital wouldn't allow them to fly the baby home and they were potentially faced with a bill for £85,000. For whatever reason, the hospital wouldn't accept their insurance cover, but I understand they went back on that decision in the end. My insurance company dealt with the French hospital directly and refunded us in total and without question. I cannot fault them. They made our very traumatic stay in France that bit easier. Thank you!

CHAPTER 6

IT'S A JUNGLE OUT THERE

By October life had definitely improved so I decided I was going to have a girlie weekend to celebrate my birthday. No, I haven't quite managed to wangle two birthdays a year like the Queen, but for my real birthday back in May I'd done very little. I was huge then and I'd been so ill. It was my friend Louisa who suggested a weekend away in Monaco that autumn to make up for it.

I love Louisa, who is definitely one of my posher friends! Real Chelsea set. It's funny because she comes from a completely different background from mine (her parents actually live in Monaco!) but we clicked the first time we met. I'd been working out at Sol Gilbert's gym in Hove while I was dating Leo and staying with Jane. Louisa and I got chatting during our breaks. We instantaneously bonded over our love of horses and exchanged numbers. We've been friends ever since. Imagine the sitcom *Birds of a Feather*. If I'm like Sharon or Tracey, Louisa is a younger, glammer version of Dorien. She's so funny.

It sounds strange, but my instinct was to invite Jane too. Despite everything that had gone on in France she was still one of my closest friends, but for obvious reasons I was hesitant. Since we'd brought Jett home, my friendship with her had cooled. We hadn't fallen out or anything. In fact, I'd come to the conclusion that while heavily pregnant I'd perhaps been oversensitive. Now things had calmed down a little, I still wanted to spend time with Jane. When it comes to friends I'm a very loyal person. But I know I put trust in people when I probably shouldn't, and I was apprehensive about how Jane would make me feel. Would all those fears about her and Kieran come to the surface again? It didn't take long to find out . . .

I regretted asking her along as soon as we met at Gatwick to catch our flight. Not long after we'd joined the luggage queue she came out with, 'You've put on a bit of weight, Kate. You're not looking as thin as you used to.'

'Oh my God, Jane! You can't say that to Kate,' Louisa gasped before I even had a chance to open my mouth. 'She's not long had a baby!'

Here we go again, I thought, but I didn't rise to it. I forced a smile and carried on through the security gate.

Rather than stay at Louisa's parents' we booked into a

hotel and shared a room. After my nightmare summer it actually felt good to be away with the girls and finally letting my hair down. I was confident too that Kieran would be fine looking after Jett. Lizzie was on hand to help with Harvey, and Junior and Princess were with Pete. Wooohooo! A weekend of complete freedom.

That evening we spent ages getting ready. Trust me, you can't hurry that kind of operation. After two months of sleepless nights with Jett I had so many bags under my eyes I needed matching shoes! You gotta love concealer . . . Not long after I stepped out of the shower I could hear my phone ringing and suspected it was Kieran checking in. 'Aren't you going to answer it?' Jane shouted through. 'It's probably Kieran, but we've got the restaurant booked and I'm nowhere near ready. I'll ring him later,' I yelled back. But when I looked, Jane already had my phone in her hand.

'How about I talk to him and tell him you're busy?' she suggested.

'Oh, sure,' I agreed, feeling a bit flustered.

I must have felt reasonably confident by then that nothing was going on between them because I don't remember thinking, Why the hell would Jane want to talk to him? Stupid me for believing she wanted to help! Whether she and Kieran were in touch that weekend independently of me I don't know, but Louisa made me stop and think when she commented that Jane had begun acting like my shadow. I dismissed it at the time, but a few things did stick in my mind.

First of all she kept asking me what make-up I was using and then taking a note of all the brands I had in my toilet bag, which was weird. And to be completely blunt, Jane's fanny stuck in my mind too. Not that I made a habit of looking, but you know what girls are like when they're together. I'd always noticed that lady topiary had never been high on Jane's list of priorities. I make no secret about being bald as a badger down there and I'd always quietly baulked at Jane's bush. I'm not even joking, it was a proper growler. But by the time we got to Monaco she'd had everything waxed off.

'When did you have that done, Jane?' I asked as we were getting dressed. 'Oh, I've had it like that for ages,' she replied casually. I thought, No, you haven't, Jane.

After we'd eaten in this lovely restaurant we hit a club. Okay, guilty as charged. It was my first night out after Jett's birth and I definitely had a few too many. That's the awful thing about not drinking while you're pregnant. When you do have a few, you've turned into such a cheap date it's not even funny. Besides: music, dancing, vodka and me in the same room? A lethal combination!

I don't remember much, but I do remember Jane saying,

'How do you do it, Kate? How come all the men look at you?' I hadn't actually noticed. I was far too shit-faced and enjoying the atmosphere too much to even care. 'You could have anyone in this room if you wanted,' she continued.

'So could you, Jane! It's not just me they're looking at,' I laughed, playing it down to make her feel better about herself.

As it happened, I got so drunk that this turned out to be our only night out on the tiles in Monaco. Jesus, did I suffer the next morning . . . I had a thumping headache and could barely lift a toe out of bed. As I was lying there, Jane brought up the subject of France and how the atmosphere had been bad between us there. 'Yeah, it was odd, Jane,' I agreed. 'But I was pregnant. I was stressed. Don't worry about it. Let's just get back to normal now.'

When we eventually stepped out to eat in the early evening I still felt like I was about to throw up. What would I do without my large pair of designer shades?

*   *   *

As soon as I got back from Monaco I had my autobiography *Love, Lipstick and Lies* to launch. So much had happened in 2013 that it seemed like ages ago that I was writing all about my relationship with Leo and my disastrous marriage to Alex Reid. The book launch was on 22 October, but if the press thought that giving birth to a fourth child would end my appetite for show-stopping outfits they were dead wrong. Plus I hadn't been photographed at all throughout the summer, so it was time to make up for that! You know me, I always want to give people something to talk about. So I had a giant red lipstick to pose next to . . . and my outfit? I loved, loved, loved my outfit. They say everybody's got a book in them . . . well, I had a book on me – around fifty copies actually! My skin-tight cat suit was plastered head to toe with images of the cover of *Love, Lipstick and Lies*, complete with plunging neckline and dusted over with silver sequins. Because I hadn't lost all of my baby weight I neatly covered my belly with a blinged-up pink feather boa, and of course I couldn't forget a tiara on top.

Later, I went on a nationwide book tour and I was so thrilled by the reception I received. I've been writing autobiographies since 2004 and it's always nerve-wracking releasing another and opening up your life to the world. I've always had a policy of being honest, trying not to cover over the cracks and pretend I'm something I'm not. I'm human and flawed just like everybody else, and I think my fans identify with that. I certainly get queues of people at my book signings who tell that me they understand the emotional roller coaster I've been on – although, to be fair, the cross-dressing husband was probably a step too far . . . even for me! But they can see that I've picked myself up, got on with life and always tried to turn a bad situation around. And I was doubly thrilled that *Love, Lipstick and Lies* went straight into the top ten bestsellers list.

Two weeks after the launch Jett was well enough for me finally to do a long-haul flight to Australia. Because we'd been in France far longer than I'd expected, the launch of my shoe range had had to be rescheduled.

Back in July, I'd been due to fly to Sydney for one week but flights were strictly off the menu by then. I hate cancelling anything to do with work and it's really unlike me to do so because I don't want to let anyone down. But I'd been forced to put the health of my baby and myself first.

The shoe range idea had come about after I'd been approached in 2012 to sign an exclusive deal with Sistar Shoes to work on a couture collection for them. As soon as I heard about the designers, sisters Connie Gerakis and Samantha Dionisiou, who run the company, I was up for the challenge. Although their business had only been going for a year they'd already designed for celebrities like Paris Hilton, someone I knew from travelling back and forth to LA. Impressive! Not only that, but they marketed themselves as a business 'run for women, by women and about women', with the tagline: 'A pair of shoes can change your life ... Cinderella is proof of that!' I've always seen myself as a real-life Cinders – come to think of it, I'm probably still waiting to slip on the perfect glass slipper and find my prince! So, if that wasn't enough to get me interested, I don't know what would be.

The range we talked about had me written all over it – creative, elegant and sophisticated but with a seriously glam edge – and I love working with people who naturally think outside the box. It's amazing too that we could do all of this with 10,000 miles separating us. It was just as well Connie and Samantha could take on board my suggestions, understand my style and run with it, because after Jett's traumatic birth I hadn't been as hands-on with the project as I'd hoped. That's so unlike me because normally if I put my name to something I want to be 100 per cent involved at every stage. I guess you could say I'm a bit of a control freak but it's only because I've got a good sense of what works and what doesn't. Though it's not a licence to be bossy! As a matter of fact, I was really pleased with the range they finally presented and itching to get over there and launch it.

Each pair of shoes was exquisitely covered in rhinestones, pearls and sparkly brooches, and the stiletto heels were studded with Czech crystals. As soon as I slipped a pair on, my feet felt so comfy, and the sisters had also designed beautiful clutch bags to match. There's even one matching shoe and clutch set in a pink-and-gold colour scheme called 'Katie'. How amazing is that?

In the end, I only had one issue. Having my name attached to the range generated loads of great press in Australia, but not so much over here. And anyone wanting to buy a pair of shoes in the UK has to order online from Oz. That's a £50 postage-and-packing charge on top of a £250 pair of shoes. Personally, I thought this would put a lot of people off placing an order especially if the shoes didn't fit and needed to be returned. You could buy another pair of shoes with the £50 you'd spend on having them delivered. While I'd love to work with Connie and Samantha again, next time I would insist that batches be shipped over and sold through outlets in the UK. It's a small gripe, but an important one, I feel.

Although I was supposed to spend six days in Sydney I actually ended up cutting my trip short by two days. My PR and the rest of my team stayed out there to finish up, but being thousands of miles away from them reminded me how much I wanted to get back to Kieran and the kids.

Don't get me wrong, I love Sydney: the harbour; the restaurants; the shops. Definitely the shops! It actually reminds me of London, only with plenty more sunshine. The promotional events were a success too but practically from the moment I arrived I suffered the worst jet lag I've ever experienced. I've done many long-haul flights in my time, but nothing like this. I felt completely frazzled and really woozy, like I was permanently drunk, and I ended up sleeping a lot of the time. It also didn't help that the minute I landed I went straight on to live TV to be interviewed!

Also, I still felt fat and insecure from having given birth three months before so I'd brought with me a suitcase filled with the baggiest clothes ever. I might as well have packed a tent! I put on a brave face, but if I'm truthful the whole trip felt so different from the times I'd flown out there to take part in *I'm a Celebrity* . . . Instead of getting out and exploring, the first thing I did when I arrived at my hotel was FaceTime Kieran and then curl up on my bed in a doze that continued throughout the whole week. Hardly rock 'n' roll!

One evening, Kieran mentioned that Jane had been up to the house for a few hours. Immediately, I felt my hackles rise. 'Why has she been to the house when I'm not there?' I snapped at him. 'I don't know. I hardly even saw her!' he replied defensively. I felt so angry particularly as Kieran knew how uneasy I was feeling about Jane. Apparently Harvey's nanny Lizzie had answered a text from her and Jane had asked if she could visit with the kids. Lizzie thought it was fine for her to pop up. I was so rattled that I even ended up having a go at the nanny which, in hindsight, was really unfair.

On the final night I spent in Sydney there was a nightclub bash to round off the week of events. My Australian agent Clarissa forewarned me the place was going to be packed full of football and rugby players. Fine, I thought.

I'm in love with Kieran and nothing will turn my head.

It's funny though, because there was one guy – a rugby player I don't want to name – who was drop-dead gorgeous: dark, muscular, and with a real glint in his eye. Not far into the evening, it was obvious he was coming on to me too. He wanted to stand by me, have a drink with me, dance next to me, and every time we spoke he'd brush his hand across my arm or down my back. If I'd been single I definitely would have thought, Ring-a-ding-ding, who's this? And I know that if I'd given him the green light, I could easily have gone back to his place that night. But I didn't.

For starters, there were cameras at every turn so I was on my best behaviour. Even though there was nothing in it, I kept imagining how Kieran might feel if he saw pictures of me and another man plastered across the internet. Or what if someone tried to make up a story saying we were all over each other? Years in the industry have taught me exactly how images can be manipulated and stories fabricated to suit the gossip columnists.

The truth was, the only man I seriously thought about that night was Kieran and it was then that I knew I was truly in love with him. Sure, I can tease for England when I'm abroad. It's always very flattering to attract a bit of attention and who doesn't like indulging in flirtatious banter? But be unfaithful to my husband? No way! Putting a ripped rugby player in front of me did feel like a test. But Kieran and I had gone through such a rough patch I came to the conclusion that although this guy was nice enough, and physically absolutely my type, I wasn't interested.

Despite his advances, that night I sloped off early to my hotel to FaceTime Kieran again. I even told him about the rugby player and how fit he was but said that all I could think about was seeing my husband. He said he was missing me like crazy and really wanted me home. By the next morning I was in a taxi heading towards the airport ready to catch my flight.

Make no mistake, though. If I'd known then what I

know now, that rugby player would have been in with a 1,000 per cent chance of kissing me that evening. They say ignorance is bliss and it couldn't be truer. There I was, thinking how amazing Kieran was for taking the week off work to look after Jett. After the trauma of our summer, it finally felt as though we might be getting our lives back on track. As soon as I touched down I felt excited to be home.

*   *   *

Not long after I'd returned from Oz I was forced to deal with another reality check. I've always had a love-hate relationship with the British press but sometimes they are completely out of hand. One great thing about being abroad is that there isn't always someone trying to cook up a story about you, or paint you in a negative light.

Being in the public eye, I accept that I have to take the rough with the smooth and deal with what's thrown at me. But there are also times I feel compelled to have my say when it's obvious that a piece has been plucked from fantasyland! I've never done it lightly, but in the past I've also been forced to get legal, especially when my marriage to Pete ended. Then the tabloids portrayed me as an unfit mother and out of control, and also claimed that my businesses were failing when they clearly weren't. Where the press were getting their diet of so-called news from remains a mystery to me but at that time in my life I felt very fragile and those stories were soul-destroying to read.

What I've found the most bizarre, though, is that throughout the whole of my career the tabloids and the gossip mags have been desperate to portray me as a super-bitch, particularly towards other women, which is something I've never understood. It doesn't make sense to me that women with strong personalities always have to hate each other and, in general, I've found they don't. I'm a tough negotiator and, yes, I am a bitch when it comes to business, but anyone who knows me will tell you I'm very encouraging towards other women. If I see that a person has a great business idea or they're pursuing success in other ways, I don't say, 'I hate her' at all. In fact, I'm the opposite. I think, Good on you! Great idea! Wish I'd thought of that! If I didn't, I'm not sure I'd have much of a social life – some of my closest female friends are very successful entrepreneurs. Like I always say, the world is big enough for everyone – it wasn't only made for me! Yet in November 2013 that's exactly what I was accused of when Amy Willerton entered the jungle as one of the contestants on *I'm A Celebrity* . . .

Back in 2012 Amy had been the winner of my television series *Signed By Katie Price*. The show had aired on Sky Living and the idea behind it was to find fresh talent – a person who was not only model material, but who had the personality, drive and intelligence to develop their own brand, all with the help of me and my management company BlackSheep, which is run by my brother Danny and my manager.

Right from the off, Amy stood out alongside contestant Rylan Clark, whose warmth and humour also shone through. Amy was a bright, very beautiful, bubbly and savvy girl. In the end, Rylan was my first choice to win in the final, but my team convinced me that Amy was everything we were looking for. I bowed to their opinion and I don't want to say 'I told you so' but . . . I think the proof of the pudding is in the eating.

Since appearing on my show, Rylan has carved out a very successful career for himself, appearing in regular slots on *Daybreak* and *This Morning* and going on to host the *Celebrity Big Brother* spin-off show *Celebrity Big Brother's Bit on the Side*. Amy, on the other hand, refused to sign an exclusive deal with BlackSheep after she won, even though it was a requirement of her contract to appear on the show. Because of that, my team and I weren't prepared to plough time and effort into shaping her career, only to have her jump ship. I wasn't being a bitch, it simply didn't make good business sense.

The reason I'd been hesitant about Amy in the first place was that her attitude seemed wrong to me. She seemed to want overnight success without doing all the hard graft necessary to get it. When she won, it seemed to go to her head and she couldn't understand why she wasn't on every magazine cover or being invited on to every talk show. Her boyfriend was even deluded enough to turn up on my manager's doorstep asking why she wasn't as big as Cheryl Cole! Seriously? Believe me, achieving fame takes time, patience and stamina, and that's a good thing. Instant success can also mean an almighty instant fall and in this business you need to be ready and steady enough to cope with everything that fame brings – good and bad.

That autumn I was intrigued to watch Amy on *I'm a Celebrity* . . . By the end of my association with her, my team were more than a little relieved that she'd decided to go it alone. In my opinion she had unrealistic expectations and we were all concerned about how we were going to manage these. But I hoped she'd learned a few lessons since *Signed by Katie Price*, grown up a bit and realised that the world didn't owe her any favours. In fact, what better chance to confound public opinion than finding yourself in the middle of the Australian jungle, having to guzzle down maggots or swim among baby crocs, and showing yourself to be a real team player.

Having appeared twice on the show, I tune into *I'm a Celebrity* . . . every year. There's no point in even talking to me while it's on. I'm glued to it. Yet that season, there were some celeb mags who wanted to drag me into the story even though I was a viewer like everybody else. Not long after Amy entered the jungle, a magazine approached my PRs wanting my reaction to a story they were planning on publishing. The story centred around me being angry because apparently Amy was copying me in the jungle and I was jealous of how beautiful she is. Snore . . . Normally I would have let that kind of rubbish go, but on this occasion my team were prompted to put out a statement. This wasn't a magazine putting a negative spin on a true story, this was a magazine blatantly making it up.

Unfortunately as the series continued Amy didn't show her best side in the jungle. It was revealed that she'd smuggled in contraband, including cosmetics that she'd hidden in her rucksack and bikinis that she'd worn one on top of the other before going through the security check. Naturally that was going to upset the other contestants. If I'd been in there I'd have been pissed off! I think it was *Emmerdale* actress Lucy Pargeter who said after her eviction that going into the jungle is all about teamwork and, when someone behaves selfishly, it is bound to annoy people. She was dead right.

If Amy was copying me in the jungle, she didn't do a very good job of it. First of all, I wouldn't have dreamed of smuggling anything in there. I always entered the show wanting to be a team player. However, if anyone wants to copy my style, I never take offence. I take it as a compliment.

As for being jealous of Amy because of her looks? Utter bollocks. What people seemed to forget was that Amy won my show. I thought she was bright and beautiful and I still hope she has a glittering career ahead of her. She chose to go it alone and I accepted her decision. Okay, she said a few things in the press at the time that weren't correct but I've never made an issue of them and I believed that by the time *I'm a Celebrity* . . . aired the press would have moved on too.

By December 2013 I was thirty-five. I'd given birth to Jett. I was in love with Kieran and my life had changed. The idea that I would compare myself to someone of twenty-one is ludicrous. What upset me the most was the implication that Amy being beautiful would make me (or any woman) angry, jealous or bitter. There are tons of pretty girls on the planet. I even know some of them! Gossip magazines are aimed at a female audience and I'm positive they would never publish a story about how a man was jealous of another man's looks. However, when it comes to women, they continuously want to pedal the myth that successful women become unhinged at the sight of an attractive girl. At the end of the day, I know conflict sells papers so I guess I shouldn't be surprised that there's always a woman being pitted against me. Sorry to burst your bubble, guys, but it's not real.

In fact, I thought it was a very irresponsible story to want to run because it encouraged Twitter trolls to fire online abuse at Amy about her looks, and that is something I do have a problem with. Whatever did or didn't happen following Amy's appearance on *Signed By Katie Price*, nobody should be made into a target.

That's exactly the reason why a year later I took to Twitter to support Zoe Sugg, otherwise known as the video blogger Zoella. Zoe has amassed a seven million strong following on YouTube. Her make-up tutorials and advice on fashion and beauty have captured the imagination of internet users worldwide, and the truly amazing thing is that she was only nineteen years old when she started in 2014.

When Zoe's first novel *Girl Online* was published it broke all publishing records by selling 78,000 copies in its first week. Yet she was cyber-bullied for admitting she used a ghost to help her write it. Immediately, I felt a real empathy with Zoe. I met her on the panel of an episode of *Loose Women* and thought she was a sparky, smart young businesswoman. So what if she uses a ghost? I've made no secret of using the services of a ghostwriter since the publication of my first book *Being Jordan* in 2004. Back then, no publisher wanted to take my story, and John Blake ended up buying it for £10,000. On publication *Being Jordan* went on to sell more than one million copies. It broke all records for an autobiography at that time. That showed them! But I could never have written it without the help of Rebecca Farnworth, my ghost for many years, who tragically lost her battle with cancer in November 2014.

When Zoella's novel came out, everybody compared her to me. I wanted to shout, *'Boring!'* I can't imagine they meant it in a positive way but, like I always do in these situations, I took it as a pat on the back. I was half-expecting reams of ridiculous column inches saying I was consumed by the green-eyed monster because Zoe was using a formula that had helped build my publishing empire. If the press can make up those kinds of stories about me and Amy Willerton, they can do it with anyone. But thankfully they didn't wheel out that old chestnut.

In Zoe's case, what people fail to realise is that it's accepted practice for celebrities to use ghosts. Lots of people in the public eye do. It's a collaborative process and, as far as I could see, Zoe had been honest about it. The worst thing about it for me was that Zoe felt the need to come off Twitter, albeit temporarily, because of the abuse she was receiving. She was branded an 'idiot', a 'liar' and a 'fake'. Cyber-bullies even hurled abuse at her ghostwriter and her ghostwriter's family. How mad is that?

I wanted to say to Zoe that I'd been there, done that, worn the T-shirt, the only difference being that when my first book came out Twitter didn't even exist! If she let those comments affect her, she may as well give up now. Fortunately, she's gone from strength to strength and I think she's got a great career ahead of her. There are things in life worth worrying about but the bad opinion of a few ignorant people is not one of them, so I pinged her over a few encouraging words to counter the crap that was swirling around the Twittersphere:

Don't worry @ZozeeBo when others criticise u it means ur doing OK! it also makes u more determined 2 succeed. ur a good girl, keep being happy.

That seemed to get Zoe some positive coverage, which is more than I can say when I put out the statement countering the claims that I was jealous of Amy Willerton.

According to some reports, I hadn't released a statement setting the record straight. Oh, God, no! Instead, I'd 'gone on a massive rant' about Amy, like I was some crazed diva. It goes to show that you can't win either way, but I'll never stop trying!

CHAPTER 7

BOOM AND BUST

In December, I started gearing up for Christmas. It's a time of year I love, although nothing could make up for the fact that I wasn't going to have Princess or Junior with me on Christmas Day this year as Pete and I take it in turns. One year they're at mine and Pete has them for New Year, and the next year we swap. It's an arrangement that's practical and it works, but to this day I've never really got used to it. I adore the excitement of Christmas morning when the kids rush downstairs to see what Santa's brought. But at least they're old enough now that I can speak to them by phone on Christmas Day. When they were little we couldn't have a proper conversation, but now they talk me through every one of their presents. And of course I always tell them how much I love them and how much I am missing them.

But in the run-up to the holiday I began to feel exhausted. I do recall wondering if I might be pregnant but didn't think I could be so soon after Jett's birth. Anyhow, I didn't feel pregnant. Granted, my body hadn't regained shape the way it used to – I put that down to age – and I was spotting rather than having a full period. But there was so much going on that I thought, Kate, whatever it is, it will pass.

But on Christmas Eve I was rushed into hospital and ended up being very poorly. One of my boobs had swelled up. Just before I'd met Kieran I'd had a boob job but because I'd fallen pregnant with Jett soon after, my boobs had never had the chance to settle. I put it down to that, but with hindsight perhaps it was the first sign of my body changing with another pregnancy. I was discharged in time for Christmas Day but all that week I felt dreadful.

Still, I wanted New Year to be really special. Forget going to a restaurant or a nightclub like I used to do. For the past few years I've really enjoyed arranging a party at home. I much prefer it, because you can totally let your hair down without having to worry about someone snapping you pissed on a dance floor. You can choose precisely who you want to invite, and besides my parties are legendary! More than anything else, it also means that for the early part of the evening anyway, the kids can run around, dance and have fun too.

As far as I'm concerned, there's nothing like a good old fancy dress party to loosen up the atmosphere and

I'd decided ages back on a onesie-themed do. I'm sure everybody thinks that I prance around the house with all my sexy outfits on and without a hair out of place, but they couldn't be more wrong. My style's not shabby chic, it's just shabby! There's nothing more satisfying than ditching the stilettos, scrunching my hair up in a ponytail, getting into my track pants or my onesie, and curling up on the sofa. As long as I've got a tub of Vaseline on hand to keep my lips moisturised, I don't even wear make-up. What mum has time? And, in my humble opinion, onesies are the best and comfiest fashion phenomenon of the decade. Oh, and my sheepskin-lined Uggs are perfect for kicking about in at home too.

Even by my standards there were some pretty amazing outfits at the party. Imagine eighty people crammed into your front room, sporting an array of tiger-striped onesies, superhero onesies, reindeer onesies. You name it, it was on show. I ordered mine off ASOS, and I think to everyone's surprise had plumped for a plain hot pink. Well, I am a creature of habit. Kieran's onesie was covered in pictures of snowboarders and I even loaned Jane one of my striped numbers, which she insisted on wearing without knickers. And I paid for her to have her hair and make-up professionally done, even though we hadn't seen much of each other towards the end of the year. From what I remember of that party, Jane was by my side the whole time. Derrick passed out early on but we carried on dancing. The next morning she and I even sat in Princess's room and laughed about what a fun night it had been.

Two weeks later, just before Kieran's and my first wedding anniversary, Jane sent me a card going on about what an amazing day our wedding had been and saying she hoped we'd have many more together.

When I read it I thought, That's such a typical Jane thing to do, because she could be a very thoughtful person. That Christmas she'd even insisted on bringing around individual tree decorations with our names on them, and that did strike me as a really lovely gesture. In fact, reading this back now makes me think of all the little presents and messages that Jane sent and I found heart-warming at the time. My interpretation of them now? I don't know if they were made out of friendship or not. In fact, I often wonder if she did those things to cover up what was really going on. Was it her way of making herself feel less guilty? She was right about one thing though. However disappointing the resort we got married in was, our wedding in Nassau had been one of the most amazing days of my life and I did want to spend more years with Kieran. Many, many more . . .

On the face of it, she also continued to be supportive of me. Around that time Kieran and I were looking at buying a house near Worthing. Kieran wasn't keen because there wouldn't be enough room for all our animals, but I was tempted. 'Kate, it's your money! He should think himself lucky. What's he got without you?' Jane would say. Sadly, I now know that at the same time she was telling Kieran, 'I think Kate's behaving really selfishly. It's not just her house. You both have to live there.'

I'm not sure how it happened, but we even ended up spending our wedding anniversary with Jane and Derrick.

We didn't do anything fancy, just a scrummy bowl of pasta at Donatello's in Brighton. Halfway through the meal I did look over at Jane and Kieran sitting opposite one another. For all I know they were playing footsie under the table. It did cross my mind to wonder: Why the fuck am I sharing my anniversary with Jane and Derrick? Why didn't Kieran offer to whisk me away somewhere romantic? Most couples are still in their honeymoon period after a year. They can't get enough of each other! I was in love, but it wasn't that all-encompassing feeling I'd had when Kieran and I first met.

Ever since France, I'd had this inexplicable feeling in my gut that we weren't going to last. Then again, we'd not long had a baby and they don't exactly make for hearts and flowers and candlelit dinners for two!

* * *

Around February another old acquaintance got in touch. It was my friend Chrissy, and let me tell you, she and I go way back. Almost as far as my friendship with Jane does. I don't actually remember how Chrissy and I met but I must have been in my late teens, early twenties. It was before I had Harvey anyway, and we'd go out clubbing together. In those days we'd dance the night away at Sugar Reef or Red Cube Bar in London and then clubs like Attica. God, I sound like such an old nineties raver!

Even though Chrissy had a job with NatWest Bank at the time, for some reason we all thought she worked in PR. She was one of those girls who knew everybody on the scene, and somehow she could get us into any club we wanted. She was with me when I met Dwight, and we'd always pile back to his place after a big night out. Anyone who knew Chrissy could tell you she wasn't the settling down type. Talk about a good-time girl – not exactly attractive but a real fitness fanatic, and I could spot her a mile off on a dance floor because her trademark outfit was always a Burberry jacket and a cowboy hat. I've seen her pick up so many guys it's unbelievable. Going to a club with her was like being out with heat-seeking missile. There was no time that girl wasn't on the pull and she landed some well-known lovers too. A chef, actors, footballers. You name it, she's had it.

Once I'd had Harvey, I stopped going out as much, and Chrissy and I lost touch for a few years. It didn't matter though, because she was always one of those friends I knew I'd meet again and we'd pick up where we left off. And that's exactly what happened. I was married to Pete when one day I was driving in Brighton and spotted her in her car. Immediately I tooted the horn. 'Hey, haven't seen you for ages!' I yelled, leaning out of the window. We exchanged numbers and stayed in touch, but it was nothing more than the odd text. She came to all of my weddings too. A few months after my March wedding to Kieran she messaged me, *Let's meet up, Kate, it's been ages!*

Again, when I think back on how stupid I was to have trusted Chrissy it makes me incredibly angry. But it also makes me very sad too. The reality that I'll never see her or Jane again doesn't feel like the slow, painful death of two friendships; it feels like the people closest to me have been murdered. That's the impact it's had on me. I'm still mourning their loss even though I hate them – it's such a confusing feeling. It's impossible for me to be objective, but if I cast my mind back to February 2014 I do remember thinking that it was nice Chrissy wanted to pop over.

As things stood I wasn't seeing Jane as much, which was a real shame for the kids. But also when you've got a family, it's easy to stay at home and drown yourself in domesticity. Old, single mates can help to remind you that you did once have a wild, carefree time before babies! Although, to be fair, my life and Chrissy's were poles apart by then. She was still hitting the clubs at weekends and I'd grown up in so many ways. But, of course, now I know that Chrissy wasn't desperate to see me at all. She was desperate to see Kieran . . .

On that occasion, can you believe I even encouraged her to train with my husband in our gym? I knew that she loved to work out and she had an athletic body too, at one time, countered only by the most hideous teeth on the planet! Kieran happily obliged. He's brilliant at creating personal work-out programmes for people and afterwards she came back dripping with sweat, saying how much she'd loved training with him. 'Did he put you through your paces?' I asked her innocently. 'He was *really* good,' she replied. She stayed for dinner, which Muggins here cooked. 'We should see each other more often, Kate!' she mentioned as she was leaving. 'Yeah,' I said. 'That would be nice.'

But it was like I'd started something. From then on she didn't stop texting me and wanting to come up to the house. Not long after that, she brought over loads of old pictures of me, her and Dwight. There were also stacks of old letters she'd received from various journalists asking her to dish the dirt on that particular relationship. I thought they were hilarious. Afterwards I even put some of them up on Twitter, tagging the reporters involved, saying: 'Do you remember sending these to my friend Chrissy, begging her for stories on me?' We had such a giggle in the kitchen while I was cooking.

'Oh my God, Kieran, look at this!' I laughed, putting some of the more embarrassing snaps under his nose. He managed to raise an eyebrow and I assumed it was because the photos were of Dwight. We all know how jealous men can get! If you'd asked me then if I thought Kieran showed the slightest bit of interest in Chrissy, I would have said 'absolutely not'. He barely acknowledged that she was in the room and yet now I know that they'd already met and had sex. It is still beyond me to understand how two people could disconnect like that.

What I did think strange was that Chrissy left the photos and letters at mine then rang the next day in a panic, saying she needed them back. 'Can you get them to me, Kate?' she asked hurriedly. 'Er . . . not right this minute, Chrissy,' I replied. 'Is it desperate?' Apparently it was. She went on to suggest that Kieran could bring them to his work, which was near her office, and she'd collect them from there. I remember thinking, I'm not sure I want you to be alone with Kieran, but I didn't dwell on it, and he did end up meeting her to hand the pictures over. I thought, Kieran wouldn't go for Chrissy.

To be on the safe side, though, whenever she wanted to come to the house after that, I arranged it but always found a last-minute excuse. She was an old friend. I didn't want to upset her or create tension between us but she was becoming so full-on and I wasn't in the mood for more mind games.

I wasn't really in the mood for anything. During that month I'd been feeling so nauseous and tired. Again I put it down to endless sleepless nights and my body not being able to recover fully and readjust after having Jett. It always takes a few months. By the time March rolled around, I can't say I felt much better but I'd been so busy and I think subconsciously may have been ignoring the warning signs. It's funny to think that I was in fact pregnant all that time and didn't have a clue. I hadn't put on any weight, for starters. I was still wearing my size 6–8 trousers, whereas I'd ballooned immediately with Jett. And none of the telltale signs were there, like the bloated belly I'd suffered before. When I think about it now, the even weirder thing is that only a few months later, Bunny was to save my sanity and eventually help save my marriage. But of course I didn't know any of that at the time.

*   *   *

Anyone who knows me knows that I'm very proud of where I've come from. I was only seventeen when I got my big break as a Page Three girl for the *Sun*. I was a model, but soon I became an author and a businesswoman, although I always say that my greatest achievement in life is being mum to my five children . . . and winning *Celebrity Big Brother*! Love or hate the fact that I posed topless for the tabloids, it made me who I am. There's no doubt that my background as a glamour model has given people an excuse to have a pop at me. 'Oh, Katie Price – she's only a brainless Page Three girl.' That kind of remark rolls off me like water off a duck's back now because, in my view, I've always had the last laugh.

I've never really spoken about my thoughts on Page Three although I've had a close association with the *Sun* for many years. In 2012 I began writing a weekly column for the newspaper. Before then, people only saw me as boobs, lashes and fake tan and I'm sure they were surprised when they saw that I actually had opinions and I'm a common-sense kind of person.

I wrote on subjects like failing schools and the controversy surrounding prenatal testing for disability. I had fun doing it, and readers saw a more serious side to the Pricey too.

In February 2012, the same month that I began my *Sun* column, I went on *Newsnight*, then presented by Jeremy Paxman, to talk about the PIP breast implant scandal. It was discovered that industrial-grade silicone, which is only supposed to be used in products such as mattresses, was instead used in the breast implants of more than 40,000 women in the UK. Although I've had many boob jobs, I did not get caught up in the scandal but I did think that it was disgusting a company thought more about their profits than the well-being of the women involved.

Believe it or not, I get a real buzz when I take part in that kind of debate because I feel I can offer a personal perspective on a range of subjects. I would have been far too shit-scared early on in my career to agree to anything like being on a panel chaired by Paxo, but I've been in the entertainment industry now for twenty years and feel I've amassed enough experience to know what I'm talking about. Well . . . on some topics anyhow. World peace is probably out of my remit!

In early 2014, when I was approached by London's Southbank Centre to take part in a discussion on the

subject of the *Sun*'s Page Three, I immediately said yes.
The event was organised as part of the Women of the
World Festival, to coincide with International Women's
Day on 8 March, and the topic under discussion was
'Does Page Three make the world a better place?' I can't
pretend I wasn't nervous. As I've said, I wasn't feeling at
my best, but unless I'm at death's door I don't say no to
anything. Besides, I was missing being fired up about
work.

I had asked Jane to come with me for moral support,
but she said she was too busy. God knows with what. It
wasn't as if she had a job. (Unless you class finding ways
to fuck my husband as full-time employment!) Kieran
was working that day too and so I did feel a bit like Billy
No Mates getting the train up to London to face a crowd
whose passions were running high. For some reason the
subject of boobs set everyone alight. I wonder why?

Sometimes I get the feeling people invite me to these
things because they think I'm going to be feisty, cause
trouble and be controversial. Actually, I'm not like that
at all. Instead, I like to tell my side of the story and talk
about my motivations for doing the things I've done. I'm
not arrogant enough to claim to speak for everyone, only
for myself.

However, I do think it's too easy for outsiders to judge
Page Three girls harshly. How many people have actually
met one in the flesh and found out why they wanted to
be there in the first place? I hoped I could answer some
of those questions and I was also interested to hear the

views of others on the panel, including the founder of the Everyday Sexism campaign Laura Bates, lads-mag editor Martin Daubney, and the columnist Eleanor Mills, who chaired the event.

Beforehand, I was panicking: Shit, all these people are really intelligent. What do I have to offer? I'd be the first to admit I was out of my comfort zone but I figured, I can only be myself, and that's exactly who I was.

It totally didn't help that I'd forgotten my glasses, so when it came to reading a speech from my iPhone, I was practically wearing it on my face.

Oh, well! After a very deep breath, I began by talking about how I got into the business. I told the story of how I'd been a teenage model when one day a girl didn't turn up for a Page Three shoot and my agent rang to ask if I'd like to step in. I did wonder what my mum and dad and my brother would say but, me being me, I thought, Stuff it, and did it anyway. I think people naturally assume that I was coerced into going, but I hammered home to the Southbank audience that no one pushed me. In fact, it was the opposite: my friends and family tried to put me off!

When I met Beverley Goodway, the man who ended up photographing me throughout my Page Three career, I also felt completely at ease. There wasn't anything sleazy or threatening about the set-up at all. In fact, I loved it even though I was only paid £90 for three hours' work. I was banned from doing Page Three after I had my first boob job, because they have a strict policy of no implants, but again, me being me, I had the surgery anyway. That was my choice too. Sadly Beverley died in 2012.

For me, Page Three became a platform. From that beginning, I was lucky enough to go on and sell millions of books, launch my equestrian and baby ranges, put my name to perfumes and fashion items, star in my own TV series, and loads more. And, touch wood, I'm still here. But most importantly, through my own hard work, determination, and by living my dreams, I've been able to provide a lifestyle for myself and my children I could never have imagined once. And for that I have Page Three to thank.

Several people on the panel had very different views from me, which I respected, and some of the audience supported the No More Page Three campaign. I had no idea how they were going to react to my being there but they let me put my view forward without harassing me. In fact everybody was completely fine with me, which was a real relief.

I went on to say that I didn't think that showing a woman's body was a big deal and that people have been admiring the female form for centuries, from caveman drawings to present-day statues. During the war men even paid a shilling to look down a telescope and see my nan, who was modelling as a topless mermaid at the time. She ended up getting the sack for smoking . . . that story got a few laughs at least! And why is it that when I take my kit off it's called cheap, yet when a top fashion model and a top photographer do the same thing it's called art?

Just because I think showing a woman's body is harmless doesn't mean I think it's okay for women to be abused within the sex industry. I am not supportive of women being abused at all. In fact, I think that's disgusting. All I am saying is, knowing how much disturbing porn is out there and accessible to anyone online these days, Page Three is comparatively innocent. It's a cheeky, light-hearted institution and I never felt exploited being part of it.

At one point when the debate was getting very heated, I even felt confident enough to inject a bit of fun into the argument. Lots of people were slagging off men for wanting to look at a topless woman, but I made the point that men weren't the only ones to enjoy the page. 'Don't forget the lesbians. They love it too!' I shouted out. Well, it's true, isn't it? I even suggested that the *Sun* go for that extra wow factor, and bring back the Page Seven fella!

And because the *Sun* sells millions of copies daily, what better platform than Page Three to raise awareness of breast cancer? The Coppafeel charity started by Kris Hallenga, who sadly has Stage 4 breast cancer, teamed up with the newspaper to run Check 'Em Tuesday. The weekly feature encourages all women to check their breasts for abnormalities because early diagnosis improves a person's chance of surviving breast cancer. Without that high-profile platform, would that campaign have been anywhere near as successful? I don't think it would. Now

I can mention Coppafeel to any woman and they know exactly what I'm talking about. And if it saves even one life, that's a very good thing.

All in all I surprised myself. I really enjoyed being part of the discussion. There were some strong arguments made against Page Three, all of which I took on board but didn't necessarily agree with. What can I say? Page Three made a better world for me. But I'm always up for learning and I'd love to do more events like that in the future.

CHAPTER 8

CAPE VERDE

On 23 March, Kieran and I, Derrick, Jane, my brother Danny and my stepdad Paul all took part in a twenty-five-mile bike ride around East London to raise money for Sport Relief. The event had been planned for ages. Other than Kieran, nobody else knew how awful I'd been feeling. My natural inclination is to tough it out when I feel like shit and I did my best to put on an act and pretend everything was okay, but it wasn't. Inside I kept thinking, I'm actually going to die!

Kieran and I were also going through a particularly rough patch. I sensed that now, more than ever, he lacked interest in me and our relationship. We didn't argue. In fact, Kieran and I never really argued, but it was those affectionate glances and lovely cuddles that were lacking.

He was so moody, too. The weird thing was we were still having sex, and good dirty sex, but with a new baby that snored for England it wasn't as if we were at it every night. Also, why would I want to have sex with someone who seemed sulky one minute and fine the next? I put it down to his ongoing shoulder problems, but his behaviour towards me was so unpredictable and that's hardly the come on most girls respond to!

Kieran had been doing more with Jett but it looked to me like he was going through the motions. He still hadn't properly bonded with his son, even though I kept pushing him. I was largely looking after Jett on my own. If I went to London, Jett always came with me. When Kieran got home from work, I'd often hand him the baby, saying, 'Here, you take him for a while,' but he'd fudge some excuse about wanting to go to the gym, or train someone, or feed the chickens. Aren't you going to do *anything* with him? I thought sadly. This isn't what I signed up for! When we'd first met Kieran had been so amazing with my kids, so gentle and attentive. I loved that about him, and all my friends had commented on it. I couldn't understand the turnaround.

On the morning of the bike ride we headed to the Queen Elizabeth Olympic Park in Stratford. Even though I felt like absolute crap I still managed to drive us and the bikes in the horse box. Originally, I'd asked Halfords if they would donate a new bike to me, which I then planned to auction off for charity following the event. After at first agreeing – at least, I thought they had – the company decided not to and no bike was delivered, which really pissed me off. They were probably thinking, Katie Price, she's loaded, she can use her own bike, but that wasn't the point. It would have been nice for whoever won to have a brand spanking new bike and, seriously, what is one bike to Halfords? The company hadn't entered into the charitable spirit at all! After some furious tweeting, the online store Chain Reaction Cycles agreed to donate a beautiful Venon road bike to the cause. I made sure I thanked them in my weekly *Now* column. See . . . what goes around really does come around.

As I remember, it was bitterly cold that morning and we all huddled in the back of the horse box to change. Yet again Jane didn't fail to disappoint. 'Ooh, Kieran, look at Jane's six-pack!' I said to him as she peeled her top off down to her bra. I wanted her to know that I was watching her closely. Alongside my determination to finish the ride, anger propelled me around the route. Before we set off I had two goals: get to the finish line and smile for the cameras. Punching Jane was high up on the list too but I managed to hold back . . . just.

Once we got to the start line, the atmosphere that day was incredible. We all wore our bright red Sport Relief T-shirts and the roars of encouragement from the crowd were much appreciated. I've done a few sporting events in my time, including the London Marathon, and I've always loved taking part and finding out about all the different causes the money helps. This was no different.

And because Sport Relief helps so many vulnerable children, including those with disabilities, it's a cause close to my heart.

I started out front, but there was no way I could keep up that pace. I'm such a trouper that I hadn't told any of the organisers I was suffering. Instead my goal was to concentrate on getting round the route. For someone who said they didn't work out, Jane shot ahead of all of us. The relief I felt when I eventually crossed over the finish line! I'd been the charity's special guest for the day. I'd got through it. I hadn't let anyone down and that was all that mattered to me.

We grabbed a KFC and headed home, but instead of me complaining of feeling sick it was actually Kieran who ended up crashing and burning! By the time we unpacked the bikes his temperature was sky-high and he'd started vomiting. I assumed it was because he was hungover. The day before, we'd celebrated his birthday and I'd taken him to a health spa even though he'd seemed really ungrateful. He was disappointed because I hadn't bought him the Breitling watch he'd wanted, but why would I? He was so off with me all the time! There was no way I was going to spend all that money on him. But I had organised a party in the evening and invited his friends and he'd definitely overdone it on the booze. Maybe that's why he was ill now. Or maybe it was a bug that had been lingering and that was why I felt so terrible too. But Kieran was *really* sick and we agreed he'd sleep in the spare room that night with a bucket by the bed. Whatever was wrong, I didn't want to catch his lurgy.

The next day I had a round of meetings in London so I hauled myself on to the train with Jett despite feeling as bad as Kieran looked. He'd taken a sickie from work first thing that morning and I'd left him in bed sweating out his fever. Just as I was pulling into London Victoria, Derrick texted me to ask if he'd left his Sat Nav in the house because Jane was claiming it was still in the horse box and she wanted to drive up to double check. We'd cleared the horse box the night before and I knew it wasn't in there, but what could I say? She was coming anyway.

When I got back that evening my cleaner mentioned that Jane had popped up to see Kieran. No sooner was she in the door than she'd asked how he was and if she could see him. My cleaner had felt uncomfortable directing Jane upstairs to the spare room, but apparently she'd not stayed long. I decided to keep that information under my hat and not say anything to Kieran for now but it did plant another seed in my mind.

Kieran ended up taking the whole week off work. I did feel sorry for him, and my natural inclination was to look after him, but I couldn't ignore the bad atmosphere between us. Other than the days I was away having meetings or doing press calls or shoots or whatever, I was at home . . . but I always have to work. Whether it's a string of phone calls or planning my next venture, it's all go. It's brilliant that I've got that freedom and can work from home, but it was as if Kieran saw this as an opportunity to forget he had an important role to play too. 'We're all part of one big family now,' I kept reminding him.

The longer Kieran's sulking went on, the more I concentrated on digging around for an explanation. Right, I thought, I'm going to get to the bottom of this. 'Can you do this? Can you do that?' I was continually asking him, to see what his reaction was. The answer was always no. 'But why not?' I said, exasperated. I was getting sick of the sound of my own voice! 'Oh, I'm too tired,' he'd say with a shrug. 'If you're tired, I'm exhausted!' I shouted back.

I wanted to return to living in a happy home and resolve all this tension between us. It was starting to do my head in. All the questions that had been raised by his behaviour in France rose to the surface again. Am I getting fat? Am I neglecting him? Aren't I good enough?

Kieran wasn't a big earner, but I've never seen that as a problem either. In my view money isn't the be-all and end-all, but perhaps he was finding it hard being married to someone in the public eye, who was a financially independent woman? Even Jane kept asking, 'Are you and Kieran okay?' and I'd reply that he was quiet and moody but I didn't understand why. On hearing that, she must have been thinking, Oh, great, Kate's relationship's is in trouble and there's a chance for me and Kieran. The conniving cow! At the time, I figured another break might do us the world of good. Even if it didn't resolve our differences, I seriously needed some sun and chill-out time.

At the beginning of April I was really looking forward to jetting off. With a sprinkling of Pricey charm I'd managed to get two free villas at the beautiful Meliã Tortuga Beach hotel on Cape Verde. Well, you've got to try, haven't you? Besides, I'd heard great things about the resort and when the owner asked if I would post some pictures of our holiday in return, I was happy to do so. I could not wait for lazy days by the pool and feeling the sea breeze against my skin, playing with the kids and indulging in some luxury treatments.

On offer were two villas, one overlooking the gorgeous white sand and turquoise blue sea and one slightly further back, on the largest island in Cape Verde, Sal. The first villa was for me, Kieran and the kids, and the second I'd got for Jane and her family. She flew with us from Gatwick with Ruby and George and the plan was that Derrick would come out four days later.

What possessed me to invite Jane this time around I'm not sure. The kids, I think. They loved playing together. But all I can think about now is how she and Kieran behaved before we'd even got on the plane. There I was, pushing the trolley through the departure lounge, piled high with luggage, and Kieran and Jane were walking in front, talking and giggling. 'Guys, wait for me!' I was shouting ahead, but they weren't taking the blindest bit of notice. And Jane had turned up wearing the same make of grey cropped T-shirt as me, with jeans and boots.

I mentioned that to Kieran after take-off. Like me, she was also wearing her rings stacked up on her fingers and had gel-polished, square-shaped nails, exactly as I have. As usual Kieran dismissed my comment. I felt like saying to him, 'Please notice me. I'm your wife, not the bag carrier!' I couldn't get over how little Jane seemed to care about me either. She flirted outrageously with my husband, as if I were invisible. I'll never forget it. At one point on the plane she bent over to give something to Ruby. Her G-string was hanging out and we could practically see what she'd had for breakfast! 'Are you telling me that's not for you?' I said to Kieran. I felt jealous and angry! How could they treat me like this?

Not long into our holiday it was obvious to me that something was seriously wrong. Kieran wasn't there and I don't mean physically. Emotionally, he was in another universe. It was like France all over again. What is going on here? I thought, frantically. I married a knight in shining armour and this is what he's turned out to be . . . an arsehole wrapped in tin foil! This Kieran was a stranger to me. And I wasn't only suspicious of Jane – I hated her. But before I jumped to any conclusions I decided to sit it out and see what would happen.

As part of the package Vera, a lovely woman, came to cook us breakfast, lunch and dinner every day. On our second morning she'd already laid out breakfast by the time we got up. Jane and the kids had arranged to join us and I watched as George ran over from their villa on his own. 'Where's your mum, is she coming over?' I asked.

'No, she's tired. She says she's got bags under her eyes. She'll be over in a bit.' That was weird. What does it fucking matter? I thought. When we're away Jane *always* comes for breakfast. When she finally did pitch up, she had on large sunglasses and a tiny bikini. 'Oh, there you are, Jane,' I said sarcastically. 'George said you didn't want to come over because you had bags under your eyes.' At that, she turned around and walked off.

Later that day she refused to sunbathe with me. Instead she headed towards the pool or sat outside her villa. She'd pop over occasionally for a chat and offer to rock Jett in the buggy. I couldn't help noticing that all the time her toe was on the footrest she was checking out her reflection in the glass doors of our villa. You're not interested in rocking Jett, I wanted to say. You want to show off your body.

*   *   *

One evening before Derrick arrived, we'd all got in from a long day at the beach. After we'd eaten and got the kids ready for bed, I suggested we play a quick round of the card game Uno. I'm a sucker for Uno. It's a game that everyone can join in. So much fun. 'Go and get the cards out of the car,' I asked Kieran, because I knew there were two packs in the glove compartment. I was on the sunbed with Jett, hardly likely to move, and so he must have figured that it was a good time for him to disappear. But after he'd been gone fifteen minutes I was on tenterhooks wondering where he'd got to, especially seeing as the car was parked right next to the villa. Keep calm, Kate, I kept telling myself.

'Where have you been?' I asked coolly when eventually he strolled inside. Underneath, I felt anything but calm. He'd been to Jane's, he admitted openly, and although I was trying not to show it, I was furious. He made up some bullshit excuse about how he couldn't find the cards in the car and he'd gone to borrow her set. I didn't want to say anything in front of the kids but I knew that was a blatant lie. I bottled up my anger for later. Then everything that had been gnawing away, making me feel so insecure, suddenly exploded inside me. I confronted Kieran.

'I've got the same feeling as I had in France. Something's going on with you two and you're not telling me.'

'Shut up, Kate, don't start this shit again,' he snapped back, but I was like a dog with a bone. I was not letting this one lie!

'Jane's looking good, isn't she? Do you think she's got a good body?' I was really goading him.

Kieran agreed Jane was looking great but ended the conversation abruptly with, 'Kate, stop ruining my fucking holiday!' *Me* ruin *his* holiday? What a cheek! The stupid thing was I actually didn't have a problem with Kieran looking at Jane. All men look, don't they?

God knows, I do too! But there's a line that's not to be crossed.

'There must be something going on,' I said. 'Otherwise you wouldn't keep denying things.' But Kieran sat there giving me the 'drop it, Kate' look.

The next day, the sun was beating down and I was lying out on the sunbed feeling awful. Chilled out holiday? Dream on, Kate! From the minute we'd arrived in Cape Verde I'd had an upset stomach and now I started to develop shooting pains up my body. This wasn't a bug, surely. I was really starting to worry. Could I be pregnant? Maybe the signs had been there all along? Whatever the problem, I *really* wanted to take things easy. All of a sudden, Jane appeared in another glittery bikini – this time bright pink. What the hell are you wearing? I thought as she sauntered up to the sunlounger and asked me whether anything was wrong with Kieran because apparently he'd been acting quieter than usual. Only moments before he'd been swimming but I noticed he'd done one of his disappearing acts.

'That's Kieran, isn't it? He's quiet,' I replied, but Jane wouldn't drop the subject.

'Do you think he likes me being here?' she continued.

'Of course he does! We love having you and Derrick here. We love your company, and when Derrick comes the boys can go off and do their thing and we can have fun,' I outwardly reassured her. But in my head I was saying, You fucking bitch. All this is obviously about Kieran. For the rest of the afternoon I sat there, rubbing my stomach, rehearsing how I was going to voice my worries to Jane. I had no proof of anything and I didn't want to ruin our friendship if I was wrong, but it was getting to the point where I knew I had to say something.

While I worked out the situation in my head, I continued to give Jane the benefit of the doubt – you don't exactly expect your best mate to make moves on your husband, do you?

That evening, after we'd eaten, Junior and Princess were begging to go to the mini-disco. Harvey had already fallen asleep. All that sea air and building sandcastles on the beach had floored him and, very kindly, Vera had offered to sit with him while we took the others out for half an hour. Jett came in the buggy and he was sparked out too.

We had a couple of drinks before we left the villa. Kieran doesn't really drink, but he seemed tipsy to me. He had that charged-up look in his eyes. Jane was already sitting in the bar by the time we arrived and as soon as the kids ran off for a boogie, Kieran offered to get more drinks in. But who did he make a beeline for when he returned? Hang on a minute! I thought as he headed straight towards Jane. Who are you here with? I felt so pissed off. I was convinced that anyone looking on wouldn't have a clue which one of us was Kieran's wife. Jane, all glammed-up and fawning over him, or me, standing there like a lemon with the buggy? I stood there analysing, analysing, analysing, and getting more and more uptight and anxious.

'I need to head back to the villa so Vera can get off,' I

said, before asking Kieran if he wanted to stay on for another drink. I was pretending to act all blasé, like I wasn't worried about anything. Inside, I waited nervously for the answer. I wanted to trust him, I really did. I've never wanted to be one of those women who stops their husband chatting to any other female. In fact, I think it's healthy if men can get on with any woman they meet. 'I want to stay out, but we're part of a family,' Kieran told me. Phew! At least he got that part right. Mind you, I would have loved to stay out too. I'm a bigger party animal than Kieran and Jane put together, but the deal was that it was the kids' holiday.

Jane announced jokingly she was taking her kids back to her villa, then going to the pool bar to 'chat up men'. Looking back, I can only think that was her way of trying to make Kieran jealous. At the time, I dismissed it as Jane's sense of humour. I was secretly pleased that Kieran had wanted to leave with us. It told me he wanted *me* – finally! And this holiday was all about us spending quality time with each other. We said goodbye to Vera and had a couple more games of Uno before Junior threw in the towel and went to bed. Kieran headed back to the pool bar to grab some more drinks, and by the time he returned ten minutes later Princess was already stretched out starfish-style on the sofa, dead to the world. 'They've run out of Coke. I'll go to the other bar to get some,' Kieran whispered. 'Okay, don't be long. I'll wait for you. I won't fall asleep,' I promised. After all, we had the villa to ourselves now . . .

So there I was, lying in bed and waiting for him to come back. Where the hell was he? I kept checking my phone. It had been almost an hour since Kieran had gone to the bar. In my head, I began making up all these excuses. I thought, He'll have got chatting to the owner at the bar and forgotten the time. But the longer I lay in bed waiting, the more claustrophobic and breathless I felt. I fired off a sarcastic message to him. *Hope you're having a good time. Thanks for leaving me in the villa with the kids . . .* but after a few minutes there was no reply, which was very uncharacteristic of Kieran. I tried again. *We're never going to work, if you're going to be like this.* Again, silence.

Suddenly, a kid's toy started going off in the villa and began drilling into my brain. I leaped out of bed to see where the noise was coming from and checked my phone one more time. Kieran still hadn't messaged back and every minute I waited was a reminder that he wasn't beside me, under the sheets. By now my imagination was running riot. He's had an accident; he's lost his phone; he doesn't want to be with me any more and this is his way of telling me, I thought. I'd had enough. I was going to look for him. I yanked on my shorts and grabbed my flip-flops. Because there was a bar next to our villa, there was a security guard parked outside. I asked him if he'd seen Jane and he pointed towards the bar. He agreed to stand in front of my door and listen out for the kids for a few minutes while I scoured the area.

In the bar it was a quiet night, with just a few stragglers

and no sign of Jane or Kieran whatsoever. I studied the few faces there and breathed hard. Deep down, I knew it all along, but it was as if the penny had finally dropped. He was with Jane. Now for my next mission. I needed to catch them together. I needed to prove to myself that I wasn't going crazy.

Back at the villa, I asked the security guy if perhaps Jane had gone back to her house? He confirmed that she hadn't returned. What kind of woman was my 'friend'? I wondered. I returned to the bar where a group of guys who had been in there all night caught my attention. 'Are you all right?' one of them called over. I must have looked distraught, searching around like a madwoman. 'No. Not really. I'm looking for my husband,' I replied. Apparently, he'd been pacing around earlier, they said, but he'd not long ago headed towards the beach.

Kate, stop worrying, he's probably on his phone and went to get better reception, I kept repeating to myself. But my heart was pounding out of my chest and my shoulders and legs were shaking uncontrollably with fear. I felt the sand crunch underfoot and slip in between my toes as I walked towards the sea. Something was propelling me further and further along the beach. I scanned the shore and saw a pile of sunbeds stacked up. As I peered harder into the darkness, in among them I saw two figures sitting opposite each other.

Every muscle in my body tensed, and this searing pain overwhelmed me, as if I'd been punched hard and was waiting for the next blow. I recognised the silhouettes immediately – my husband and my best friend – the two people I should have been able to trust. I watched silently as they leaned closer together and kissed passionately in the moonlight. As their lips touched, Jane's hands slowly reached down towards Kieran's shorts.

I stood there, frozen, for around thirty seconds. As much as I wanted to, I was unable to look away. My eyes were fixed on Kieran and Jane. How I made it across the beach I still don't know, but something snapped in me. I'd rehearsed no words. I had no clue what I was going to do as I tiptoed towards them. Without a moment's thought, I reached out and grabbed Jane's hair from behind. She had no chance to hear or see me before I dragged her from the sunbed. I yanked her hair tighter as her legs and arms flailed around desperately. She looked completely horrified.

'I knew it! I fucking knew it,' I yelled as I jolted her neck back hard. Suddenly, I heard it click. *Shit*. I've broken her neck! I thought. I freaked out momentarily as Jane lay trembling on the sand. But within seconds she'd stumbled to her feet. I was screaming at her again. 'I think I'm pregnant, you fucking whore!' My fist clenched tight. Adrenalin was surging through my body. I was so *fucking* angry. I punched her hard in the face and watched her reel backwards. I had no idea then, but I'd dislodged her front tooth and it dropped out soon after. Fucking hell! I had no idea of my own strength.

By now the resort owner and a few customers from

the bar had run over. 'We weren't doing anything! It's not what you think!' Jane and Kieran were shouting, but who were they trying to kid?

'I'm *fucking* divorcing you,' I roared at Kieran as they rushed to hold me back.

'Kate, calm down, we were only cuddling because I was crying,' he said calmly. Far too calmly for my liking.

'What the fuck were *you* crying about?' I snapped back.

'I needed someone to talk to and you've not been feeling great. I haven't been able to talk to anyone,' Kieran was moaning.

'You weren't cuddling, you were *kissing*!' I screamed back at him.

A crowd had gathered. 'I knew they'd been at it. I knew it,' I was saying, in between telling everyone to fuck off back to the bar. Wave after wave of anguish washed over me. I felt like a wounded animal. Then I remembered the kids. 'Shit! They're alone.' So I turned and ran back towards the villa.

'It isn't what you think it is, Kate,' Jane was whimpering as she ran to keep up with me.

'Shut the fuck up, you bitch!' I screamed. I didn't want to hear anything from her. I didn't even want to look at her ugly face, but along with Kieran she followed me back and even kept repeating that line during the phone calls I made to Derrick and Kieran's mum, to tell them both what had happened. When I looked over at Jane, her eyes were red and puffy and she had that 'Oh, fuck' expression in them. What did she expect? How could my husband and my best mate do this to me? How could I ever trust the pair of them again? My life had been suddenly blown into a hundred million pieces, and the worst thing is that now I know she sat there that night and told me a bare-faced lie.

For the next day neither Kieran nor I saw Jane. It was a relief, too. Thank God the kids were around to lighten the mood, but I was still shaken to the core. I hadn't slept and the next morning lay in bed with a terrible sinking feeling, replaying the sequence of events over and over in my mind.

'How long has this been going on?' I asked Kieran. He swore that it was the first time he and Jane had kissed. Every part of me wanted to believe him, and every part of me now mistrusted him. Maybe the friends and family I'd confided in were right. Maybe everything leading up to this point *had* been in my imagination, and this was the first time anything *had* happened. I wanted to believe that. Kate, don't let him talk you round, I kept thinking, but I felt so conflicted. I wanted to hate Kieran. I wanted to pack up everything, take the kids and run as far away as possible. I told him how I was feeling and how I suspected that I might be pregnant. I was miles away from home. I wanted to get back there straight away. I even tried to book flights to London, but I was told there was no availability for eight whole days!

It sounds mad too, but there was also a part of me that wanted to make things up with Kieran, cuddle him, and even make love to him. He swore on his granddad's life it was only a kiss and I almost believed him. No one had been closer to him than his granddad. Kieran would never lie about that, would he? Over the next few days he wore me down. What can I say? I loved him.

The bizarre thing was that when we did have sex it was so passionate, like when we'd first met. I can only think it was my way of proving that Kieran was still mine. It was as if I was saying to Jane, 'You might be the fit one, but I'm the one he wants to be with. Take that, you home-wrecking slut.' How messed up is that?

When Jane and I talked, I wanted to know every little detail. Was it the first time they'd kissed? How did it feel? But she gave no reply. 'Don't you remember kissing him?' I kept hassling her.

She was sitting on our bed with her head in her hands.

'No. I don't remember. But if we did kiss, I'm so sorry, Kate. I was drunk,' Jane replied in the softest voice.

Appealing to her woman to woman was my only option.

'Jane, I've known you for almost twenty years. Please tell me the truth. If it was more than a kiss, you owe it to me to tell me. If he's done this I need to know, because if he has then he's no fucking good for me,' I pleaded. Again, she stayed completely tight-lipped.

As soon as Derrick arrived there were heated discussions around the dinner table. 'Do you fancy my husband, Jane?' I kept asking, but she was still denying everything. Then I turned to Kieran. 'Do you fancy her?'

I shouted. Eventually they both admitted they fancied each other. 'See, we were right to be suspicious in France,' I said to Derrick.

By now, Kieran must have known that I'd stop at nothing to get to the truth. I'd told him as much. That evening, I even lied and said I'd phoned a guy who did lie detector tests and pretended he'd given me a list of questions for Kieran to answer. (When we got home, I did end up calling a proper lie detector guy and found out that I could only ask three questions per test. In Cape Verde I had sixteen! Thank God no one was testing me!)

'Did you have sex with Jane in France?' I grilled Kieran.

'No,' he replied. 'In England, have you had any sexual contact with Jane other than a kiss?' 'No,' he answered. He said 'yes' to texting Jane and telling her he fancied her, but said he'd never thought of leaving me for Jane, and that he only wanted to be married to me. At the question, 'Are you having an affair with Jane?' he replied 'No,' and he also denied having sexual contact with any other girl. I kept on firing question after question. Go, Kate! I was on a roll.

The next morning I marched over to Jane's villa. She looked a mess. She'd obviously been crying and, by now, had a gap where her tooth had fallen out. Derrick was beside her when I asked, 'Why didn't you tell me Kieran was texting you? Why were you texting him back?' Again, she sat with her head in her hands. 'Kate . . . Kate. I don't know, Kate,' she kept repeating.

I couldn't get my head around that at all. How could she do it to me? Not only that, but Jane had always been the sort of person who, if we were talking about sex, would say: 'Well, I'm shit in bed. I'm nearly fifty and I don't know what it's like any more.' I was beginning to realise that was all one big cover-up. I'd been right all along. She was besotted with Kieran.

'Come on, Jane, why don't you tell Derrick the truth?' I carried on. 'You don't want to be with him. I always hear from you about how you don't love him. You owe it to him to be honest,' I said, getting more and more wound up.

Now Derrick was asking Jane if this was true? She turned to him.

Then she said something that was really weird. 'Does Kieran still fancy me?' she asked. Derrick and I stood there dumbfounded. 'Are you for real?' I gasped. I demanded that Derrick go and fetch Kieran. As he left, Jane sat at the kitchen table rearranging her top and tidying her hair, presumably for Kieran's benefit. I couldn't believe what I was seeing.

The minute Kieran arrived with Jett in his arms, I asked again. 'Tell me the truth. Who was texting who?' But instead of either of them answering, Jane looked at him.

'Why are you doing this to me?' she asked, all puppy dog-eyed. Kieran announced that he didn't want to get involved and was going back to the villa. But as he started walking, Jane leaped out of her chair. 'Kieran! Kieran!' she began shouting after him.

Out of everything that had happened, that finally pushed me over edge. I snapped. I'm not proud of what happened next but I lost control. I grabbed Jane's hair, pulled her head towards me and repeatedly banged it off my raised knee. I punched her from underneath with the other fist too, cracking a nail as I made contact. 'Stop! Stop!' Kieran shouted. Derrick was pleading with me to get off her too. 'Kieran, help me!' I could hear Jane screaming out.

Kieran rushed to get Security. They were the ones to pull me off Jane. As soon as I released my grip she ran into the bedroom, quickly followed by Derrick. The door slammed shut and locked behind them. 'Calm down, Kate!' Kieran screamed at me, but how could I? 'Open the fucking door!' I yelled, and hammered on it, but I could hear Jane telling Derrick not to. In the end, Kieran persuaded me to go back to the villa and that was the last I saw of Jane and Derrick until the day we were due to fly home.

For the rest of that day, and for our remaining time in Cape Verde, I was such a mess. I didn't eat and I didn't sleep. In the early hours of the morning I was pacing up and down the beach and even lying on the sunbed looking up 'men who cheat' on my iPhone. I felt so alone. I didn't know whether I wanted to kill myself, or kill Kieran, or kill Jane. One minute I felt love for Kieran and the next I despised him. The only people who made the stay bearable were my beautiful children, but I felt in no state to enjoy my time with them, which made me feel even more of a failure. The day after our almighty row I made an extra-special effort to have fun with them, but that turned out to be a disaster too.

The sun was shining but it was windy down on the beach and the sea was choppy. All of us were lined up, laughing and jumping over each wave before it crashed against the shore. But I was caught off guard and one ginormous wave caught me, toppled me over and sucked me under. It knocked me out because all I remember is coming to and tumbling round and round underneath the surface like I was stuck in a washing machine. No amount of struggling helped me. I was barely conscious and in danger of drowning. Apparently Kieran ran over and yanked me up by the hair but the force of the water sucked me under again and he had to pull even harder to drag me out. When he eventually got me on to the sand blood was streaming down my face. The impact of the water must have caused a nosebleed. It was terrifying but Kieran had saved me which, after everything that had happened, made me feel even more confused. I didn't want to feel grateful to him. I wanted to hate him!

The worst thing was, a deal's a deal and I still had to do the shoot I'd promised the hotel owner. As happy as I was to promote the resort because our villa was wonderful and we'd no complaints whatsoever, the last thing I wanted was to play Happy Families with Kieran for the cameras. I cannot tell you how sick that made me feel, but I'm a professional so the resort got their snaps: me in a pink beach dress with Kieran on a four-poster bed and champagne chilling; Kieran and me kissing; us with the kids on the beach . . . all of which I tweeted soon after.

As hard as I tried to shield the kids from what was going on, it was impossible to hide it. But the last thing I wanted was for Harvey, Junior and Princess's holiday to be ruined too. Of course, the newspapers back home reported it as a sign of how happy and loved up Kieran and I were. And, looking at those pictures now, the whole scene looks so romantic, but that couldn't have been further from the truth.

In the end, I changed our seats for the flight home so I didn't have to look at Jane. And when Derrick came over on the day we left Cape Verde I told him so. 'You're not going to go for Jane again, are you, Kate?' he checked worriedly. As long as Jane didn't pass me to go to the toilet on the plane or even so much as look at Kieran there would be no trouble, I said. 'If I catch a glimpse of her, I don't care whether it's on a plane or in public or whatever, I *will* go for her,' I promised him, but they stayed well clear of us and that didn't happen.

I was sad to say goodbye to Cape Verde, it's such a beautiful place, but as soon as we touched down in London I made a promise to myself – that I was going to get the whole truth, no matter what.

CHAPTER 9

HOME TO ROOST

Back in the UK, Kieran remained unforgiven for ruining our holiday. What I couldn't fathom was how he could be attracted to Jane in the first place. He's always had a thing for older women, but Jane wasn't just old, she had two kids, a husband and nothing whatsoever to offer him.

It also dawned on me on the flight back that although I'd known Jane for sixteen years, I actually knew nothing about her. If you'd asked me to name a friend of hers other than me, I'd have drawn a complete blank. 'Oh, I'm boring, I keep myself to myself, Kate,' she would say. Other than the times she stayed at mine, I had no clue what Jane did during the week or while her kids were at school. When we talked, she was always digging the dirt on my latest drama but she never gave away any information about herself.

As much as I tried, I couldn't get that image of Jane and Kieran kissing on the beach out of my head. 'It was only a kiss, Kate,' he kept reassuring me. He wanted me to drop the subject. He seemed embarrassed, but there was something he was hiding, I knew it. The minute we landed, I made plans for us both to see my therapist Gaylin. 'Make no mistake. I *will* find out everything,' I threatened Kieran, thinking that would make him confess. Even my stepdad told him he may as well tell the truth because I wouldn't let it lie. In fact, everyone told him!

At Gaylin's he sat there with his head bowed and swore that the only contact he'd had with Jane was a few texts and the kiss on the beach. I wasn't convinced but I did feel relieved. Whatever's gone on, thank Christ he hasn't fucked her, I thought. That would be unbearable.

That evening I did a pregnancy test, and the result couldn't have been clearer. I was pregnant. I didn't know exactly how far gone but I figured it must be early days. If I'm brutally honest, I felt a mixed bag of emotions. My relationship with Kieran was under so much strain. Of course, I was optimistic about carrying a new life but physically and mentally I felt drained. When I told Kieran, we were upstairs sitting on our bed. He hugged me.

'That's great news, Kate,' he said softly.

'Are you happy, Kieran?' I asked him.

Nothing was right between us. I'd just caught him kissing my best friend! Also, I do think men are different. However connected they are to their children once they're

Growing up so fast! Jett giving Daddy a hand mucking out Benjamin the goat.

Above: I love how Junior and Princess both love riding as much as me.

Our family and other animals, Angel and Benjamin.

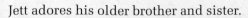
Jett adores his older brother and sister.

My two chocolate covered monsters after a homemade cake-eating competition.

Captain Harvey reporting for duty! A day on the high seas in Cape Verde.

Junior and his first footie medal.

Princess tries my mate Louisa's horse Alicante out for size.

A moment of
father and son
bonding.

Jett loves his bath-
time bubbles –
almost as much as
Mummy!

FACING PAGE

Top: Out with
my girls Michelle
and Claire. A few
champers too
many, perhaps?

Expecting again.
This time I had
no idea if Kieran
would be at the
birth.

A pre-op selfie on the morning of Bunny's birth.

There's never a bad moment to strike a pose.

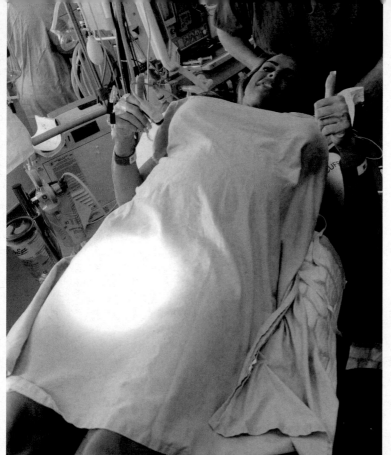

Even if I was
unsure about me
and Kieran, I was
desperate to meet
our little girl.

Hate hospitals,
hate needles, but
adore my babies.

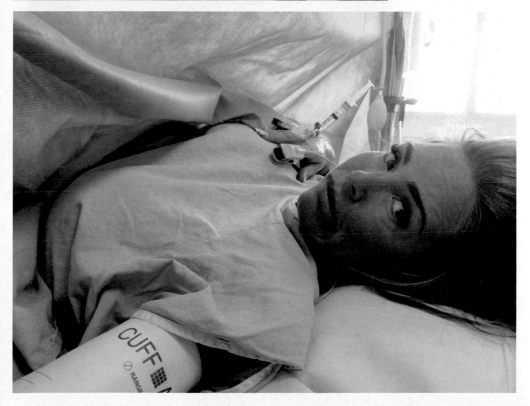

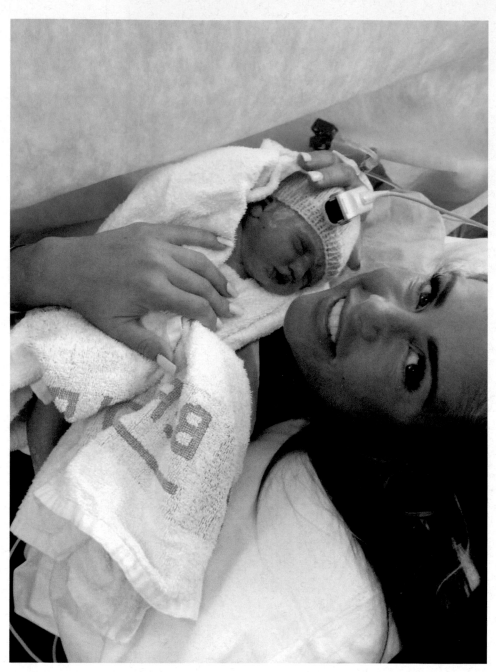

A brief cuddle before Bunny was rushed to an incubator with breathing difficulties.

born, they never actually carry a baby or worry about every stage of pregnancy. I'm not suggesting for one moment that they don't care, it's that the whole experience is different for them, I guess. 'I'm happy,' he said, but Kieran's always so quiet that I didn't know whether he was hiding how he really felt.

The following day we were en route to London. My stomach had been such a mess in Cape Verde that the day we'd flown back I'd texted Dr Gibb to tell him that I thought I was pregnant. I admitted that I didn't know by how much. Now I was sure, he advised me to come in for a check-up straight away.

Memories of the devastating miscarriage I suffered in LA when I was with Pete are never that far from the surface with me and I kept rubbing my belly, praying that this little one was going to be okay, but an even bigger surprise awaited us when we got to the clinic. By Dr Gibb's reckoning I was around five and a half months pregnant, which was way more than I'd first suspected.

'Fuck! We're that far?' I couldn't hide my shock . . . and utter dismay. I could be giving birth to this baby far, far sooner than I'd imagined. How could I be five and a half months? I wasn't ready!

'Let's have a look,' he went on. 'Do you want to know the sex?'

I didn't know what answer to give. There were too many questions swirling around in my head. What if Kieran and Jane had done more than kiss? If we found out its sex, then the baby stopped being a baby and became our son or our daughter. What if Kieran was lying to me?

Would I still want him to be part of this pregnancy? I felt completely torn.

In the end, I gave in and said yes. If there was a problem with the baby, I needed to know. 'I'm sure it's a boy,' I kept saying as Dr Gibb spread the warm gel on my belly and placed the scanner on it. When the baby's grainy outline appeared on the screen I saw its silhouette for the very first time. It was huge! He moved the scanner around, looked closer and then smiled. 'No, Kate, it's a girl.' At that, Kieran burst out crying. He was completely overwhelmed.

'I've got a girl,' he whispered as the tears streamed down his face. Steady on! I thought. Don't get me wrong, I was completely over the moon too, but I did wonder why Kieran was visibly moved to hear about this baby in a way that he hadn't been with Jett.

Stupid me. I was still under the impression that he and Jane had only kissed. Now I know it was so much more. My reading of that moment now? I think it was the first time Kieran realised that he had the perfect family: a king's choice. A baby boy and a baby girl on the way plus a wife who loved him. Who knows? Maybe guilt hit him then. Maybe he was thinking, Shit. I've completely fucked up!

To be on the safe side, Dr Gibb wanted to check my cervix. But as he examined me, his voice was worryingly hesitant. 'Right . . .' He paused.

'What is it?' I asked, my body tensing with fear.

'Hmmm. I don't like the look of this,' he continued.

Apparently my cervix was dilated by 40mm when it should have been 20mm. It appeared as if I was carrying full term. My waters could break at any moment. My heart almost stopped. 'Please, not another nightmare pregnancy,' I panicked. No way could I go through something as awful as Jett's birth again. No way.

Dr Gibb demanded that I take it easy and come back in five days, but the following day I felt horrible. We were in Tesco doing a massive post-holiday shop when Kieran found me creased over the trolley holding myself in pain. It was shooting right through me and, worryingly, I was short of breath too. 'I've got to lie down,' I told him, but even after a few hours stretched out on our bed nothing had changed. *Sorry for texting late*, I messaged Dr Gibb at around 10.30 p.m. *Something feels wrong.*

By Friday, Kieran and I were back in The Portland. If I'd popped there and then our baby would have had little chance of surviving. The news was devastating. Apparently I could opt for an emergency stitch in my cervix to stop my waters breaking. I'd never even heard of the procedure before but Dr Gibb calmly explained everything. From what I could gather, the operation didn't guarantee I would carry to full-term but it could buy me a little more time. Just like in France, I could feel myself retreating into my shell. Were Kieran and I a couple or not? Were we going to have this baby together? The worst thing was I couldn't share my anxiety with him. I felt scared and alone.

The operation, called cervical cerclage, was not without risk, I was warned. The stitch can become infected and in a worst-case scenario may cause a miscarriage, but it was my only option. I was booked in for the next day. Under general anaesthetic I would be tipped upside down so all the water in the amniotic sack could drain back and Dr Gibb could insert the stitch. It was a day procedure, fortunately. I was counting down the hours until it was over and I was safely back home.

After that I would be on a strict regime of duvet days, which obviously I'd be rubbish at. My urge is to be on the go all the time, but needs must. The night before the op Kieran sat next to me in my hospital bed. Every time I caught his eye, anger with him and Jane welled up inside me. I was so anxious about the operation that I needed to get the past few weeks out of my system. Foremost in my mind now was the prospect of losing the baby. I had to focus on that. So there was only one thing for it. I drafted Jane a letter.

What I wanted to tell her was how much she'd upset me, that best friends don't do this to one another. And that she might have kissed Kieran, but she never got to fuck him. (Mind you, now I feel like a complete dick for even entertaining the idea that Kieran had been honest about that with me.) Once I'd typed out the letter on my iPhone I read it aloud to him, watching him at the same time to gauge his reaction. 'It's a good letter, Kate, you should send it,' he said, nodding. The devious bastard.

To sit there and say that when all along he knew they'd been fucking for months! Jane must have been laughing up her sleeve when she received it.

Jane,

I'm writing this to you as you need to get mental help as you have a very serious illness. You're a dangerous woman. I've been friends with you for sixteen years and became ultra-close to you six years ago. I've always trusted you and basically you became family to me. I transformed you from an average-looking mumsy, dumpy housewife to a much better-looking person in the past two years. A year ago, you changed dramatically. I wonder why?

I've never, ever had a problem with you talking or hanging out with any of my boyfriends or husbands. Why would I? You were my best friend: loyal, trustworthy, and had my best interests at heart. We were there for each other and you even made me godmother to your children.

But when I met Kieran, I saw a different look in your eye, a different aura, a different Jane. Although your look had changed dramatically – lost weight, had teeth done, hair extensions, nails, Botox – I thought it was fantastic that you looked amazing. But when you got on the table to dance in the Bahamas my mum and me looked at each other with the same thought.

'What is Jane doing?' I said to myself. 'This isn't like her.' Then I thought, Wow, she's getting confident, good for her. From then, till our wedding in England, I noticed you dressing more like me and thought, Ahhh, I'm flattered, so I didn't say anything, even though people were commenting on it to me.

Every other weekend you would come to my house and live there with your kids and I would cook and do everything, like it was a hotel. But, what I'm saying is that I welcomed you. You used to slob around in track pants like me but then you started dressing rather too sexy for slopping around. You did make me feel uncomfortable. I was thinking, Why is she doing this? She never used to. I was getting bigger and bigger and you were cloning into me. In the summer you dressed like you were going clubbing. You looked old and mutton but I thought it was a phase so I didn't say anything.

You used to ask questions about Kieran that you'd never asked me about any other boyfriend or husband and it made me think, What's Jane's point? It then crossed my mind, Does she fancy Kieran? Then I thought, No, it's in my head. She wouldn't, would she? She's my best friend and if she did, she'd say, 'Kieran's fit, Kate, you've done good.' But you didn't.

France: before we left you hurt your arm so you said you couldn't drive. I was heavily pregnant with a bad back, but that didn't stop me. But instead of sitting in the front with me you spent more time in the back with Kieran. I did think that was odd but like everything else I ignored it. The morning after our arrival you came out of your room all made up in Hello Kitty shorts and a top – yet again something I would wear. I remember thinking, What the fuck are you doing, Jane? All made up in shorts and a vest and you're nearly fifty!

I have been away with you enough and had you around the house with enough exes with you not caring how you look. At this point I said to myself, She fancies Kieran, she has to. I said to him, 'I'm pretty sure Jane fancies you.' He said, 'No, of course she doesn't,' but I was convinced. It wasn't just my hormones. I know it wasn't. From then on I analysed everything and I'm afraid to say, Jane, it was pretty obvious. I didn't say it to you, as I didn't want to embarrass you.

When my waters broke you know it was a horrible time for me and Kieran, and on top of it all Kieran's shoulder was infected. You would all visit me in hospital but every time you came I was shocked that you dressed as you did. Obviously I now know that it was for Kieran. You might as well have said to me, 'Look at you, Kate, all fat. It's okay, I'll show your husband a bit of glamour.' As time went on I was saying to you, 'Is Kieran okay? What's Kieran doing? How're the kids?' You would say, 'Yes, he's good, playing with the kids,' so I thought, He is doing okay. I kept saying to Kieran, 'Come spend time with me.' I kept questioning him and saying, 'Jane definitely fancies you.' He said you cried to him and told him that Derrick was being horrible and so he cuddled you. I guess you were thinking, Yes, yes, Kieran's cuddling me!

You knew I had it tough in hospital and knew it was hard on Kieran and that's when you thought, Pow! Yes! Kate's not about. I'm going to flaunt it. Even when Derrick was still at the villa I would send you messages about my concern over why Kieran wasn't spending time with me at the hospital. You never passed on these messages to him.

In fact, this is when you started your massive manipulating head games between me and Kieran and yourself, for your own gratification. You knew I wanted Kieran with me all the time. You knew I was really upset. At the same time, you knew Kieran wanted to be at the hospital with me too, but you knew you had the power to control this whole situation so you could try your best to get him away from me.

Why would you not pass my messages on? Why would you not tell Kieran I was missing him? I am in love with him and needed his support. More to the point, you were saying the opposite to him. When he said, 'I'm going to see Kate,' you would say, 'You need to rest. Kate will understand if you don't go.' Or, 'Wait for Derrick. We will all go.'

In other words, Jane, you didn't want me to see him alone. You wanted him around you all the time, to flaunt, flirt and get him to fancy you. You knew we were struggling with the pressure, but instead of helping you would act all fun, someone he could talk to, and make him think, Ahhh! Jane's so nice, so understanding, when in fact you were being a cunning bitch behind my back because you wanted my husband.

When my kids went home, why didn't you go too? There was no need for you to stay. That was a big sign that you didn't want to leave Kieran. When Derrick went, why didn't you go home with your husband as a family instead of staying in a villa, paid for by me, with my husband, son and nanny? Why? Because you were besotted with Kieran.

Even Derrick picked up on it. What made it obvious was that when he went, you hardly ever came to see me. But weren't you supposed to be there to be my supportive friend? No, you were there to pull my husband and get in his head. I actually hated you and wanted you to go. Why did you decide to leave when I came out? Because you wouldn't have had Kieran to yourself. It was obvious you weren't there for me and you dressed like a mutton slut to the airport.

When we got back to England you texted Kieran first saying you fancied him. Why? For the next seven months you were slagging me off all the time to him by text and by phone, because Kieran has told me and Gaylin everything. You would slag Kieran off to my face, saying I deserve a better man who supports me and that I could do better. Even when I told you how I felt about Kieran and that I wouldn't be unfaithful, that I'm happy and I wanted to dress up for him, you would tell him the opposite, saying, 'You're one of many. She's not that into you. You deserve better than Kate.'

Jane, what I'm trying to say is that you manipulated me and Kieran because you are jealous of me, jealous of my life, and jealous of my husband, so you tried to destroy things for me. Well, I'm sure you've had a wake-up call. You have lost us both. It might have taken me seven months to catch you but even then, you still never got to fuck my husband. He now knows what an evil, twisted woman you are and feels totally sick that he fell for your game. He says it wasn't your looks or body he was attracted to, that you have no tits and your face is old with bags, but he was attracted to your personality which he now knows is fake. He hates you. I hate you. Everyone hates you. The fact you have not said sorry shows how guilty you are.

Thanks to you I now have my Kieran back, my husband back, and we are stronger than ever. We are having amazing sex with a new baby on the way and re-doing our wedding vows. And do you know the best thing about it? You're not part of it or our lives so go and take your baggy, haggard face, tea-bag ugly tits, and remember you're fifty years old and behaving like a desperate bunny boiler.

I hope that Derrick wakes up and smells the coffee and realises you are with him for the wrong reasons and he actually deserves better than you. And if your mum were alive she would be ashamed of you. You're a disgusting human being.

Kate

Perhaps I shouldn't have been surprised, but on that occasion I got no reply from Jane. Not a sorry. Not an explanation. Nothing.

As soon as I came round from the operation Dr Gibb reassured me that the stitch had held, but I know exactly what I'm like. As soon as we left the hospital I was in the car frantically googling 'babies born at 23 weeks', 'what do they look like?' and 'do they survive?' Our baby wasn't a nameless foetus with a heartbeat any more, she was my little girl. She's going to come early, I kept telling myself. My belly felt so knotted up. If she survived, I'd have so many happy times to look forward to. But I'd caught Kieran and Jane kissing. There was so much to lash out against! My mind was continually lurching from heartbreak to hope. It was excruciating.

As the days went on I was realising that the story that Kieran had concocted simply didn't add up. Let me say one thing here: time on your hands does nothing for your sanity. So . . . if Kieran and Jane had kissed in Cape Verde for the first time, why had their behaviour been so strange in France? And why had Kieran been so off with me since then? Why hadn't he bonded with Jett? If he could kiss Jane, was there anyone else he'd kissed? And probably the most important question . . . who the fuck did I marry?

I kept returning to that night in Cape Verde. I thought, There's no way you would kiss someone so passionately on holiday, at midnight, on a beach, if you weren't fucking them. There's no way you would meet someone knowing that your wife was waiting for you in the villa, and that she had a problem with the person you were meeting, unless things were serious between you. 'It's all in your head, Kate,' one voice inside kept telling me. Then another would interrupt, 'Duh! Get real, Kate. He's been fucking around from day one. It's so fucking obvious.'

That week, I insisted that Gaylin came to see us every single day. The more I cried and the more we talked, the more I hoped Kieran might confess, but he didn't. For hours at a time he sat there not saying anything or else denying any accusation I threw at him. I was getting impatient. Fuck therapy, I figured. This is going nowhere. I'm pregnant. I need proof. And fast.

As random as it sounds, I'm an avid watcher of *The Jeremy Kyle Show* and I'm glued whenever a serial cheat is exposed. I love it when someone's been bare-faced, denying their infidelity throughout the whole episode, and then the results of the lie detector test come in and ... ta dah! ... they're caught red-handed. There was only one thing for it. Instead of firing off the questions as I'd done in Cape Verde, I'd get in the real McCoy. So that's exactly what I did. I got hold of the details of the man who conducts all of Jeremy Kyle's polygraph tests. My stepdad wasn't wrong when he told Kieran I'd leave no stone unturned.

'This is what's going to happen,' I explained to Kieran very matter-of-factly. To my surprise he agreed to go through with it. But as soon as the guy arrived Kieran announced he was going to the gym while the equipment was being set up. Now I know he'd read up on ways to cheat a lie detector test. He'd escaped to neck Red Bull and run on the treadmill so he could get his heart rate up and change his breathing. Talk about deluded! Even the lie detector guy commented on how bad it looked that he'd gone to the gym in the first place. When he did reappear Kieran looked casual, like he didn't have a care in the world. He even had me fooled. Why doesn't he look scared? I kept thinking. I'd be shitting myself!

Next was the pre-test interview where the polygraph test was explained. We also discussed the questions that I wanted to ask as I'd been told I was only allowed three. That was frustrating. I had so many going round my head. In the end, I narrowed it down from ... ooh ... around 100! Overall I was pleased with the questions I chose and Kieran ... well, Kieran didn't have a say in the matter.

When it came to it, I wasn't allowed in the room while the test was being conducted. Apparently, everything had to be done in a controlled environment. Obviously I was the least controlled person there, so I sat outside with Gaylin by my side. I swear to God, it was the longest hour of my life. A monitor was clipped on to Kieran's finger to measure his pulse, and a strap placed around his chest to measure any changes in his breathing. Attached to his upper arm was an inflatable cuff, like doctors use when they're measuring your blood pressure, and all the wires fed into a laptop computer. The guy told me afterwards that Kieran was calm and collected throughout the whole process. He answered clearly and with no hesitation. So here's what I asked:

1. *Apart from the one time Kate knows about, have you passionately kissed Jane?* Kieran answered 'No'.
2. *Apart from kissing, have you engaged in any sexual activity with Jane?* Kieran answered 'No'.
3. *Since you've returned from Cape Verde have you had any contact with Jane?* Kieran answered 'No'.

The results were analysed on the spot and I was told the outcome there and then. The expert's conclusion read: 'It is the opinion of the examiner that Kieran Hayler was not being truthful during this examination.'

Gotcha!

CHAPTER 10

I WANT A DIVORCE

It was late afternoon by the time the lie detector guy left but nothing had changed. Despite the results Kieran refused to tell the truth. As a last resort, Gaylin suggested that we try working with another therapist – a man called Kevin whom we ended up flying in from Gibraltar. First Kevin the dog . . . now another bloody Kevin in my life! Apparently, he'd worked with serial killers and psychopaths and was an expert at unpicking the criminal mind. Kevin turned out to be a very serious guy but after three days of intensive ten-hour sessions even he lost his rag with Kieran and I don't blame him. The last session finished with Kevin telling Kieran, 'I'm sorry. I'm going home. You've wasted my time. I can't help you because you don't want to help yourself. You're untreatable.' At £2,500 a day I was willing Kieran to cut the crap and 'fess up. This therapy was costing me a fucking fortune!

To be fair, Kevin had really tried to help Kieran and even stayed in touch with him via email after he went back to Gibraltar. During the sessions he said that he thought Kieran had a sex addiction and that he needed to seek treatment. For the first two days Kieran refused to say anything other than he hadn't done anything. Not once did he say he was sorry for how much upset he'd caused me. I wanted to slap him across the face and shout, 'Tell the fucking truth!' Unbelievably, I managed to keep my anger inside.

Then, the minute Kevin told us he was going home, something shifted. It was incredible! In front of me, Gaylin and Kevin, Kieran made an announcement. 'I want to confess and I need help,' he said.

'Phew! Thank fuck for that!' I exclaimed, because I really couldn't take another day of him lying.

Mind you, I knew whatever he was about to confess would be devastating and I wasn't wrong. At first Kieran admitted to having sex three times with Jane . . . then, within minutes, he'd upped it to six. He promised that they'd only ever had sex in Jane's car and that they'd first kissed each other the night before we were due to leave for France, but had not had sex by then. It was the same night they'd left me outside, heavily pregnant and packing up the horse box alone. Apparently, they'd arranged to meet in my cinema, but Jane had pulled Kieran towards her in the utility room.

I couldn't believe what I was hearing. France was months ago! 'Stay calm, Kate. It was only sex,' I was saying to myself. 'It wasn't as if they were having an affair.' I know it sounds bonkers, but the fact that Kieran told us that it was 'just sex' made it easier for me to accept. If he'd said he and Jane had fallen madly love with each other that would have finished me off, I guarantee it.

But I still didn't believe that he was revealing everything.

'Fuck you, Kieran!' I said. 'Tomorrow you're doing another lie detector test,' I promised him, because now we were on a roll I wanted to keep going. Even though I knew the answers would kill me, I needed to know every single detail. 'If I find out there's more, that's it, Kieran. It's over. I mean it,' I added.

Although I was pregnant and needed to keep healthy, eating was the last thing I felt like doing. My belly was churning and there were times when I was bent over in agony desperately trying to catch my breath. Kieran was whizzing me up fresh fruit protein shakes in the blender so at least I was getting some goodness into me, but I could hardly drink them. I'd also been prescribed a four-day course of Valium to steady my nerves and stop me falling apart entirely, but for someone who was supposedly on bed rest I was failing miserably.

The next morning, the lie detector guy arrived again. Kieran was upstairs in the shower while he set up. 'Get down the stairs, we're ready to start,' I shouted up to

Kieran. I paused . . . then listened, but I couldn't hear any movement so I marched up to see where he'd got to. He'd been ages! As I slowly opened the bathroom door, I could just make out Kieran through the steam. He was naked and curled up in a foetal position in the shower tray while the water bounced off his body. He was sobbing his eyes out. 'I'm ill, Kate,' he cried.

Wait a minute. This was a side to Kieran I'd never seen before. The cool, calculating man of the past few days had gone. Instead, he seemed like a helpless puppy. 'What kind of an excuse is that?' I said, hand on hip, struggling to control my temper. He didn't deserve my sympathy, and he wasn't going to get it either. Only medication not illness can affect the results of a test and this was Kieran making excuses for what he knew would be an obvious outcome. 'I don't fucking care how ill you are, what headache you've got or how tired you are. Get your fucking arse down those stairs NOW,' I screamed.

Again, I put three pre-arranged questions to Kieran. I wanted to know if he and Jane had kissed any time before the night we were packing up for France. He answered 'No' and the result showed that he was telling the truth. Then I asked if they'd had sex before our holiday. Again he answered 'No' and he was telling the truth. Finally, I needed to know if, other than myself and Jane, there were any other women Kieran had slept with. His reply left me completely gobsmacked.

'One,' he replied. And yes . . . he was telling the truth.

I couldn't control myself. I grabbed the nearest thing

to me, which happened to be a hardback copy of my sixth autobiography, and lobbed it straight at Kieran's head. Frustratingly, he ducked and it missed him. 'You fucking cunt!' I yelled as I stormed out of the room. With a sick feeling in my gut I climbed the stairs towards the spare room. All I wanted to do was shut myself away from Kieran and from everybody else in the house and take in the grim truth about my husband and my marriage. I felt destroyed by Jane and Kieran's betrayal.

I didn't cry. I couldn't allow Kieran to see me crying. I'd spent the whole week crying and, at that moment, I didn't want to give him the satisfaction, but I was a broken woman.

Kieran raced after me. 'Kate! Wait!' he pleaded.

'Just fuck off!' I kept shouting. My whole body was shaking. I was still reeling from what I'd heard and I needed to vent my anger somewhere. Anywhere. Deal with it, Kate. The man's a born liar and your best friend isn't your friend, I was telling myself. My fingers were trembling so much that I was barely able to press my iPhone keys, but before I could stop myself I fired off a tweet.

Sorry to say me and Kieran are divorcing, him and my best friend Jane Pountney have been having a full-blown sexual affair. I didn't mention the other woman. I didn't know who she was, and besides, I'd run out of characters.

I spun around to face Kieran. Suddenly, I had an overwhelming urge to hurt him, as he had me. 'I want to be with *you*, Kate,' he pleaded, but it was far too late for that. Violence of any kind is not in my nature but in the heat of the moment I pushed past him and ran back downstairs. Snatching a Yankee jar candle that Kieran had me bought me from the nearby garden centre, I opened the front door and hurled it at the windscreen of his new Land Rover.

'Fuck you!' I yelled again, but the worst thing was that neither the windscreen nor the candle smashed! The jar bounced off the glass and thudded on to the gravel driveway. Fuck! That was so annoying. I guess that model of 4x4 isn't called a Defender for nothing!

Once we'd packed the lie detector guy off, I texted Jane. *I know everything. I'm coming over*, I told her, and with that my phone immediately started ringing. It was Derrick. I had no idea what he knew but Jane must have said something because he asked me to stay put. He said he was coming over with my friend Neil. Then I rang my sister Sophie. I needed her there for moral support. Then my friend Melodie arrived and one of Kieran's friends. I knew it would only be a matter of time before the press kicked off big time too. Although I'd impulsively tweeted my heartbreak, and I make no apologies for that, I wasn't up for talking to anyone, especially as I didn't know the whole story myself.

Everyone pleaded with me not to go to Jane's. 'Calm down, Kate. Think of the baby,' they kept saying because by now the tears were pouring down my cheeks and I was doubled over on the sofa with terrible cramps. But strength came from somewhere inside me. I'm stubborn. Once my mind's made up, there's no going back. Given my distress, remarkably Kieran remained as calm as anything and Derrick was still trying to play down the whole thing, defending Jane and saying he was convinced that she and Kieran had only had a drunken kiss. I don't blame Derrick at all for openly trying to protect himself and his family. Deep down I think he knew that something else had been going on.

Derrick, Neil and Kieran took one car and Sophie and I piled into mine. As we drove through the security gates and on to the main road I was amazed to see that the paps had already started setting up. How did they get there so quickly? The last thing I wanted was to be photographed, but they followed us down the dual carriageway and set up camp again outside Jane's house.

The worst thing for me was that confronting Jane turned out to be such a disappointment. I wanted her to crack and tell me everything, but in fact she continued to give nothing away about her and Kieran and, to this day, has revealed no details of what went on between them. But she was supposed to be my best mate! Surely she owed me some kind of explanation?

'Kieran. Tell Jane what you told me,' I ordered him, but he was subdued and, to my mind, even sounded apologetic when he spoke to her. 'I'm sorry. I'm not in love with you, Jane. I want to be with Kate,' he mumbled. That wasn't convincing at all! He could at least sound genuine, I thought. Still, he'd given me enough rope to hang Jane with. I leaned towards her. 'How do you feel now you've been dumped, Jane?' I said cuttingly. But there was no reply. 'Come on, Jane. How do you feel?' I continued, glaring at her. 'You've been fucking him so you must have thought you were going to be with him!' I added.

'Come on, Jane! Answer the question!' Derrick chipped in, but her reply was astonishing.

'I hated you, Kate,' she admitted. 'I hated that every time I came to your house you had my boyfriend . . .'

'Your *boyfriend*?' I gasped. I wasn't sure if I'd heard it correctly, but suddenly Derrick shouted, 'What are you on about, Jane?' and I knew she was for real.

'*Jane!* He's my *husband*. Not your fucking *boyfriend*,' I yelled, but she sat there in silence. This is totally fucked up, I thought. Was this the reaction of someone who'd shagged my husband only six times? I seriously had my doubts. 'Kieran's told me you fucked six times and he never wore a condom once! Is that true, Jane? Was it six times? And why would you shag my husband without a condom?' I confronted her. But again, Jane had no reply.

Mmmm. Someone's telling big fat porky pies, I reckoned. But it was a waste of time me quizzing Jane. It was obvious she was either protecting herself or Kieran or both. Halfway through the conversation Kieran walked out, saying he'd had enough and eventually, as I turned to leave the house, I looked back at her. 'Why did you clone yourself into me, Jane?' I asked.

'Look at me, Kate,' she replied. 'I'm fifty. Do you think I wanted to wear thigh-length boots and little dresses? I dressed like you because I knew that's what Kieran wanted.' It was probably the only question she answered honestly.

On the journey home I was driving myself crazy thinking about what had really gone on. None of what Kieran had said made sense. So I began calculating . . . if he and Jane had their first kiss the night before we went to France, and I caught them on a beach ten months later in Cape Verde and Jane thinks Kieran's her boyfriend, did they seriously have sex only six times in ten months? Er . . . pull the other one, Kieran.

Over the next few days we continued to see Gaylin, but when I think back on that week now it's a complete blur. The more time we spent in therapy the more Kieran drip-fed us details about his meetings with Jane and the more confused I felt. He revealed that he was the one who had started to text Jane. When she replied, the whole affair snowballed. I'm no Miss Marple, but I was at least reassured that my instinct was spot on. Kieran and Jane had shagged way more than six times.

There was also the question of the other woman Kieran had admitted to, but I'd made the decision that I wasn't going to beg him to reveal her identity. There's only so much a pregnant woman can take and it was better that Kieran admitted everything himself instead of me dragging the answers out of him. I had my suspicions anyway. There was a girl Kieran bought his protein shakes off sometimes. He was always texting her and arranging to meet her (although, in the end this *was* innocent). The truth will out, Kate, I promised myself. For now I needed to concentrate on Jane.

Apparently, the first time Kieran and she had had sex was two days after I'd been admitted to hospital in France. Can you imagine it? Your wife is in hospital, having your baby, and you're in a villa getting off with her best mate.

What kind of sick person does that? According to Kieran, Derrick was even downstairs when they pulled each other into the bathroom, locked the door and fucked doggy style. Kieran was very quick to tell me that he never saw Jane's boobs because, quite frankly, they're rank and she always insisted on keeping her bra on. Seriously, though. What difference did it make? I wasn't exactly going to say, 'Oh, well, if you didn't see Jane's boobs, all is forgiven!' Boobs or no boobs, he still managed to stick his dick in her!

Then two weeks after we came back from France, when Jett was only weeks old and still poorly, they arranged to meet ten minutes away from home in the carpark of Tesco Extra. They had sex in the passenger seat of Jane's Ford Fiesta. He'd gone out saying we needed shopping done! *Tesco Extra?* They're not kidding!

He also admitted meeting her at a nearby country pub. He'd go straight from his plastering job, park his 4x4 next to her car in an overgrown corner of the car park. His car shielded hers from view and they'd shag in her front seat. And they had sex at her house in Storrington. She had an annex and they'd fuck there. Thank Christ they never did it here, I thought, looking around the living room. The house and the kids felt like my only refuge, the safety net to keep me sane in all of this madness! But it wasn't long before that was destroyed too . . .

It emerged that every other weekend, when Jane was at my house, they had sex in either the cinema or the utility room. Aha! It was all clicking into place now. I'd be upstairs bathing Princess or Junior or Jett. Kieran would always come up to check on us, because he knew I'd have to get them out, dried and dressed, and he'd have enough time to go back downstairs where he and Jane would be at it. He'd pop his head round the door to ask if I needed anything so I wouldn't suspect anything.

There were even times when I'd go to Tesco to buy food for our fun evenings in and, while the kids were outside playing, he and Jane fucked. There was another occasion when we ran out of sweets during a marathon film session and I offered to stock up at the supermarket. As soon as my car disappeared from view, Kieran and Jane left the kids glued to the screen in the cinema and shagged in the utility room.

New Year? Another corker! They even fucked at my onesie party! I have no idea how because all I remember is Kieran making me Porn Star Martini cocktails all night and him getting hammered too! But, according to him, at around 1 a.m. he and Jane had sex standing up in the stables still dressed in their onesies. The really weird thing is that I remember Jane being with me all night and then Kieran going to bed. I slipped under the duvet next to him and cuddled him before we both slept. He wasn't interested in having sex, which I did think was odd. Now I know that probably less than an hour earlier he'd been outside fucking Jane. Ugh!

Oh, and then there was the day after the Comic Relief bike ride, too. That was the day that Kieran had supposedly been throwing up and I'd struggled around London having to carry Jett. It was the day my cleaner had told me Jane had come to the house seemingly to look for Derrick's Sat Nav, and how the cleaner had felt uncomfortable that Jane had gone to see Kieran in the spare room. She'd stayed for fifteen minutes then left. But of course Jane didn't leave. Instead, they planned that Kieran would leave the house to let the dogs out and she would follow. All along they'd been upstairs secretly arranging how to meet in the stables again . . .

I decided I wanted to see the evidence. It was like I was torturing myself, but I had to know. One evening after Gaylin had gone and we'd fed the kids, I sat in the kitchen and started running through the tape from our security cameras. 'What are you doing?' Kieran asked me. 'The camera doesn't lie,' I said bitterly. He looked horrified but left me to it. I found the footage from New Year but there was no sign of Kieran and Jane leaving the house. I also rewound to the day after the bike ride. Kieran did go out of the front door to let the dogs out and he did head towards the stables. Jane followed around ten minutes later but I lost track of her as she walked towards her car.

At this point, Kieran returned to the kitchen looking anxious. The kids were watching telly and he gestured for me to step into the living room. 'Kate, I need to tell you something. You won't find anything,' he whispered.

I was confused. 'Why not?' I asked. 'If you went to the stables it should be on the tape!'

'We found a way to dodge the cameras, Kate. There's no evidence.'

'You devious cunt,' I spat at him. Sure enough, they'd walked separately along the boundary fence, up through the back of the stables and jumped through the rear stable door that he had opened earlier so no camera would pick them up. It was pointless me trawling through the film, I wouldn't find a single thing.

'You're like a cross between Ted Bundy and Alex Reid,' I said to Kieran. Okay, when I think about it now, I was probably overdoing it comparing Kieran to the 1970s serial killer Ted Bundy. But what I meant was, he had a split personality. Ted Bundy charmed women. He was this good-looking professional who used his charisma to groom, pick up, torture and kill girls. Alex Reid had a split personality too. I fell in love with Alex the gentle giant, but at the flick of a switch he wanted to dress as a woman, act like a woman and be fucked like a woman. Again, I'm not suggesting that Alex was in any way violent or wanted to physically hurt women.

179

With me, Kieran was quiet, thoughtful and perfect, but I was finding out there was a whole different side to him.

'You've got this side to you that needs to pick up women even though you've got everything on a plate at home,' I said. 'It's like a drug. I don't understand it!'

I openly blamed Kieran for what had happened but the worst thing was that I blamed myself too. Gaylin told me not to. She reassured me that Kieran's behaviour was not a reaction to anything I'd done, but I couldn't help it. At first I'd been so strong. I'd told Kieran that whatever the outcome, I was divorcing him. I didn't want to be with a man who cheated on his wife. To me that person was dead. But there were times when all the hurt and insecurity began creeping back and I became consumed by self-doubt. 'Everyone is right. It's your fault for marrying him too soon,' I told myself. Then again, everything had seemed so right. I had no reason to believe Kieran wasn't a genuine guy until our holiday in France. Perhaps he'd done all this because I'd been pregnant virtually from the moment I'd met him? He'd never seen the real Kate – the girl who can be fun and sexy and carefree. Instead, I'd been fat or sick or in hospital or giving birth!

True, if a friend of mine had come to me in the same situation, I'd have said, 'Fuck him! That's disgusting! Get rid of him!' But no one was feeling what I was feeling. And none of my friends had sat with us for days in therapy, and they didn't know about the horrific event that had occurred in Kieran's childhood either. My mum, my manager, everybody was telling me to get rid of him. In fact, the atmosphere between me and my mum was awful. I felt this intense pressure to kick him out. Even Kieran's mum said she couldn't understand his behaviour and she wouldn't blame me if I didn't want to stay with him. I got on well with Wendy and I respected her for saying that, because she could easily have taken Kieran's side no matter what. My manager warned me that staying with Kieran might impact on my career. But this had nothing to do with my career! 'You don't understand,' I told him. 'This isn't about my career. It's my fucking life! It's reality!'

I had so many decisions to make. Most importantly, I had the kids to consider. I'm their mother and I didn't want their lives ruined too. They adored Kieran. They loved spending time with him, but that was no reason to stay in the relationship. And now there was a baby on the way!

One thing was clear. I didn't want to stay in the house. Every time I walked through a room I had a picture in my mind of Kieran and Jane there. I even had the sofa professionally cleaned! There'd been a time when Kieran and I had toyed with the idea of buying a dilapidated property near Haywards Heath to develop, but that project was now on hold. Instead I instructed my estate agent find me a new house. He came up with one near Orpington. It was off the M25, had been newly refurbished and, when I timed the journey in the car, was exactly the same distance away from the kids' school as my current property. I asked for a survey to be done and even started packing some of the kids' belongings into plastic boxes and piling them up in the centre of the living room. And I asked my solicitor to begin divorce proceedings. I told Kieran that while I wanted to continue with our therapy, there was no way I wanted to be married to him a moment longer.

And, on 12 May, I wrote Jane another letter:

Hi, Jane,

Since I last saw you, loads has happened again, and trust me, this is the calm before the storm as it's gone public. I'm glad it has because you should both be ashamed of yourselves. It's not a nice time for any of us as I'm sure you'll know. We are all emotional wrecks. I could write this letter and abuse you and be horrid to you as I have every right to, but I won't. I'm not like that, even though you have made my life and world fall apart. I'm a decent, kind person and that's my problem. People take my kindness as a weakness and that's what you both did to me :-(

I've gone from pure hate to confusion to questioning: Why this? Why that? Why did it start? So far Kieran is the one who has been totally honest with me and the reason is that he wants to be with me for ever and he is doing absolutely everything he can to prove this – not just with what he is telling me but with his actions too.

As the friend that I really thought you were, why could you not be honest with me? Even if it hurts me, please tell me your side! Please tell me how you think it started. What made you start texting Kieran back? What was so strong about his texts that meant you crossed that line where you couldn't resist? Why did you not tell me that his texts were crossing the line? How quickly did you fall in love? Were you really in love with him? Did it never cross your mind what his real intentions were?

There were so many questions and still so few answers.

CHAPTER 11

ADDICTION, WHAT
ADDICTION?

I've never been one of these celebrities who wants to spend their life banging on about how long they've been in therapy. I've always counted myself a strong person. Rightly or wrongly, I've prided myself on the fact that I've never sought treatment for drug or alcohol addiction and never, ever set foot in a rehab clinic. Without my family to keep me grounded I'm absolutely sure I would have done, though.

However, I can't deny that talking to a professional has been brilliant at times. Like so many people, when I first sought therapy I thought I was being weak. Now, I realise it's helped me overcome some massive hurdles in my life.

When I suffered post-natal depression after Junior's birth I had no idea what was happening to me. But talking to someone who understood not only lifted me out of that depression but helped me to discover that I wasn't alone. Many women go through the same feelings after childbirth, yet there's still so much shame attached to saying 'I need help'.

Likewise, after Pete and I split, I found that discussing my pain and insecurities helped me refocus my life and move on. Although I had accepted that the marriage was over from early on, I still felt completely devastated. I had three children to take care of and I had to be strong for them. They'd already lost the stability of having a mum and a dad together full-time so the last thing they needed was a parent who was unable to give them the love they needed. With the right help, I started to see the bigger picture and I was able to concentrate my energy on them, not just myself.

Don't get me wrong, I'm not suggesting that therapy is some kind of magic bullet because you've got to put in a lot of work yourself. And I've only sought help when I've really needed it because I'm also a firm believer that whatever life throws at you, time is a great healer. But, in my experience, therapy has been a valuable tool in my armoury – albeit a staggeringly expensive one!

When Kieran and I came back from Cape Verde I didn't just want to see my therapist, I *needed* to see her. And I needed to take Kieran with me. Trust me, had I not been able to express my hurt and confusion in a calm environment, Kieran would have had many more Pricey-inflicted injuries to nurse. So far only his car windscreen had taken the brunt of my anger – although I'd even managed to mess that up!

Talking through my anguish was hard, but it was something I had to do. I'd trusted Kieran. We were married. We had a son together and I'd found out he'd been cheating on me with my best friend. I'm not exaggerating when I say that my heart was shattered into thousands of pieces. What I couldn't understand was how both he and Jane could hate me so much that they wanted to hurt me that badly. I know many of you will be reading this and thinking: Why didn't you listen to your family and friends and chuck him out? But it's never that easy once you are married. Somehow I also felt that this relationship was worth saving.

Whatever anyone says about me, I'm a fighter. Instead of running away, I wanted to confront the situation head on. Had I not found out I was pregnant, I might have felt differently. I'm sure the first thing I would have done then would have been to call my girlfriends and arrange a wild night out. Usually there's nothing like a truckload of vodka and a good boogie to get a dickhead out of your system. Strangely, this time I didn't even feel like doing that. Anyhow, I wasn't sure who out of my girlfriends I could trust any more! Maybe you're getting old, Kate, I thought. Katie Price gets old? A shocker, I know! And if I gave it my all then no one could knock me for trying.

As I've mentioned elsewhere, I was expecting Kieran to sit in a room with me and Gaylin, put his hands up and do the big 'I'm sorry' number. When that didn't happen I assumed the reason was that he was secretly in love with Jane but was too scared to admit it. Why else would he not show any remorse or give away any details of their affair? I found that especially painful. As I saw it, as much as Jane was protecting Kieran, he was doing the same with her even though people have suggested since that the only person Kieran was protecting was himself.

The minute Kevin suggested that Kieran showed all the signs of someone with a sex addiction, I thought, My self-esteem's at rock-bottom and suddenly Kieran's got a sex addiction? This can't be real! 'Are you taking the piss?' I exclaimed. 'Isn't that what celebs say when they've been caught with their leg over one too many times and they want to save their flagging careers? Or get people to feel sorry for them? Surely sex addiction's an excuse for bad behaviour rather than a serious condition!'

I even mentioned the addiction theory to some of my male friends to get their reaction. 'He hasn't got a problem!' one argued. 'All that's happened is that he's been playing away and he's made the mistake of getting caught. That's not an addiction, that's bad luck!'

Even my mum asked Kieran's mum how long we were going to keep the 'addiction' line up for. 'Why isn't he man enough to apologise and get on with it?' she said.'He's not ill, he's a shagger!' No one could ever accuse my mum of holding back.

Once everything was out in the open I remained 100

per cent sure that I wanted to continue with the divorce. But I had to listen to my heart too. I wanted Kieran to be a part of mine and the kids' lives, especially Jett's. However much I hated him for what he had done, I would never deny him access to his son. It's unfair on them when children become the weapon in a war between parents.

So I guess there was a large part of me that wanted (and still wants) to believe that Kieran does have a problem, because starting up a ten-month affair with your wife's best friend soon after getting married isn't exactly normal! Then again, there are still days when I don't know whether to buy that explanation. Men have affairs all the time but it doesn't make them addicts. They're being idiot men! What's the difference between those men and Kieran? Is treating him as someone with an illness letting him off the hook? Back then, I wanted him to lose everything! I wanted him to suffer! I wanted him to feel pain!

I felt like I was stumbling around in the dark looking for an explanation. On top of that, as ever, I had to face the lies that were being printed about me too. I tried not to read any of them but avoiding the papers is easier said than done. What people say to sell a story is unbelievable! Jemma Henley – another contestant on *Signed By Katie Price* and certainly not a friend of mine – was even quoted as saying that the reason I hadn't thrown Kieran out was because I needed a man so badly, stemming from never having got over the break-up with Pete. What utter rubbish! Pete and I were over five years before this. We have both moved on. Why can't people understand that?

As far as I could see, some parts of the media even wanted my marriage to fail. It was like they were rubbing their hands and enjoying my heartbreak. It felt as if they were saying 'I told you so', but what they couldn't seem to appreciate was that there was a family's welfare involved, a family that I was fighting hard to keep together. I could not understand why I wasn't being given credit for that.

What made things a whole lot easier when Pete and I split was that my kids weren't old enough to understand what was going on. Harvey doesn't grasp the impact of a divorce, although he did understand that Pete wasn't going to be living with us any more, and Junior was four and Princess only two at the time. Of course, I had to explain to them in the simplest terms that Mum and Dad weren't going to be together, but that we loved them and we would both stay a part of their lives. They accepted it because that's what little children do. But I knew that it would change their lives for ever.

With Kieran, at first I decided not to sit the kids down and tell them because I didn't want to stress them out. They're not stupid, though. It was impossible to hide the fact that something was seriously wrong. For starters, they'd witnessed all that upset in Cape Verde, Gaylin had been at the house every day and the paps were camped on the roadside whenever the children left for school.

Also, I was so on edge that I kept snapping at them over the smallest things and I really regret that now. My home is such a positive place I can't bear arguments, especially when the kids are involved. Standing by Kieran was tearing me apart, but if there was anything that made me want to work through our problems it was the children. Give me all the designer clothes and diamonds in the world, none of it would match up to my family. They are, and always will be, the most important thing in my life.

At times I tried to see the funny side too, especially when a few secret admirers crawled out of the woodwork. I don't want to say who, but I received some very flirtatious texts from several high-profile men. 'I might be a mum of four, pregnant with a fifth, but I've still got it!' I laughed. Even Leo dropped me a line, followed by Alex Reid. Bloody hell! They both wanted me to know how sorry they were to hear about my marriage and that they were there for me if I needed them. I only had to say the word. God, between the pair of them they've sold so many stories on me, I wouldn't touch them with a bargepole. Sorry, guys, I was heartbroken, not desperate!

After Kieran began to confess, Gaylin gave me stacks of material to read on the subject of sex addiction. There were reports from American psychologists and articles written by people with all sorts of letters after their name, which made a change because my bedtime reading is usually *Hello!* But for Kieran's sake, I ploughed through it all. Some of it was really heavy, but the weird thing was, I could recognise his behaviour in many of the traits that were being described.

I learned all sorts of facts. Apparently sex addiction has only been discovered in the last ten years and it affects far more men than women.

The effects on the brain are similar to the buzz experienced by people who are addicted to cocaine or gambling or even bodybuilding. The high only lasts so long before the addict needs another fix. And as the addiction progresses the person wants to take more and more risks. It's completely normal for sex addicts to cover up or make excuses for their behaviour because most of the time they don't think they're doing anything wrong. I read all these case studies of people who'd sacrificed their health, their home, their work, their relationships and their families because of their addiction. In most if not all cases Kieran's behaviour resembled theirs.

Gaylin had also explained to me that sex addiction isn't really about sex. Instead, it's about adrenalin. According to her, the sex Kieran was having with Jane wasn't about fancying her or even about wanting to be intimate with her. Kieran would have done anything to get any woman into bed. And he was always on the lookout for someone else to fuck! If I hadn't caught him he would just have carried on. Shutting down as he did and refusing to tell the truth was also a classic symptom of someone with an addiction problem. And there was me thinking that was Kieran being a twat!

I couldn't understand it. I even asked Gaylin, 'What has Jane got that I haven't?' All I could imagine was the whole time they were together, they were laughing at me behind my back or taking the piss out of me. The humiliation was unbearable.

Even more baffling to me was that the whole time Kieran and I were together we had a good relationship and great sex. There was nothing off bounds. He knew he could have whatever he wanted at home, so I didn't understand why he needed to look elsewhere. 'It doesn't matter if he has dirty sex with you, Kate. You're his wife,' Gaylin explained.

'For him it's about the fact that he's doing it with someone he isn't married to. It's about the danger and the thrill.' And the more I kept banging on about him fancying Jane, the more exciting it was for him to meet and have sex with her, because he knew it was wrong.

In some ways, I had been relieved to hear that there was another woman involved. I know, I know! It sounds absolutely crazy, but at least if he was sleeping with other women it proved he was using Jane for sex and wasn't in love with her. I even texted Jane telling her that he'd fucked another woman. I felt great satisfaction in breaking that news to her. I thought, Up yours! Let's see how you react that! Mortified is my guess.

After a week of talking, we agreed that Kieran would start treatment. If he had my support that would help his recovery. And, even though I still wasn't convinced, I wasn't ever going to say that to him. Apparently, most addicts relapse far more quickly if their partner isn't with them every step of the way, encouraging them to get better. It would mean I'd have to put my own heartbreak to one side, which was the hardest thing in the world to do, but if there was a possibility it could save our marriage then there was no harm in trying.

Once his treatment started Kieran would have to move out of the house. He was warned that he'd probably suffer withdrawal symptoms too. Anything from tiredness to depression to shaking or vomiting. To begin with he'd go through several sessions of learning various relaxation techniques. Or to give the treatment its proper name, Autogenic training. During each session he would learn special mind exercises to help his body totally de-stress because anxiety is often one of the triggers for sex addiction. Admittedly, there was a part of me thinking, Hang on a minute. None of this sounds like he's being punished for anything, but again I kept my thoughts to myself. Reluctantly, I knew I was going to have to get used to it.

Plus Kieran did have to give lots of things up. He was banned from going to the gym. He was banned from having sex with me . . . or anyone else. And that meant all sex. No oral. No anal. Come to think if it, he wasn't even allowed a cheeky wank and, worst of all, he was banned from kissing! I was under strict instructions only to kiss Kieran on the cheek and never on the lips. We weren't allowed to sit on the sofa and watch TV together. He wasn't allowed to use the internet. He couldn't watch porn. He couldn't ring, text or tweet any woman other than me. He'd already given up his plastering job when he did his shoulder in and he'd not continued stripping either, so he wasn't working.

I couldn't help thinking that only one month before, Kieran had a beautiful house, a family who loved him, he was having sex with two women … maybe even more. Now he had no job, no money, no home, no children to come back to, and his name was splattered all across the newspapers as a 'love rat'. He'd lost everything. More importantly, what the fuck was he was going to do for the next sixty days? His treatment sounded like solitary confinement. That would drive me nuts!

We had one last weekend to be with each other, but after that his new regime would kick in and Kieran would have to leave. Knowing that he wasn't going to be living with us made me surprisingly sad. Other than the times I'd been in hospital in France, we'd hardly spent a night apart from each other. Don't you dare have sex with him, Kate, I kept telling myself. Don't you dare give him what he wants. At the same time I had this overwhelming urge to be close to him. As much as I was supporting Kieran in his treatment, it felt like I was being punished for something he'd done. I wanted cuddles, I wanted kisses and I wanted sex. I was pregnant and craved the love, attention and security that women need when they're expecting, but I was having to rein back all my feelings even though I'd done nothing wrong! And, in spite of everything, I was still in love with Kieran. If not, I figured I would have kicked him out weeks before.

In a moment of weakness we did have a quickie on the Friday morning. All the time it was happening I felt as though I was exacting my revenge on Jane. In my head, I was saying to her, 'You might love him, but I get to touch him.' People might find it absurd that I even wanted to have sex with him, but it's a feeling I can't explain. It's just something I had to do although afterwards I felt like I'd let myself down, and Kieran too. He also admitted he was disappointed in himself and we promised each other that it wouldn't happen again. If Kieran was to see out his eight weeks, we both had to be strong.

On the Sunday, Kieran went to his mum's. There are some moments in my life that replay in my head like a film and that day is one of them. All the kids were with me and I had the unenviable task of explaining to them fully what Kieran had done and why he was going. I tried to be very matter-of-fact so as not to ramp up their distress. I told them that Kieran had been seeing Jane when he was supposed to be married to me and, because of that, he had to leave the house. As soon as I'd finished my speech, Junior and Princess burst into floods of tears. Thank God Harvey didn't really get it and Jett was far too little. I hugged them tightly and told them that everything was going to be okay, but nothing I said seemed to help at all. There's nothing more gut-wrenching than watching your kids cry like that.

Kieran has since told me that leaving us was the worst day of his life. He had to climb into my car (bizarrely, I insisted he take it!) with only a holdall full of clothes and drive off with all of us, his mum and Gaylin standing by the door watching him disappear from view. I could barely hold back my own tears and it took me a long while to calm Junior and Princess down. They're absolutely besotted with Kieran!

That evening the house felt so strange. It was great to hear the kids playing, but it also felt like I'd lost everything. Princess insisted on sleeping with me. As I lay there I thought, This isn't right. Princess is in bed with me. Jett is in a cot beside the bed and I'm lying here heavily pregnant. I wanted Kieran there so badly it hurt, and texted him to tell him that, even though I wasn't supposed to.

For the next few days Kieran was on his phone non-stop texting me. He was constantly asking me if I wanted him to be there, but I didn't know what to say. I know he wanted me to reply telling him, 'I love you. I want you back,' but as much as I wanted to reciprocate, I realised that would be feeding his addiction. I wanted to stick to the rules, but it was so hard. He even sent a picture of himself from his mum's house, which looked like he was in the dingiest bedsit ever. According to her, he wasn't eating or showering. He'd turned into a caveman, not talking to anyone. But I wasn't going to feel sorry for him. Actually, all I kept thinking was that a pregnancy had been fucked up yet again. It was fucked up with Jett because we'd been in France. Now, Kieran was at his mum's because he'd cheated on me so badly that he wasn't even allowed to be at the house. In fact, the whole situation was fucked up!

One morning when I was lying awake at 4 a.m. I texted him a picture of us from when we went to the hospital together and saw the first scans of Bunny. I wrote: *Look how happy we are. Look how innocent I am, not knowing you were fucking my best friend.* No sooner had I pressed send than he texted back: *Go to sleep. I know you don't believe me, but the sex with her wasn't good. It wasn't about that. I just wanted sex . . .* He was right. I didn't believe him.

Soon it became obvious that with Kieran away I would not be able to cope with the kids on my own. Dr Gibb kept ordering me to rest, but Jett was teething and I was losing sleep. Kieran had gone from his mum's house to his nan's, which was worse for him as he couldn't even get a proper signal on his phone. And it was a good forty minutes' drive away. But the bottom line was that I really needed him to help out with childcare. Because of my stitch I couldn't lift anything, including Jett. So we went back to Gaylin, who agreed to change the treatment.

Kieran was now allowed to come to the house between 2 p.m. and 8 p.m. every single day. Jett wasn't walking then but, like any nine-month-old he was crawling around and into everything, and he needed constant supervision. He wasn't yet sleeping through the night either so eventually Kieran asked if he could stay over to take some of the pressure off me, although he was banned from sleeping in our bed.

For two nights in a row he slept in the spare room and fed and bathed Jett first thing in the morning. He also gave me a hand getting Harvey ready for school. Then for two nights I'd take the spare room and Kieran would sleep in with Jett so I could catch up on my forty winks. We were very, very good. We stuck to the regime completely. That wasn't as difficult as it sounds because Kieran said his therapy had really messed with his head. For the whole eight weeks he couldn't even get a hard-on! Even after the eight weeks ended we didn't have sex straight away. It was like we had to relearn how to be intimate with each other. But I'm pleased to report that we're now completely back on track.

Do I believe that Kieran has an addiction? He's convinced that he does and I have to believe it to get through each day. Not only that but as our therapy continued there were more revelations to convince me that he definitely had a problem.

CHAPTER 12

NEW REVELATIONS

As soon as Kieran's addiction treatment kicked in I was due for another scan. So far my stitch had held and the doctors were pleased with my progress but I was being closely monitored. Whether it was in London or at my local hospital, I needed regular check-ups and the prognosis wasn't brilliant. At this rate, I was unlikely to carry the baby for longer than thirty weeks.

Kieran came with me to all my appointments, despite what the newspapers would have you believe. They all picked up on the fact that in late May I'd arrived at hospital in East Grinstead by myself and that I cut a lonely figure entering the outpatients' unit. The picture taken then looks like I was trying to win their sympathy, but the truth was a lot less pathetic. Kieran wasn't far behind. In fact, I think he was parking the car and he came through the unit's rear door to meet me.

Still, I might as well have been alone. I wanted to be anywhere but in the UK. If I could have been magically transported to a desert island away from the press, I would have been a very happy girl. Let's face it, no one wants to be snapped outside a hospital in boiling hot sunshine, looking fat and frightened. Although I hadn't given any interviews, the level of speculation about our marriage was insane, but I'd held off talking to any journalists. I was still taking the news in. I didn't know what to say to other people about it.

In all the confusion, I still hadn't made up my mind about whether or not I wanted Kieran to be part of my pregnancy. It was one thing him helping me out at home and us going through the therapy, but quite another him being there at the birth. That smacked to me of planning a future together. After everything he'd put me through I didn't trust him one bit and I wanted to take things very, very slowly.

Having said that, it felt cruel to deny him the opportunity to bond with his baby daughter. Jett's birth had been such a disaster and Kieran had told me that he wanted this one to be different. He wanted to feel connected to me and the baby. But why had it taken me finding out about Jane for him to want that? It was bullshit! In a way, I needed him there. But I wasn't sure whether I wanted him there . . .

As May galloped on I didn't even have the head-space

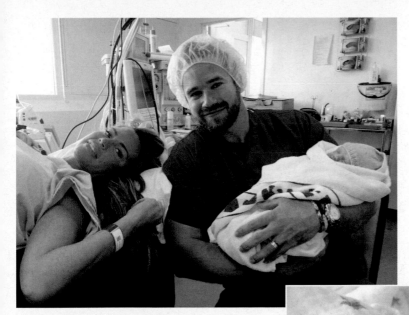

This time, it really felt like Kieran was a part of our family.

Baby Hayler's tiny feet and toes.

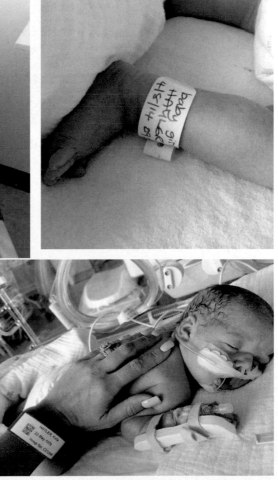

My mum gives Bunny her first cuddle.

My little 'runner bean'. Bunny was so tiny when she was born.

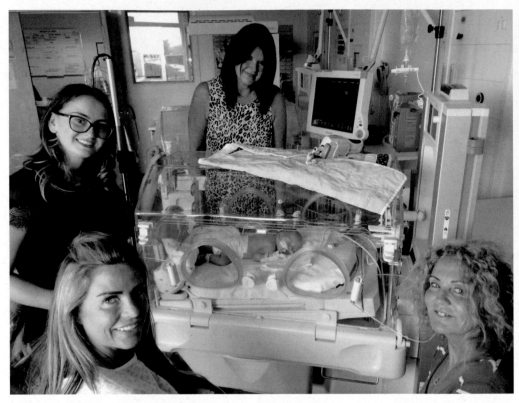

My sister Sophie, me, Mum and Kieran's mum Wendy but all eyes were on Bunny.

Jett meets his baby sister for the first time.

Harvey and Bunny are inseparable.

Above: Multi-tasking with Jett and Bunny.

Left: Roll over Superwoman!

Sleepyheads me and Kieran with our little brood.

It's all too much for Bunny!

Daddy's new tractor is enough to send any girl to sleep.

Enjoying a rare moment of rest.

What the hell did I let
myself in for? The minutes
before I entered the Big
Brother House – I had no
clue I would win!

No going back now…

They could watch me, but I missed Kieran and the kids like crazy.

I won? I won! I still can't believe it!

to think about my birthday. My thirty-fifth had fallen as flat as a pancake because I'd been heavily pregnant with Jett, although I'd made up for it in Monaco later in the year with Louisa and Jane. Now my thirty-sixth was looking even more problematic. Originally, I'd thought about having a party, something fun and blingy but reasonably low-key, but that was before we'd gone to Cape Verde. Now I could hardly face people, let alone entertain them.

When Kieran arrived on the afternoon of 22 May, he insisted on tweeting me a birthday message. *I love you. I will repair your heart*, it read. And he bought me more flowers than I could fill the kitchen with. And presented me a ring set with a turquoise gemstone heart. He told me that he wanted to show everybody how serious he was about us. Normally I'd love that kind of attention but this time I felt horribly empty. I thought, If you loved me, Kieran, you wouldn't have cheated on me. As for repairing my heart, I didn't know how to respond to that; each time I saw him, I was reminded of how badly he'd broken it.

On the evening of my birthday he covered my eyes with his hands and led me through to my cinema. He'd made a special meal and set up a table for us there amid a sea of candles. Each and every one was flickering away in the darkness. It was very romantic – the sort of date night every girl wants with their hubby. But it didn't feel romantic or special. In fact it felt fake, even though I could see that Kieran had made an effort. Please God, don't have a chick flick lined up for us to watch, I thought. I'm not big into romantic films anyway and I definitely wasn't in the mood for anything soppy. Thankfully Kieran knows me well enough to realise that I prefer a good scare, so we ended up seeing the remake of *Evil Dead*. As if there wasn't enough horror in my life!

That night actually reminded me of when I first met him and we'd sat up until 4 a.m. watching scary movies. Instinctively, I wanted to cuddle up with him again like we'd done so many times before and since. It felt so normal, so familiar. But every time I felt the temptation to nestle my head on Kieran's chest or wrap his arm around me, the voice inside my head pulled me back. Reality check, Kate! This isn't the man you married. You can't trust this man.

I'm sure that's why, the next day, I splurged £185,000 on a beautiful white Bentley convertible. I felt so vulnerable I wanted to treat myself. The more Kieran was around me, the more danger there was of him wearing me down. I needed to keep reminding myself that I was a beautiful, successful woman who can have anything I want ... well, within reason ... and I've never needed a man to provide it.

And, let me tell you, there's nothing like a spot of retail therapy to clear the cobwebs. My new car was a dream to drive. Next I went out and replaced all my knickers and bras at La Senza. New undies, new me! Well, it was enough to boost my self-esteem for a few hours anyway.

I'm sure everybody expected me to lock myself indoors, throw myself on my pillow and cry, but I'm not like that. Believe me, there had been tears . . . loads of tears . . . but in private. I'm not into over-the-top public displays of emotion. That doesn't mean I don't have feelings. I think it's important to be strong in public and I'm not going to blub just because there's a zoom lens pointing at me!

Despite the doctor's advice, I'd decided I still wanted to keep working. I remembered how, in the weeks following the split from Pete, throwing myself into various projects kept me sane. Although now I was much more limited in what I could do, there was no way I was staying indoors. I wanted to be out and about, moving on with or without Kieran.

When I thought about it, there were actually so many positives for me to look forward to. Not long before we'd gone to Cape Verde I'd agreed to be the global ambassador for the first hair colour remover, ColourB4. The product has actually been around since 2009, but it's gone from strength to strength over the past few years. I don't normally endorse anyone else's products except my own, but this was a brand I was really excited about. If there's one thing I do know about, it's hair. I've been dyeing mine for years. I get bored really easily. If I want the blonde beach-babe look, hey presto! Or sultry red? I'll give it a whirl. Besides, I once went to a hairdresser in LA who burned my hair off because he overdid the peroxide so I've never let anyone else near it again. I always do it myself.

In the run-up to the press-call in June, my manger asked me whether I still wanted to go ahead with the launch given the state of my personal life. Of course I did! I'm a professional and it's not in my character to cry off a commitment. But I hadn't anticipated the debate that followed over the outfit I wanted to wear for the shoot. My suggestion was a multicoloured gypsy dress worn with a long Technicolor wig. Pink, yellow, blue, green, purple – I had a vision and nobody was going to tell me otherwise! Had it been my own product, I probably would have been much ruder and said 'Stuff the lot of you'. Believe me, you only have to ask my manager and my brother how often we've been at loggerheads in the past over my various get-ups. The time I dressed as a pink pantomime horse to celebrate the fifth birthday of my equestrian range was the one that probably turned them both grey! But the bottom line is, if you don't stand out nobody will run the pictures. And that's a brand fail.

Initially, the marketing team had wanted me to go blonde and then dark to show off the product, but how boring is that? When I talked them through the design I had in mind for the dress they came back with, 'It's too out there.' I explained that the launch would have no impact whatsoever if all I wore was a girlie dress and dull hair, holding a packet of ColourB4. If ten years of doing press-calls have taught me anything it's be brash, be bold and get noticed! They tried to talk me round but I stayed firm.

It took several phone calls, but eventually the team

did come round to my way of thinking and I knew I wasn't wrong. Okay, I'll be the first to admit that I looked like a cross between Coco the Clown and Barbie, but who cares?

It's not every day that you can go to work looking like an idiot and every newspaper and magazine will run the shoot. I loved doing it too. Work is so much easier when you believe in a product and use it yourself.

The next day I drove to see the house I'd planned to buy one more time. As I turned into the driveway I had this overwhelming feeling that this was my chance for a fresh start, even if it was bittersweet. I'd first seen the house in the evening. Now, in the sunshine, I realised it wasn't my dream home either, but it would do until I worked everything out. There wasn't enough space for Junior to play football in the back garden. I wouldn't be able to keep my horses there either, but I came away thinking that if I surrounded myself with all the people and things in life that I loved that might be the best form of therapy.

I'd warned Kieran I wasn't going to continue paying for his therapy either. Why should I? It was costing me shit-loads and if he wanted to sort his head out he was going to have to do it with his own cash. And pay for my therapy too! If it hadn't been for him, I wouldn't have needed it in the first place. So far, he'd been approached by the *Sun* to do an exclusive, but he'd refused. Now I told him, 'I don't care. Take the money. Do it. It's not like the world doesn't know what a dirty fucker you are!'

In spite of the terrible press coverage Kieran was bound to receive, he deserved it as far as I was concerned and he even said so himself. In the piece, which ran in the *Sun on Sunday* on 25 May, Kieran admitted to twenty-five secret meetings with Jane. Some of it was very hard for me to read, and people should appreciate that when I first saw the interview I was learning some of the details for the first time.

Although Kieran and Jane had sex in her car, they mainly did it in his Ford Focus. They never took their clothes off. Kieran would meet her on his way home from work, still dressed in his skanky overalls and long johns. They had straight sex. Oral sex. Everything. And he never wore a condom once because it added to the risk. How could I even look at a Ford Focus again?

But I think the hardest thing for me to read was that Jane had told Kieran she was falling in love with him, and that she wanted to have children. That cut me so deeply. And Kieran reciprocated because, according to him, he was telling her what she wanted to hear.

Afterwards the journalist who'd interviewed Kieran called me. 'I don't think you should take him back, Kate,' she said. 'My feeling is he's done way more than he's letting on.' As if what he'd admitted wasn't bad enough!

I have no idea if Jane saw the *Sun* piece, but something prompted her finally to get in touch. Was a 'Sorry I've ruined your life, Kate' too much to ask for? Clearly it was, because again she didn't apologise. In fact, I couldn't believe what I was reading. Jane said she'd felt 'raped' and that a man like Kieran 'shouldn't be allowed to walk the streets'. She said he'd turned her into a monster, and then described herself as a victim of Kieran's 'slow, methodical grooming'.

I was under no illusions. I knew that Kieran had charmed Jane into cheating on Derrick and having sex with him . . . but calling herself a victim? I thought, Are you fucking serious? I don't remember Jane looking like much of a victim when she was prancing round in her skimpy dresses, batting her eyelashes. And what kind of victim fucks their best friend's husband while his wife is in hospital giving birth to a premature baby or at her New Year's party? Kieran had confessed to first texting Jane but hadn't she ever heard of the word 'no'?

I even thought back to my fling with Mr X before I'd married Kieran. Maybe this was my karma for ever getting involved with him. You reap what you sow and all that. But I did behave properly! I did call things off! As soon as I realised he was playing me, I ended it. But Jane knew me, knew my family, knew how besotted I was with Kieran. How could any woman do that to a friend?

And what an insulting suggestion that Kieran had 'raped' Jane too. I actually felt offended on his behalf! Rape is such a serious offence. For women, including myself, who really have gone through that horrendous ordeal, it's not a term that should be bandied around lightly. Was Kieran a charmer? Yes. A manipulator? Yes. A complete dickhead? Absolutely. A criminal? No.

As far as I could see, Jane wasn't taking any responsibility for her actions. And the extent of her mind games were about to become even clearer . . .

After the *Sun* story broke, my friend Louisa came to see me. Funnily enough, Kieran had been in touch with Louisa before we started going out. It's so ironic but, in the beginning, she was the friend whose number he had got hold of to ask how he could win me over.

She told me that Kieran had started texting her around the end of September 2013 when we'd not long got back from France with Jett. I was shocked to the core. 'Please, please, tell me nothing happened?' I said, bracing myself, waiting for the bombshell to drop. Thankfully, it didn't. Instead, she'd screen-grabbed all of the messages exchanged between her and Kieran so I could see them for myself. And the funny thing was, at first there was nothing in them really. Kieran started the conversation very innocently. *Hi, how are you doing? Thought I'd drop you a line . . .* But that's apparently exactly how his texts started with Jane! When Louisa texted back, *Does Kate know you're texting me?* he told her that he loved me, but that he hadn't told me. Then the texts got more serious. One time, he was sitting with me while I was having my extensions done, and he'd texted her saying, *Kate's having her hair done. What are you wearing?* Or if she'd been to the gym, he wanted her to send him a picture of her all hot and sweaty. And if she didn't reply, he'd write, *Louisa, where are you? Why are you ignoring me? Louisa . . . Squeeeeza . . . Where are you?* He was so, so persistent. She ended up cutting him off because she didn't feel comfortable at all.

Soon after that, the night before Bonfire Night 2013, he'd messaged her and asked her not to turn up to a fireworks party we were throwing. *We don't need people like you around*, he'd written. But she did come and, apparently, Kieran blanked her. And who was the one person she confided in over the texts? Surprise, surprise, it was Jane. 'Don't let Kate know,' Jane had advised her. She added that both of them needed to put their heads together and plan how to handle the situation. Yes, it all makes sense now . . . telling me might have ruined Jane's bit of fun. Louisa had no idea that Jane had already been fucking Kieran for three months!

You're probably reading this thinking, If Louisa was such a good friend then why didn't she warn you? I wasn't angry with her at all, but it's actually the first question I asked too: 'If I were in your position, I would have said something,' I added. 'I didn't think you'd believe me, Kate,' she replied. We are such good friends that she was terrified if she told me about Kieran's approaches it would jeopardise our friendship. She had phoned my mum and asked to meet her, but my mum had been busy at the time and the discussion kept getting postponed. 'But if you'd shown me the evidence, I would have believed you,' I said, sadly. Then it struck me that maybe it's not so easy to break that kind of news to a friend after all.

After that my old PA Catherine came forward. Kieran

had been texting her too! He'd started sending her messages as far back as after our wedding blessing at Rookery Manor. Christ! Was there a friend of mine he hadn't contacted? But Catherine also chose to ignore him and he stopped pursuing her. That far back, Jane had already received texts from Kieran and had even shown them to Catherine. 'Don't you think this is a bit weird?' Jane had asked her, showing her the messages. 'Yes. I've had some too. Keep the messages and show Kate but don't reply,' Catherine said, but Jane obviously ignored the advice . . . and that's my point. She had a choice all along. She could have said, 'No. Kieran's Kate's husband. I can't do that to her.' But she didn't . . . and look where her choice led.

Although I'd promised myself that I wasn't going to ask Kieran about the identity of the other woman involved, I now felt I needed to know. I had to be sure that I was doing the right thing by allowing him in my life and the kids'. Was he really the monster Jane described? Should I go it alone? Or should I stay and continue to work things out? Was the texting all part of Kieran's addiction problem? Or was he really a Jekyll and Hyde character?

I also couldn't understand why he'd been protecting this other woman. I even said to a couple of friends, 'Either she's an old friend of Kieran's or else she knows me.' And, as I mentioned before, I did have my suspicions about another girl. Either way, not knowing was eating me up. 'I can pay for another lie detector and you can fail it, or you can tell me the truth, Kieran,' I said to him one afternoon during therapy. He was sitting on the sofa. He seemed nervous and thought hard before looking straight at me. 'It's someone you know,' he said, hesitantly. I was silently willing him, Say it, Kieran. Just say it, but he could barely get the word out of his mouth. Eventually, he took a deep breath.

'Chrissy,' he said.

'Chrissy?' I repeated. My whole body went completely numb. *'Chrissy?'* I said again in complete disbelief. It was as though someone had smacked me in the face. I did not see that one coming at all. Okay, she'd been to the house a few times but I couldn't understand how they had even met each other. Apparently he'd got hold of her via her Twitter account directly after our March wedding, which was where they'd met for the first time. He was going from stripping in the evening to fucking her, and then coming home to me. They even fucked in the gym that time after I encouraged Kieran to train her, and came back saying what a great session it was! I was speechless. Now it felt like Chrissy, Jane and Kieran were all laughing at me behind my back. It was excruciating.

After I'd had time to take in the news, I admit that there was a tiny part of me that was relieved it was Chrissy. She's no stranger to shagging married men. She really is a filthy slapper. There was no way she was ever in love with Kieran either. But because Jane had given me no information, I had to confront Chrissy. I felt compelled to know the most graphic details: how it started; why she agreed to meet Kieran, knowing he was my husband; what the sex was like and whether she enjoyed it. Bizarre . . . but there you go. I had to know and Chrissy didn't disappoint.

The next morning I got hold of her by phone. I was in my car with my sister Sophie, and Kieran was there too. I hoped that he was squirming listening in on our conversation because I'd put it on speakerphone purposely.

During our forty-five-minute chat Chrissy admitted that she had been having sex with him. I didn't even have to force the information out of her, she sounded so blasé about it. It was as if she'd pulled someone in a club, not fucked one of her oldest friends' husband! Put yourself in my position. Imagine you're someone's wife, hearing these revelations about your husband from a friend you've known since you were eighteen or so. Someone who was such a good friend you didn't even question whether they had your back.

Chrissy revealed that Kieran's texts had started harmlessly, but soon she was receiving messages like, *I'm so in love with Kate but we haven't had sex in months. I'm so down and I need a hug.* How pathetically sad was that? And absolutely not true! When they eventually did hook up, he 'sorted her out quick'. On every occasion, no sooner had they finished than he'd pull up his trousers and go. She had no expectations of him staying because he always had to get home to me. They met at her place, they had sex in my house, but their regular meeting place was in a lay-by outside Guildford. She didn't say no when I asked her if the sex was good for her. And I know Chrissy well . . . if it was a crap shag, she'd be the first to tell me!

'When are you going to see your psychiatric person, Kate?' she interrupted me. How dare she insinuate I had mental issues? How insulting was that?

'Chrissy,' I replied calmly, although secretly I was furious, 'do you think my head would be so messed up if two of my best friends hadn't fucked my husband?'

As much as Chrissy had told me in that conversation I had to know more, so we messaged back and forth that evening too. But once again she had the cheek to suggest I was the one who was ill! I replied:

I'm not ill, Chrissy, so how dare you say that? If you and Jane didn't fuck my husband my head wouldn't be fucked. Think how you would feel: you're in love, just got married, pregnant, and two of your best mates have been fucking your husband. You will never know the pain I'm going through and how it's affected my children too. And you and Kieran must have been laughing behind my back when I innocently recommended that he should train you. You took the piss and fucked him at my house . . . How did it get from you wanking and sucking him in the car to fucking him at yours and then mine? How could you believe I didn't want him? Please! You should have told me.

I'd never laugh behind your back, I promise, Chrissy replied. She admitted it was the worst mistake she'd ever made and one she would regret for ever, but I didn't believe her at all. She kept wishing me and Kieran 'a great life together', but how could that happen when she'd helped ruin it? Livid? I was beyond livid! I texted her one last time: *Looking at your messages you actually don't give a shit about what you have done to me. You have no consideration for my feelings and you would never have stopped fucking Kieran. You are exactly the same as Jane. You are a disgrace of a human being and more of a slag than Jane as all you do is shag married men.*

Two weeks later I sold a story to the *Sun*, naming and shaming Chrissy. I figured I might as well benefit from my own misery. To this day, I have no regrets whatsoever about doing so.

CHAPTER 13

MOVING ON TOGETHER

'I *really* love you and I want to be with you, Kate,' Kieran said in one of the many heart-to-hearts that we had over the next few weeks.

'You want me, but look what you've done to me,' I replied because I still couldn't understand how he could say that after the revelations of the past few weeks.

Jane and Chrissy occupied a very different space in my brain – the space that was torn apart by the fact that two friends could behave with so little respect for me. Jane's lack of communication and Chrissy's responses only proved to me how little they cared. I thought, Where's the sympathy for me? Why don't they give a shit about what I'm going through?

But Kieran? He had made me feel deeply unattractive. He'd shattered my self-confidence so badly that there were days when I felt at rock-bottom with no clue as to how I would recover. Pregnancy is supposed to be an amazing time in a woman's life. A time when it's okay to flaunt your belly, eat a whole tub of Häagen-Dazs cookies-and-cream ice cream and not feel guilty, indulge in lovely massages and relaxing bubble baths. And have months of sleeping, dreaming and planning . . . Instead, I was terrified of putting on weight. I wasn't blossoming, I was sinking. I was overly anxious about my life, about the baby, about whether Kieran would cheat again. It really wasn't normal.

The strange thing was that now everything was out in the open, Kieran wanted to be with me all the time. It was like living with my shadow. And he'd become so involved with the kids. Now he continually wanted to feed and bathe Jett. I couldn't get my head around it. Why couldn't he do all of those things before? Why did it take my finding out about his sordid affairs for his attitude to shift? Nothing whatsoever made sense.

Although he was doing everything to make me trust him again, I continuously pulled myself back from losing myself in Kieran in the way that I'd done when we first met. With hindsight, every time I felt myself softening towards him, I pushed him away. What's more, the nicer he was to me, the more I rejected him. It was as if I was testing him.

'You're twenty-seven,' I said to him bluntly. 'You can leave. You can go back to your flat. You can go back to stripping and being admired by women every night. I'm not stopping you.' But Kieran reassured me that was the last thing he wanted to do.

Instead of his answer making me feel safe, all it did was set off another barrage of questions. We were in a horrible vicious cycle. I asked him, 'Why do you want to be with me? I'm suspicious of everything you do and everywhere you go! Why do you want to be in a house with five kids among all this chaos?' I told him that he was free to go out, meet someone single, fitter, and without children. I wouldn't stop him seeing his kids every other weekend.

'Kate, all I want is to be with you,' he repeated over and over.

I was also beginning to hate our therapy sessions together because I sounded like a broken record. I couldn't stop myself but I didn't want to keep stamping over the same ground, week in, week out. As soon as the session began I brought up all my unanswered questions about Jane and Chrissy again . . . and again . . . and again. They were the same questions I'd been asking for weeks. Negative thoughts flooded my brain. As far as I was concerned we'd reached a stalemate. If this was going to work, I needed to make progress.

While I decided to take a step back from our couples counselling, Kieran continued to see Gaylin, and he still goes to therapy now. True, there were days when I wanted to give the whole thing up and kick Kieran out, but Gaylin pulled me back. She told me how impressed she was with Kieran. He turned up for all his sessions.

He was doing his relaxation exercises and, best of all, we'd both made a commitment to stick to the rules during his eight weeks of intensive treatment. I had to believe from that evidence that he wanted to change, otherwise I don't think we'd be here today.

'Please don't move house,' Kieran begged me as I was poised to exchange contracts on the place in Orpington. What a nightmare decision to have to make. I could see two clear paths in front of me: the fresh start without Kieran or the life that included him. The first felt filled with hope, excitement, nervousness and fear. The second was like being on one side of a river filled with the stickiest tar, knowing that I'd have to wade through it to reach safety on the other side.

In the end, I agreed to put the move on hold and to put a halt to divorce proceedings. I promised to review the situation in a few weeks' time. Despite my impulsiveness, perhaps that kind of fresh start wasn't such a smart idea while my pregnancy was touch and go. I still wanted to move house though. The urge to rid myself of every reminder of Jane and Chrissy was overwhelming at times. I couldn't stop moving the furniture around so that the place felt different. It was like every room had an evil spell cast over it and the longer I stayed there, the worse the things that might happen . . . as if my life wasn't jinxed already!

By early June I needed to face the world again. Other than for the odd business commitment I'd been hiding myself away, not talking to anyone publicly about the situation. That had to change. If I was going to do anything to help myself and rebuild my confidence, work had always been the place where I felt most at ease.

Halfway through that month I secured my first-ever radio show as a co-host on Fubar Radio, sitting alongside the comedian and presenter Mark Dolan. Apparently the word Fubar is a term from World War II, which stands for 'fucked up beyond all recognition', and the station reaches listeners through a subscription-based app. Because the station falls outside the broadcast regulator Ofcom's rules and regulations, it's completely uncensored and irreverent – like me, I guess. I reckoned we were made for one another.

I'd had several initial meetings with Fubar and they seemed like a really great team. Mark made me laugh from the off so I knew we'd make good on-air partners too. I'd spent many years doing TV – from my early reality shows with Pete to my own series – so taking on a radio show was a way of branching out and really broadening my broadcasting experience. Of course, at the start of our discussions Kieran's affairs hadn't hit the headlines so when my first day at the station rolled around on 17 June, I was pretty nervous. Me being me, I knew that I wouldn't be able to hold back from airing my dirty laundry in public. In my opinion the station was pretty brave to hire me. I bet loads of people out there were shitting themselves about what I was going to come out with.

As it happened, the shows were an instant success. No one had the slightest idea what Fubar was until they hired me. Once we started the programme the station got masses of coverage every week because all the newspapers and gossip mags were listening and running stories based on what I'd talked about for three hours every Tuesday. Doing it was such a laugh too: loads of light-hearted banter which is me down to a tee. Obviously Kieran didn't come out of it too well, but I think he had to expect that. There was loads of speculation about whether we were back together too but as I didn't know myself, I found that a very difficult question to answer.

Thankfully, it wasn't all Kieran and Jane and Chrissy. Each week we talked about so many other things. Like ... my ginormous £600 a week shopping bill to feed a family of six; the various drawbacks in the bedroom department of having an older or younger lover; my feet and how they're probably the best bit of my body; my love of *Antiques Roadshow*, Friday night curries and raisin-filled Danish pastries ... You could say that we had all of the important issues covered.

One of my favourite moments was when the producers got in a guy called Alex Karidis who's one of the UK's most well-known cosmetic surgeons. I'd had my last boob job before I gave birth to Jett. With another baby on the way I wanted to know how long I should leave it before my next MOT. There and then, I asked him to have a peek at the puppies! I wasn't asking for a discount. I made it clear that I could pay my way, but as we were both in the room it seemed like an opportunity not to be missed. What's the harm in getting a free consultation, even if it is live on air?

Sadly, I only did six weeks' worth of shows with Fubar because, in the end, I was forced to take early maternity leave. As I write, I haven't done any since having Bunny but I enjoyed myself so much I'd love to rejoin the team. Who knows? Maybe by the time this book's published, I'll be gracing the airwaves once again.

Three days after my debut on Fubar I also did my first stint as a co-host on *Loose Women*. Although I've appeared on the lunchtime show on many occasions to publicise my books and sometimes appear as a guest, I'd never actually sat on the panel. Beforehand I joked that I had a better body for radio because, seriously, I couldn't find an outfit big enough to wear. In the end I plumped for a plain but stylish metallic top. Let me tell you, it's not easy to bling up a growing baby bump, and as it was my first live appearance after Kieran's affair I wasn't exactly brimming with confidence, but I did relax on set. I even told our special guest, the Irish dancing star Michael Flatley, that he looked 'ripped' under his shirt. Actually, for an older man I thought he was very fanciable indeed . . . but he didn't half looked shocked by the comment!

Meanwhile back at home Kieran and I continued to work through our differences. It had been great focusing my mind elsewhere but the daunting task ahead of us still remained. Not only did I have the kids to look after and a baby to give birth to, but I had to pick up the pieces of my broken heart and get up each morning with the man who'd broken it.

Even my mum said that whenever she looked at Kieran she couldn't believe he was capable of doing what he had. He was always such a quiet and gentle man and he'd seemed so loving. My idea of love is the kind that's depicted in the film *The Notebook*, one of the few romantic movies I like. No matter what happens, no matter what life throws at you, you love one person and you're so focused on them that you don't give a monkey's about anyone else.

But our love brought with it a kind of hurt, self-loathing, hatred even, every single day. There were times when I'd look at Kieran and think, Kate, how could you lower and degrade yourself so much as to want to be with this man? I felt very down.

Then, on other days, those black clouds cleared and I looked at Kieran through a completely different pair of eyes. I really fancied him again, we started talking more and more about our future and about how we'd like to renew our vows to each other. I couldn't help feeling that he was actually a good person, the man that I'd fallen for in the first place.

It sounds crazy but the one thing that still bothered me was that when Kieran and Jane started their affair, he was in amazing physical shape. He was still stripping.

He was toned, ripped, waxed, shaved, he didn't have a hair out of place, he smelled amazing, and every time I looked at him I thought, Wow, how lucky I am to have such an Adonis as a husband. Now, he'd not been to the gym for weeks. He'd grown a beard that made him look like a farmer. Jane and Chrissy got to enjoy Kieran at his peak in a way that I never did. I'd been pregnant for close to two years and I felt cheated. I would have loved to have had a secret rendezvous in a car park with Kieran or a quickie in the stables, even though he was my husband!

I'm always up for experimenting and enjoy a sex life filled with excitement and variety. I think it's even better when you love and trust someone and you both know each other's likes and dislikes. There comes an age when one-night stands don't cut the mustard! But with one bun in the oven, followed in quick succession by another, I'd never fully been able to express myself with Kieran in that way. I still can't help thinking that's why he looked for sex elsewhere although I know I shouldn't punish myself this way.

There were also days when I told Kieran all I wanted to do was go out and pull another man so I could feel attractive again. I was totally upfront with him about it. To this day, I don't know whether I would have done. In my heart I know that two wrongs don't make a right, but the temptation was, and sometimes is, so strong. I think that's partly why Kieran stuck to me like a barnacle. I remember one evening when he was due to go out and

223

play poker with his friends and I said, 'Well, if you're going out I'm not going to stay in on my own. I'll get a babysitter, call the girls and go out for dinner.' Within seconds, he'd changed his mind. 'Oh, let's stay in together, Kate.' It was nice that he wanted to spend time with me, but I thought, Really? Is this how our relationship's going to be? We can't even go out separately because we don't trust one another? I didn't want Kieran to stop having his time with the lads because I think that's something guys need to do once in a while. By the same token, I wanted to be free to have a girlie night out too.

By the end of my relationship with Pete, we were both miserable. I didn't want to live in that atmosphere with Kieran so I knew we needed to break the deadlock.

That evening after we'd bathed and put the kids to bed we settled down to a night watching the box. There wasn't much on so I suggested we put on one of my shows. I had all the episodes of the *Katie* series backed up on my Sky box so I picked out one randomly and pressed start.

Funnily enough, it was an episode filmed directly after Leo and I split. I felt so down and I'd gone to see my book agent Maggie. 'You've known me for years,' I said to her. 'Do you think I'll ever find the right man? All I want is someone faithful, loyal, and who loves me. I'm not asking for much.' I promised her that the next man I married would be the one I loved and trusted and the person I'd spend the rest of my life with. At that line, I looked over at Kieran who was staring at the screen. So I paused the episode to ask what he was thinking.

'The weird thing is, I love you, Kate,' he said.

I couldn't believe what I'd heard. 'The weird thing is, Kieran, you cheated on me too. You fucked me over. You're like the rest of them,' I said, sadly.

He sighed. 'I know I've been awful. I've been out of order. I'm doing everything I can. I can't change the past. I'm a completely different person now. I'm not that person.'

I thought, It's all very well saying that, Kieran, but how we can rebuild trust in our marriage?

Knowing that everybody close to me also hated Kieran for what he had done made life so much worse too. I felt like I was constantly being judged for making the decision to stay with him and work things out. I kept saying to people that it wasn't only about me. I was trying to see the bigger picture for the sake of the children too.

Some of Kieran's friends were so upset with him that they weren't talking to him at all. They said he'd been a dick for cheating on me and actually blanked him for ages. They didn't even turn up for the baby shower I threw on 12 July. I was a bit disappointed because I thought they could have at least come to give me some moral support, but I did understand their decision.

As it happened, it turned out to be a really lovely afternoon. I invited around forty people for a barbecue in the summer sunshine. Nothing over the top – just family and friends. Right, I thought, I'm going to insist that the men understand what it's like to be fat and pregnant. It took me a while to track one down, but I hired a pregnancy suit and asked the male guests to take it in turns to wear it throughout the party. As a few of my female friends were expecting too, their partners we're totally up for joining in. What a laugh!

Of course all the blokes began by being ultra macho: all slugging each other in the gut and saying, 'I bet I can keep it on longer than you!' In fact, none of them could take the weight for more than an hour. What a bunch of wusses! I thought. Try nine months of carrying a baby! And while I do think pregnancy suits give men a good idea of what it feels like to be pregnant and hopefully make them empathise more with what their partners are going through, until they experience all the hormones whizzing around their system as well, the experience is a pretty poor second.

CHAPTER 14

OUR TINY PERFECT MIRACLE

I started this book with Bunny's birth and there was a good reason for that. If there's one thing that kickstarted the turnaround in the relationship between Kieran and me it was my little Bunny's arrival into the world.

In lots of ways she became the fresh start we both needed. Normally I wouldn't recommend having a baby to save a relationship. More often than not the strain breaks an unstable marriage, but I guess because we had kids already it wasn't such a shock to the system. If she'd been my first and Kieran had behaved as he did, I wouldn't have coped. But it's funny how good things happen when you least expect them.

During July I'd been really hard on Kieran. I'd told him that if the baby was premature, brain damaged or harmed in any way, I'd lay the blame at his, Jane's and

Chrissy's door, and I'd sworn I'd make him carry out another lie detector test too.

My actual due date was 14 September but the date of my Caesarean had been set for 16 August. That was the earliest doctors wanted to deliver her safely although they were surprised I'd carried the baby for as long as I had. So I wanted Kieran to do the test a couple of days before my op. If he passed, he could be present at her birth. If he failed, he'd be out of my life for good. It's not like I wanted to keep threatening Kieran with a lie detector test, but I didn't see any other way to let him know that if he'd played away I was serious about our relationship being over.

In the end, I didn't even get to arrange the test because on the first Saturday in August, when I was out shopping with my mum in Brighton, a dull ache began spreading through my whole belly. I was struck with the same shortness of breath that I'd felt before. Immediately, I got Dr Gibb on the phone to ask his advice on what to do. 'If you're in Brighton, Kate, you won't have time to come to London. Go to your local hospital straight away,' he said.

Fortunately, I was also being monitored at St Richard's Hospital in Chichester, which wasn't too far away. My mum kindly offered to pick up the kids while I headed there. It's not like my waters had broken or anything, but as I got closer the pain was getting worse and worse. I thought, Bloody hell! What is wrong with me?

I managed to get through the outpatients' unit in double quick time and once Dr Tipples, my obstetrician at St Richard's, had examined me, she confirmed that although my stitch had held, I should expect to have the baby sooner rather than later. That meant she could be more than six weeks premature.

As with Jett, and all other premature babies, a steroid injection was needed to help the baby's lungs. Premature babies are so tiny that the steroids improve their breathing capacity at birth and can also reduce their chances of developing lung disease. I would need two injections within forty-eight hours, and they were going to start now by injecting the steroids right into my bum. Glamorous or what?

'I'm needle-phobic,' I explained again. At least this time, unlike in France, the doctors could understand me.

'I have to inject myself,' I told them. 'Are you sure, Kate? Because it would be much easier if we did it . . .' the nurse replied, nervously. Before she could persuade me otherwise I was already squatting down with my bum cheek in the air, gesturing for them to pass me the syringe. 'Give it here,' I said. 'It's better if I do it.' Instead of jabbing myself quickly, they watched me slowly ease the needle in. Afterwards, all of the staff said that I'd made a straightforward injection look 100 times more painful, but I didn't care. I hate needles so much that I much prefer to be in control.

Although Dr Tipples said I could inject Sunday's dose at home myself, I opted to come to hospital. As it turned out, I needed to be rushed in anyway. An hour or so before I was due to leave for Chichester I'd run myself a luxurious bubble bath. Moments before I was about to step in I felt this gush of water down my legs. I thought, Oh my God, what the fuck? Straight away, I called for Kieran and told him to take a photo. 'Have my waters broken?' I kept asking him. Neither of us was sure because once I'd wrapped a towel around myself and sat on the bed I'd pretty much stopped leaking. Whatever the problem was, we both knew that this wasn't the time to be taking any chances.

We arrived at the hospital where I showed Dr Tipples the picture. 'Kate, this stitch is not going to hold much longer,' she warned me. 'You'll have to stay in overnight and we'll take her out tomorrow.'

'What . . . really? Tomorrow?' I gasped. Shit! This was like Jett all over again!

Despite my panic, I cannot fault St Richard's Hospital one single bit. They made me feel so welcome and took complete care of me. Given the experience I'd had less than a year ago that was one weight off my mind. Kieran drove back and picked up an overnight bag for us both. We had a little room with a bed for me and a sofa bed for Kieran. The way the staff checked in on us to make sure we were comfortable made me think I wasn't a patient in an NHS hospital at all – it was no different from going private. My only complaint was that our room was right next to the delivery suite. That night we were kept awake by the sound of women screaming. 'Is that for real?' Kieran asked. He hadn't been in theatre with me when Jett was born so he was still clueless about what women go through. 'Kieran, that's the sound of real pain!' I said, forcefully. In fact, as soon as he said that, I half wished that I was giving birth to the baby naturally so he would feel even more guilty about what he'd done to me. Having said that . . . remembering Harvey, perhaps not. Ouch!

Even so, a C-section is still a major operation. That evening I texted my mum and stepdad and Kieran let his mum know we were having the baby the next morning. But I couldn't sleep at all. Apart from the noise, every few minutes I was tossing and turning thinking about the needles that they were bound to want to stick into me.

First thing the next morning a nurse arrived to apply numbing cream to my lower back, which was just as well because without it they wouldn't get me in the same room as a needle! Once I'd got kitted out in my gown and stockings I felt petrified about what lay ahead, and really excited too. Unfortunately, at around 8 a.m. another emergency C-section had to be slotted in before me, so we had another whole hour to wait, which feels like a bloody long time when you're about to have an op. Well, there's never a wrong time to strike a pose so I got Kieran to whip his phone out and take pictures of me in my gown and we even did a few selfies together.

Again, I'm not sure what I expected from Kieran, but I longed for him to kiss me or hug me and tell me how proud he was of me for having his second child. He owed me that at least! But all he kept saying was, 'Oh my God, we're going to have her soon.'

It's funny because I've spoken to lots of Kieran's male friends who've all said that having children was a life-changing experience for them. Most of all, being there at the birth changed their relationship with their partner. Although I think most women hate the thought of anyone's head stuck down at the business end, a surprising number of men want to see what's happening. Some of Kieran's mates even said they fell in love with their partner all over again as a result. Watching the birth made them appreciate what women go through. But Kieran's never said anything like that to me.

I guess I'm going to have to get used to the fact that he's a man of few words. He doesn't show his emotions easily and, at that time, I think we both felt incredibly unsure about whether we were going to be together. Though I did think it was another opportunity to redeem himself that he'd missed.

If the maternity nurses expected an easy time with me once I'd got into the operating theatre, they had another thing coming. I was so paranoid that as soon as they gave me the epidural I thought it wouldn't work, just like when Jett was born. Unusually, the final injection wasn't half as bad as I'd anticipated. It just goes to show how you can build things up in your imagination. The main problem was that I could still move my right leg from the hip even though the left side was completely numb. Eventually they tried tipping me up so the anaesthetic would move around my body. But when they cut me to bring out Bunny I could feel exactly the same burning sensation as before. That same fire was moving through my body. I soldiered on despite being in agony.

Beforehand, we'd been told that if there were any complications and they needed to put me to sleep, Kieran would have to leave the room. With hindsight, I probably should have been out for the count but forced myself to keep going. 'Come on, Kate,' I said inside. 'Be brave and take the pain.' There was no chance I was going to let Kieran leave me this time and miss out on this birth too. Plus he was poised with his phone at the ready to film her coming out.

If there's one memory I have from three of my children's births it's the moment they've been wrapped and handed to me to hold. I still very much regret that I wasn't allowed to do that with Jett. And as soon as I saw Bunny I fell hopelessly in love with her. It struck me that her eyes and nose looked like Princess's when she'd just been born. Kieran was emotional but I wanted him to behave like a character in a movie. I wanted him to break down and take all the pain of not being there for Jett and for fucking up my whole pregnancy. But, as I said, he doesn't show his emotions in that way.

All I kept thinking was, Thank god she's not been whisked up to the intensive-care unit. She was absolutely tiny, like a little sparrow, but she was healthy. Of course I spoke too soon. As I've already described, the minute she was brought into our room, her breathing almost stopped and she was rushed upstairs by the nurse, with

Kieran following close behind. I couldn't believe it. Why does this always happen to me? I kept thinking as I waited anxiously for news. All I wanted to do was hold her, bond with her, take in her gorgeous little face and wrap her tiny fingers around mine. Instead I was left alone, frantically wondering where she was, how she was, and whether her father and I had a future together.

Not long afterwards Kieran re-emerged. He'd watched as an oxygen tube and a feeding tube had been inserted into Bunny's nose and down her throat. He'd taken photos of her lying in the incubator to show me. Awwww! She had a little sign above her bed that read 'Baby Hayler'. Everything had been so rushed, we'd not even had time to discuss what we wanted to call her.

Thankfully, it wasn't too long before I was allowed upstairs to see her too. I hated the fact that I couldn't feed or cradle her. All I could do was look at her through the glass. The nurses were reassuring me that she was going to be fine, but they predicted she'd need to remain in the incubator probably for another couple of weeks. Kieran and I both commented on what a difference it would have made if the French doctors had communicated with us in the same way.

For the first week I was kept in the maternity unit and Kieran didn't leave my side. We simply called Bunny 'Runner Bean'. I don't know why but she reminded me of a stringy green bean with those long legs and a tiny body. After a few days I was able to pick her up. She was so small that Kieran could hold her with one hand.

Overall I felt blessed to have another healthy baby when I thought about what could have been. However, I couldn't rid myself of my insecurities. Two days after her delivery my ankles swelled up like balloons and my scar stitches felt so uncomfortable. Instead of admitting to Kieran that I was in pain, I kept saying, 'I'm okay. Don't worry about me.' I was even purposely walking down the corridor at a quicker pace than I could actually manage so that I looked fighting fit and full of energy. More than anything I wanted to get back to the healthy, toned and confident person Kieran had met in the beginning. No one need remind me that it wasn't normal to think that way!

When it came to leaving Bunny in hospital, both Kieran and I found the experience awful. Honestly, I could have sat with her all day and all night. Both of us kept looking back at her alone in her incubator as we left the ward, knowing that there was a whole night ahead of us before we'd be back to help take care of her.

I'd also been really disappointed that Princess and Junior were on holiday in Africa with Pete at that time. Again, I'd wanted them to be there to see her after she was born. We did bring Jett in to meet her but I think he was a bit too young and Kieran had to take him home the minute he started kicking off, so as not to disturb the other families and babies.

My brother brought Harvey in too. The first thing he shouted when he saw me was, 'Mummy's bump's gone now!' He even drew a picture of Bunny so I knew he'd acknowledged she'd been born. Now he adores her.

Harvey knows that Junior and Princess go to Pete's every second week and he also knows that Jett and Bunny are always at home with him. Every night when he goes to bed, he'll ask me, 'Who's waking up with me tomorrow?' I reply, 'Who do you think's waking with you tomorrow?' Then he says, 'Kieran, Jett, Bunny and Mummy.' It's a little game that we play between us.

Because Bunny's birth had been so stressful and things were still unclear between me and Kieran we wanted the press as far away as possible. Having the other kids to juggle too, we were making the journey back and forth to St Richard's at least two or three times a day. The last thing I wanted was the paps to catch on that Bunny was in intensive care for three weeks.

We even found a route which involved driving the 4x4 off-road, round the back of our property to join the dual carriageway at a lower point so we weren't seen exiting our driveway. It's one of my greatest fears that one day I'll be pursued by paps and there will be an accident. Some of them can be very aggressive and I always have the Princess Diana tragedy in the back of my mind if I know they're on my case.

Poor Jett, we even had to postpone his first birthday party because Bunny was still hooked up to all her tubes. Although the nurses said we could bring her home with the feeding tube still attached, we both agreed we wanted to wait until she was 100 per cent okay. She was in the safest place possible. When we did eventually celebrate Jett's birthday with a party at home, complete with a cake handmade by Kieran's mum in the shape of a jet fighter, she was sleeping soundly upstairs.

I shouldn't have been surprised, but Princess and Junior were totally brilliant with her. 'Where is she? We want to see her!' they both shouted when they ran in from school. Princess especially loves having a little sister to play with. At first, though, Jett was an absolute nightmare. I don't think he understood that Bunny was a living, breathing baby because every time he went to stroke her head he'd dig his fingernail right into her face, or I'd find him throwing toys on to her in her crib. It did occur to me that perhaps he was a bit jealous because every time I went to pick her up, he'd grip my leg and beg for me to pick him up too. Fortunately, that was a phase. He seems completely fine with her now.

For the next few weeks we drew a complete blank over what to call her. Initially I'd wanted the name 'Duchess' – like Duchess Kate – and that name went well with Princess too, but Kieran reckoned it sounded too harsh. At one point I even wanted to name her Disney, but I didn't really want my daughter growing up thinking she'd been named after a theme park! Then there were Bambi and Precious, which Kieran also hated. I liked old-fashioned names like Ethel and Peggy too but the danger was that she might sound like one of the characters in *EastEnders*. When Bunny came into my head, it seemed right and Kieran agreed it was cute. We'd left it so late we'd had a letter through the post reminding us to register her name! I'd been close to writing back to ask for more time. But that's me. Lastminute.com all over! Then I couldn't decide whether to spell her name Bunni with a heart above the 'i' but Kieran pointed out that that probably wasn't even part of the English language. So Bunny it is.

Did I give a toss what other people thought of her name? Absolutely not. I know my mum didn't like it at first, but she didn't like Princess's name either. She's come round to it though because Princess suits her name so much. And yes, I did read the columnist Katie Hopkins's comment about Bunny. She tweeted that she thought the name was apt seeing as her dad had been 'going at it like a rabbit' with all of my mates. Actually, I thought she was bang on about Kieran, but to say that about a six-week-old baby was simply vile. I wouldn't mind but she named one of her children India. Geography's not my strong point, but that's a whole subcontinent, for God's sake. Hasn't she ever heard of the phrase 'pot calling the kettle black'?

On the back of us naming Bunny, the press even reported that Princess had told Pete she hated her name . . . and the colour pink too. I have no idea whether that story is true or not, but he and I chose Princess's name together, just like Kieran and I chose Bunny's name together. Besides, Princess has never complained to me about it once. As for the colour pink . . . As soon as we moved into our new house at the end of last year, Princess had the choice of what colour she wanted to decorate her room. And what did she choose? You got it . . . pink.

CHAPTER 15

A FRESH START

I always say to Kieran, 'I can't forgive and I can't forget. What you've done is just "there".' That's true today, and was even more so after Bunny's birth. Kieran didn't leave my side but I didn't yet know if we were in this for the long-haul. So I did my first *OK*! magazine shoot with Bunny on 23 September alone. Kieran accompanied me to the studio, but I didn't want him in the pictures. For Jett's birth we'd been pictured as a happy family. I can't look at that issue now, knowing that Kieran's smile is completely false. He was already in the throes of his sleazy, disgusting affairs with both of my friends.

How I managed to hold it together during that September shoot I don't know, because I'm sure Bunny was making me pay for all the upset during my pregnancy. For the first few weeks she cried non-stop.

We even joked that we wanted to take her back to the hospital and trade her in for a new baby. She was a nightmare! We were taking it in turns to get up to do her night feeds but there's nothing like constantly interrupted sleep to make you feel completely washed out. Fingers crossed that hair and make-up and a big fat airbrush would work their magic.

Though it is weird how you forget the stress and pain of giving birth so quickly. As soon as we brought Bunny home, I said to Kieran, 'I want another one, but not right away.' I had to let my body recover first! I don't know what it is about newborns, but I adore having them around. In fact, I want as many babies as the doctors will allow me, and I'd even consider freezing my eggs if it comes to the stage where I'm told I can't have any more. My doctor thinks I'm bonkers, but I don't care.

Admittedly, Kieran did make those first few weeks of looking after Bunny much easier. I could see he was being determinedly hands-on. He'd said that as a result of his ongoing treatment he'd refocused his life and was discovering who he truly was: the family man I knew he had in him all along. And yes . . . he'd convinced me that he was sorry. I've always had a feeling that deep down Kieran is a good person, but I'm still upset that I had to uncover all that I did before I forced him to change.

After a while, my long succession of bad days gave way to some good ones. It was as if Bunny had breathed life into our relationship and I will always see her as my little ray of sunshine.

True, I didn't stop dwelling on the bad stuff completely. That kind of betrayal is not something you get over easily or quickly. And I still questioned why Kieran had wanted to stay with me. Perhaps he was taking advantage of my good nature. I'd given him nowhere near the hard time he'd deserved. He hadn't had it easy, but he'd had it comparatively easy compared to Jane and Chrissy. I don't see why I shouldn't batter them. They're not worthy of my kindness.

I also kept reminding myself that Kieran was jobless. He was living in my house, paid for by me. He had his family with him and a quality of life most people dream of. What's not to like? Unfortunately, I think I will always find it hard to accept that Kieran has chosen to be with me because he loves me. Trust me, I've been with so many guys who've only wanted me for my money and the life that I can offer them that, sadly, it's my default assumption.

Underneath I still wasn't feeling physically at my best. Not only had I gone through my fourth Caesarean but I'd found it hard to bounce back. I really was trying, because I desperately wanted to feel fancied by Kieran again.

I was due to be a bridesmaid at my friend Kerry Katona's wedding at Totworth Court Hotel in Gloucestershire in mid-September, but when I tried the dress on in the run-up to her big day it had been tailored in a size too big. It was too much hassle to have it altered so close to the wedding, so we agreed between us that I would attend as one of the guests instead.

Annoyingly, the press latched on to that story, claiming that I'd thrown a hissy fit and refused to be a bridesmaid because I didn't want to look fat. As if I'd spoil my friend's day like that. But, yes, as a matter of fact I'd just given birth, I'd had the shittiest summer on record and it was my first public appearance since Bunny had arrived. I also knew Kerry had secured a deal with *OK!* magazine so I didn't want to ruin her snaps by looking shit. I think any woman in my position would have felt exactly the same.

I was so pissed off with the journalist who wrote the piece. I wanted the focus of the day to be on Kerry, not me. She was a gorgeous bride and it was an amazing wedding. We left after the first dance and the speeches were great. End of. There was no strop, no falling out and no drama. Why make it up? And why, after everything I'd been through, put a downer on someone else's wedding and use me to do it? Just fuck off!

I'd made a promise that I'd review my house move after Bunny was born and I kept to that promise. After a lot of talking, Kieran and I decided that we wanted to make a go of things, and move house together. The dilapidated property near Haywards Heath was still on the market and Kieran and I did consider looking at it again but coincidentally, one evening when we were browsing on PrimeLocation, another house jumped out at us that turned out to be nearer. As soon as the estate agent gave us the guided tour we knew we'd struck lucky. I think a house chooses you, you don't choose it.

You know that feeling when you step through the door and you can almost hear the walls whispering 'Buy me'? Everything about it had such a warm feel.

It did need a lot of renovation though. And I mean *a lot*. If we concentrated on gutting the nine bedrooms inside plus three living rooms then we could move on to the outdoor swimming pool, tennis courts, paddock and the two-bedroomed annex. As I write, I am making plans to transform the algae-covered pit of an outdoor pool so the kids can splash around in the summer but . . . I won't hold my breath.

Of course I was so impatient that as soon as we exchanged contracts I wanted to move in and get the kitchen refurbished in time for Christmas but . . . reality bites! And I think we both realised pretty quickly that we'd bitten off more than we could chew. I don't regret choosing the house at all but it has become something of a money pit.

For example, the first thing we did was to board up all the overhead beams. If there's one thing I hate it's those old-fashioned cottage beams. I much prefer clean lines and a super-modern feel. Then we knocked the existing kitchen through to the dining room. For me, the kitchen should be at the heart of any home. I had a vision of the preparation area opening out on to a beautiful dining room overlooking our twelve acres. The builder's guesstimate turned out to be half of what it eventually cost us to have a huge steel reinforcement put in between the rooms when the wall was eventually knocked through. I was quite pissed off. The £18,000 extra we'd had to splash out could have been put to good use elsewhere. Like I always say, money doesn't grow on trees and now I'm the bread-winner with the sole responsibility of looking after a family of seven, I keep a tight hold on the purse strings!

I think one of my favourite features is the original Aga oven, which I had resprayed a lovely deep grey. It makes the kitchen feel so homely. And I love our big oak front door too. It reminds me of the entrance to a castle.

From the minute we moved in early in October we set to work. Whereas before when I'd had work done to one house, I'd had a luxury log cabin built in the grounds while renovations were underway, this time we all piled in and took over the top floor. As well as living among stacks of boxes, I spent most of the end of last year breathing in never-ending clouds of brick dust. I won't lie. It really started to do my head in after a while.

Fortunately, with Kieran's plastering skills he's been able to do a lot of the work himself and I love that he's building a home for us and the kids. It feels as though we're being protected and looked after. He's even decorated Junior's bedroom to look like a proper boy's room with all the furniture from Kieran's old flat: a black sofa and black leather sleigh bed. Junior chose his own black and grey graffiti wallpaper. And Princess . . . she always has a room to fit her name complete with a pink double bed studded with crystal buttons.

Downstairs we've also created a little snug room with

a beautiful log burner, which we got going not long after we moved in. It's so cosy and it's become our TV room where we curl up with the kids and watch *Strictly Come Dancing* together. We've even toasted marshmallows on the fire!

True, Kieran does tell me all the time that he reckons he's doing the house up for my next man to live in. He's paranoid that I'm going to dump him, but I only have one answer to that. If Kieran proves he can behave, we'll have years of happiness to look forward to. Perhaps my brother wasn't too far off the mark when he suggested buying us a vice as a housewarming present, in case Kieran steps out of line . . .

Neither Kieran, nor I, nor the kids, miss our old house one bit. It had been the house I'd bought when I was with Leo and not exactly the happiest place for all of us once I'd found out about Kieran; the children also told me that they were glad to leave. I think it was important to them that we were all embarking on a new life together, even if the actual move was a complete nightmare. Take one seven-and-a-half-ton lorry plus a mountain of stuff. Mix that with one afternoon to pack everything up and transport it, a wife who can't lift anything, two kids under the age of two . . . I could go on. Not exactly the perfect recipe for playing Happy Families. God, were we glad when the last load was delivered!

And with the new house taking shape, I wanted a new me to go in it. I'd been thinking about it for a while, but I vowed that once I felt halfway human again I was going for a full-on hair-colour makeover.

Earlier in the year, before we'd gone to Cape Verde, I'd taken out all of my extensions and had a shoulder-length bob for the first time in years. I absolutely loved it and I did toy with going back to that. But Junior kept saying to me, 'Mum, I really want you to go black,' so I thought, Why not? I did it around a week before I was due to launch my tenth novel *Make My Wish Come True*. I didn't do it on purpose at all but Storm, the main character in the book, has long raven hair and green eyes, so perhaps something wormed its way into my brain. I thought it was a touch too dark, but Kieran loved it and so did the kids. And anyway, nothing's ever permanent. The minute I'm bored with my hair I always spontaneously think, What colour do I want to go next? I'm sure I'll start lightening it as soon as the weather starts getting brighter.

In early October there were so many upheavals in the house that I was relieved to have a packed diary. On one day I recorded a hilarious episode of *Catchphrase*. My aim was to win money for Vision Charity, the charity for blind and partially sighted children that I'm a patron of. I was up against my old pal Christopher Biggins and the actor Warwick Davies. 'Don't knock it till you've tried it' is my motto because when you're on the podium with your hand poised on the buzzer that game is a lot harder than it looks. After each animated sequence, the panellists have to guess what well-known phrase is being acted out, but some of the clues are really obscure! At one point I took the lead with £1,300 but it didn't last. I must have been having an off day because I didn't even buzz correctly on the saying 'Diamonds are a girl's best friend'. And the most difficult phrase to work out was 'Christmas is coming and the goose is getting fat'. It took us around ten attempts to guess that one! I am so grateful to Warwick Davies for answering the bonus question correctly and doubling the money for my chosen charity. And when the episode finally aired the week before Christmas I couldn't stop laughing!

On 17 October I was invited to appear at my first-ever literary festival event on the Isle of Wight. I know! Check me out! Well, with seven autobiographies, ten novels, and ten children's books under my belt, I do know what I'm talking about. During the afternoon session I was due to be interviewed by the showbiz journalist and brother of Simon Cowell, Tony Cowell. Sadly, hc had to pull out at the last minute because of a family emergency so it was left to my agent Maggie to do the honours. It was a bit of a flying visit. I even had to put my rollers in on the Red Funnel ferry crossing, which amused the captain no end. Nothing was going to stop me injecting a bit of glamour into proceedings. Plus the Isle of Wight is famed for being an old folks' paradise so I wanted to get the audience's pacemakers skipping a beat. PVC trousers? Tick. Thigh-length boots? Tick. Gorgeous black fur gilet and matching black hair? Double tick. Well, I do like to make an entrance!

Overall I was really pleased with the event. There'd been so much speculation about my private life that I was worried the Q&A session was going to descend into loads of questions about me and Kieran, but you'd be amazed by what Joe Public wants to know. Maggie even asked me, 'Do you think your beauty made you one of the most famous women in the country? Or your searing honesty? Or your very large breasts?' Er . . . now . . . let me see!

After my whirlwind tour, it was a quick dash back across the Solent to the mainland. I was due at the press call for *Make My Wish Come True*. Back in June when I'd first seen the proposed cover for the novel I'd got really excited. My publisher had gone for a sexy snow queen theme, which was brilliant in the run-up to Christmas and fitted in so well with the film of the year, *Frozen*. So I ran with the fairytale look and wore a plunging sparkly white bodice with a hooded fur-lined lace cape, white fishnets and Perspex heels. And although no one knew it at the time I was already booked in for a boob reduction at the end of that month in Brussels, so I knew it was the last time I'd be officially photographed with my 32FF breasts. I made the most of it, slipped on my best push-up bra and got those bad boys on show.

Later that week, Kieran and I even had our first night out since Bunny had been born. Wooohooo! Believe me, people think I'm out on the razz all the time because that's usually when the paps snap me but, honestly, I could count on one hand the number of times I went out last year.

That night, I think all the stress of moving house got to me because I turned into a bit of a demon on the white wine. Embarrassingly so . . .

We'd gone to the Big Reunion Boy Band concert at the 02 in London. Never mind that some of my exes were all up on stage together, it was a really great night. Dane Bowers, my first true love who I was with for two years, performed, as did Gareth Gates whose cherry I popped not long after Dane, even though he refused to admit it publicly for ages. God, all that seems like a lifetime away. Anyhow Kieran knows everything there is to know about me and my past. That night he even had a selfie taken with Dane, who seemed totally up for it. And the great thing about Kieran is that he doesn't mind me going out and letting my hair down once in a while. It's great not to have to ask someone's permission to have the occasional drink. And it was hilarious all my exes being there together . . .

It shows how much Kieran and I had come on in our relationship because the following day, when he mentioned a girl we'd been talking to, I didn't think anything of it. She was a girlfriend of one of the guys in the band for the reunion tour. She was very friendly and I'd been drunkenly saying, 'You've got to come to the renewal of our vows!' Kieran wrote down her email address and promised we'd drop her a line in the week. As I was a bit the worse for wear when I woke up I didn't really register who he was talking about, but a few days later she did start to prey on my mind.

Suddenly I was gripped by insecurity and did something that was totally out of character – not something I'm proud of at all. Kieran had made me so paranoid in the past that I checked his phone – something I'd never done before. Sure enough, she and Kieran had been emailing each other. I felt paralysed by fear. Please don't do this to me again, Kieran, I was praying. We've only just moved and decided to build a life together!

On the surface the messages were innocent, but didn't Kieran's messages always start innocently? *It was a great show!* he'd told her. *Did you enjoy it?* she'd replied, adding, *How was your head in the morning? How was Kate?* Then he told her that I worked a lot and he didn't get out much. He said he lived with five kids and even described our new home and all the animals he had started farming on our land.

There was no way I could stay silent. When I confronted Kieran about it he played the fool. 'What? We haven't been emailing!' he lied. 'Kieran, I've seen around ten emails, don't treat me like an idiot,' I said, thinking, How could he do this? I was so pissed off. And Kieran knows me well enough to be aware that when I accuse someone of something, I've always got proof. He was fighting a losing battle.

'Kate, you wanted to invite her to the vows ceremony!' he reminded me, but I pointed out that there wasn't a single mention of that in the emails, let alone much mention of me! And if it was so innocent, why hadn't he CC'd me in? Now I wanted to trawl through all his private messages and accounts. When I looked at his Instagram page he'd posted pictures of himself, our animals and the kids. Okay, there were no pictures from when he was stripping but he was following eighteen women, and some of them were glamour models.

'Why are you following these women?' I asked him.

'You know what it's like, Kate. To see what they're up to,' he replied nervously.

'No, Kieran! I don't know what it's like . . . and you don't need to know what they're up to!' I yelled back.

Suddenly it felt like all the progress we'd made had been ripped to shreds. I didn't want to have to police his every move. I've got five kids who demand less! I didn't want him to come off Facebook, or Twitter, or Instagram either, but for this to work I had to be able to trust him. How could I live with the everyday stress of knowing that within seconds he could destroy my life again?

'I can't keep forgiving you, Kieran,' I told him, and when I spoke to Gaylin she agreed that I should stand firm and insist that one more slip up would mean we were over.

'He will make mistakes. Addicts do relapse,' she warned me. 'You have to decide what's best for you and whether you can handle this.'

I kept thinking, Can he be that ill in the head that he doesn't know right from wrong? Sadly, I don't think addicts do. But we'd made a promise that we were in this together through thick and thin and, in my heart, I wanted to stick to that. But could I cope? Kieran promised he'd not met this girl at all and agreed that until he'd progressed more in his treatment he was going to come off social media altogether. Now he has all of his accounts back, but he says he doesn't want to use them. It's a choice that he has made for himself, not one I have forced upon him, which I think shows that his therapy is working.

CHAPTER 16

HARVEY

Back in November 2013 Harvey and I appeared on the front cover of *OK!* magazine. It was by no means the first time Harvey had featured in a cover shoot with me, but on that particular occasion I felt it was very important. I'd been asked to do the interview following comments made by the ex-*Apprentice* contestant turned columnist Katie Hopkins. Ignorantly, she'd said that 'behind every fat child is a fat mother'. I didn't know at the time that one day I would live in the Big Brother house with Katie and, although when I did I saw a softer side to her, my hunch about her turned out to be bang on. Another disgusting human being. During my three weeks in the house she kept banging on about fat kids. Perhaps she was trying to get a rise out of me? Harvey is fat and there's a reason for it, so how someone could be so cruel is beyond my understanding. In 2013, when she first made the comment about fat parents, my reaction was to tell her to shove it.

I went so far as to place her in the same category as the so-called comedian Frankie Boyle who, in 2010, had made the most vile and disgusting 'joke' about Harvey during his Channel 4 programme. It prompted more than 500 complaints to the broadcaster although, to this day, they have never given me an apology. I can hardly bring myself to repeat Boyle's words but, for those who missed them, I'll reproduce them one more time. In an apparent attempt at 'comedy', he said, 'I have a theory that Jordan married a cage fighter 'cause she needed someone strong enough to stop Harvey from fucking her.' Yep ... you read it correctly. And, yep, it's still not funny.

Despite asking several times, I have also never received a personal apology from Boyle, even after I made the documentary *Standing Up For Harvey*. During its filming, I invited Boyle to meet me and witness for himself exactly what Harvey has to cope with on a day to day basis, in order to understand something of how we, his family, deal with Harvey's complex disabilities. I can't say I was surprised when I heard a big fat nothing from the comedian. Like most people who launch verbal attacks on disabled, defenceless and vulnerable children, the man is a true coward.

However, when it came to Katie Hopkins, I expected more from a woman and a mother of three herself, so I felt I had to hit back at her comments about childhood obesity. Granted, there are some parents who overfeed their kids or who feed their kids the wrong foods and they need to be educated, but not every obese child has a fat mother or father. Among the many problems Harvey suffers from is the rare genetic disorder Prader-Willi Syndrome, which means he will always have a chronic feeling of hunger. No matter how much he eats, he never feels full and so he is prone to obesity. Even though we watch over Harvey constantly and strictly control his diet, the urge to eat never goes away. I often think how horrible it must be for him to experience that feeling every single day of his life.

Katie Hopkins's comment struck a particular nerve with me too. Back in 2007 *Heat* magazine was forced to apologise and donate to Vision Charity after they ran a cover featuring Harvey against the slogan: 'Help, Harvey wants to eat me!' The cover deeply shocked and upset me and attracted a large number of complaints to the Press Complaints Commission.

And the last time Harvey's biological father Dwight Yorke saw him, which was around eight years ago, the first thing he asked was why Harvey was so big. Why was I overfeeding him? Even though I'd explained Harvey's condition to Dwight many times, he refused to understand it and kept going on about him being fat.

It's sad that he is unable to accept Harvey for who he is and seems unable or unwilling to work within his limitations. On that occasion, I think Dwight wanted to blame someone for the fact that his son is disabled.

I have always said that if Dwight could see what a courageous and talented boy Harvey is then he would enjoy being with him so much.

Throughout the years that Dwight has been absent from Harvey's life I've sent him little videos of Harvey taken on my phone, thinking that one day he'll acknowledge how amazing his son is and be moved to spend some time with him. For me, it's impossible to understand why a little boy's dad wouldn't make contact at the sight of his son opening his birthday presents, or learning swing ball, or giggling his head off on the back of the quad bike. To me, they are such precious moments. Any man can fill a pram but it takes a real man to be a father. But I guess for some men, the word 'biological' doesn't mean much at all. Let's face it, they put the same word in front of washing powder! Dwight's actions are so disappointing and I have come to the conclusion that, like Boyle, he is another true coward.

Over the past few years, I've continuously had to defend Harvey from cruelty and ignorance. Most of the articles featuring us together appear after someone has made a stupid and hurtful comment. It really shouldn't be like that. But the idea that people see Harvey as an easy target makes me want to shout louder on his behalf. It's such a shame that so much progress is made through celebrating ground-breaking events like the Paralympics, but the momentum is short-lived. I'm sure I'm not alone in thinking this. Every family coping with disability must feel that from the day a handicapped person is born it's an uphill battle for acceptance. Thank God I know such an amazing network of families, all fighting the same kind of prejudice, and a dedicated team of teachers and medics who look after Harvey so brilliantly. He's my little prince. I love him so much and want him to enjoy every moment of his life.

And, over the past couple of years, Harvey has come on in leaps and bounds, even though there have been huge challenges to overcome. Although I've never once said that I can't cope with him, there have been moments when I've felt exhausted and isolated by caring for him. But I'm one of the lucky ones. Without my mum, I would have broken long ago. She is my support system and I cannot tell you what it means to have someone there that I can rely on. I'd be super-human if I hadn't shed tears over Harvey, but if that ever happens I give myself a good talking to: 'Pick yourself up, Kate, be strong and get on with it.' And I have. Like many parents in my situation, I don't want sympathy or pity but do wish for more empathy and understanding.

One of those heart-sinking moments was in 2013 when Dorton House, the school Harvey had gone to since he was a baby, closed down. It was such a stressful time, worrying how he'd manage the switch to another school. And, as if that wasn't bad enough, I was doubtful whether we'd find another place nearby that could even manage all of his complex needs.

Harvey's main condition is called septo-optic dysplasia. In a nutshell, he suffered brain damage at birth and all his medical and behavioural problems stem from that. His pituitary gland, which regulates all the hormones in the body, does not function properly, which means Harvey lacks the correct balance of chemicals other people have. Also part of the condition is an underactive thyroid, a cortisol deficiency that makes it hard for him to fight illness or cope with shock, and diabetes Insipidus, which means he's permanently thirsty and has to wee a lot. He is registered as blind, and he has the Prader-Willi Syndrome I mentioned earlier, which means having a constant desire to eat. To add to that list, he's also been diagnosed with autism, and more recently doctors have found Harvey has Attention Deficit Disorder (ADHD) and Oppositional Defiance Disorder (ODD).

Imagine the anxiety that most parents go through with one able-bodied child and then multiply that by 100. With a special needs child you can't stop agonising over whether that child is comfortable, happy, taking the right medication, properly cared for ... and the future is even harder to contemplate. You name it, you worry about it, but I guess with Harvey I've never known any different.

I've learned over the years that his autism means he is a stickler for routine. He likes to know exactly where he's going to be and what he's going to be doing on any given day. Sudden change can be very upsetting for him. As soon as Harvey gets up I have to map his day out for him: 'Harvey, we are doing this, this and this today,' and then he's absolutely fine with anything that happens. When I did finally find him a new school, I spent weeks preparing him for his first day. 'Harvey's going to big school soon,' I kept reminding him.

But, as I'd suspected, finding a place for him wasn't plain sailing. There were a couple of schools close to us that we visited but I didn't get the impression Harvey was going to be challenged there at all. One didn't even have desks in the classroom and my mum and I thought, What are they going to teach him? When we visited another school there was an autistic child in the class and one of the staff warned us, 'He's going to kick off.' Great, we both thought. We can see exactly how the teacher handles it. But instead of dealing with the situation, the teacher turned to us and said, 'You've gotta go now.' How could I leave Harvey with staff who wouldn't know how to cope with him? That school was a non-starter.

All the teachers at Dorton House, which was run by the Royal London Society for the Blind, had been absolutely brilliant with Harvey. I have nothing but praise for them, but in the last couple of years he went there it was obvious that the school was being run down for eventual closure. Every time I walked through the gates it felt like a ghost school. Instead of Harvey's regular teachers, many of whom had been made redundant, supply teachers came in and out and Harvey had no consistency in his routine. We've always said that he shows real progress when he has a regular structure and is properly stimulated. When he's not, he becomes easily distracted and has a tendency to kick off. Unfortunately, at Dorton House that had started happening more and more, and in the mornings he'd make it crystal clear that he didn't want to go and that he wasn't happy.

As soon as we knew the school was closing, all of the families of kids there floated the idea of trying to save it but it wasn't a goer. Next, we looked at the possibility of setting up a Free School for children with special needs. We got some way to raising the money needed but, in the end, we were turned down on the grounds that there weren't enough pupils and there wasn't the commitment from the local authority to send children to it. It was totally gutting for everyone. Not only had we put lots of work into getting the school approved but now I knew that I had to start the search for a school for Harvey all over again.

Fortunately, one school I visited did make a lasting impression. Some time ago I met a group of children who had raised £2,500 for a special school in Wimbledon in South London, by doing a sponsored walk in fancy dress, apparently inspired by watching me run the London Marathon! The children, who were from a nearby school in Twickenham, raised the money to help build a Performing Arts and Movement Development Centre at the school, which is state-run and caters for multi-disability and visually impaired children like Harvey. I accepted the cheque on behalf of Vision Charity and spent a day talking to the children who'd fundraised as well as meeting those who would benefit from the new centre. Just walking around, I was so inspired by the enthusiasm of the teachers and the amazing facilities there: soundproofed classrooms, a special trampolining room which Harvey now LOVES, a sensory garden and a fantastic library catering specifically for blind and partially-sighted children. Soon after the Free School plan fell through, I approached the Wimbledon school to see if they would take Harvey even though it was way out of our catchment area. They agreed, provided no other school nearer could accommodate him, which we'd proved they couldn't.

Even though I'd spent ages preparing Harvey he did have a few tantrums in his first few weeks but he soon settled in. I think in part that was him adjusting to the change, but also Harvey always pushes things with new people and new surroundings. Despite his disabilities, in some ways he's no different from any strong-willed, naughty boy. Harvey constantly tests the boundaries to see what he can get away with!

The one thing that did bother me about the school was how far away it was from home. Although Harvey is used to travelling, it's a 120-mile round trip, which means he spends three hours in a car every single day. Again, I honestly don't know what I would have done without my mum, who travelled with Harvey for the first year or so. Every morning she was at my house by 7 a.m. along with Harvey's driver, ready for the daily commute.

Harvey is now old enough to dress himself, but I still have to shower him and make sure he's on time. He's in the car by 7.15 and, without fail, demands that the radio is tuned to LBC. He loves listening along to the chat and the adverts and it seems to soothe him. See what I mean about routine? Before he leaves he puts his toast in a special container and won't start eating it until the car is past the turn-off to London.

Harvey's so precise about when he does things. He even went through one phase of telling us that there was no way he could go to school until he'd played the whole house a tune on his keyboard. In the middle of summer we were treated to 'We Wish You a Merry Christmas' every morning. 'Are we going to school now, Harvey?' my mum would keep asking, but he insisted he had to finish the song.

My mum would also walk with Harvey to his classroom, but the corridor leading to it was too noisy for him and he ran down it, shouting ''Bye, Nan' at the top of his voice. In fact, Harvey still finds the whole school too noisy. There are far more pupils there than at Dorton House – 145 in total – so if he's eating his lunch in the noisy dining hall he knows to put on his ear defenders. Loud banging or shouting really disturbs Harvey but different noises upset him at different times. For ages he hated the sound of the kitchen cutlery drawer being opened so I'd stick notes all around the house reminding people to open drawers and doors very quietly. He was also very upset by Princess crying or screaming when she was a toddler. I think it's because the sound was so high-pitched. Poor Princess! He really took out his anger on her, but he only occasionally does that now. When Jett came along and then Bunny, I had no idea how he was going to react but, touch wood, he's welcomed them into the house, even though Jett does wind him up by hitting or poking him. Now Harvey knows to say to him, 'No, Jett. Harvey doesn't like!'

When my mum said she wouldn't be able to accompany Harvey to school any more I was concerned we'd have another battle on our hands although I completely understood why. By the time she arrived back in the morning and left again in the afternoon, she was doing six hours of travelling every day, five days a week. She'd not long had an operation on her knees and it meant that sitting in one position for any length of time became really painful. But, once again, Harvey surprised us all. My mum even thinks that the escort who now travels with him and who's trained to give him his injections, gets him on his best behaviour because, believe me, Harvey knows exactly which buttons to press with family, especially his nan! But, so far, so good. He knuckles under and does what she tells him. Long may it continue . . .

Let me say a few more words here about Harvey's journey to school. It's not something I ever thought I would have to justify publicly but, unbeknown to me, a public row blew up about his taxi run while I was locked in the Big Brother house in January 2015. Even my brother and my mum got involved! Perhaps I shouldn't have been surprised given Katie Hopkins's previous comments, but the row exploded after she and I had a conversation in the kitchen about Harvey. I mentioned that a state-funded driver and a nurse take him back and forth to Wimbledon. It's no overexaggeration to say that Harvey's condition is life-threatening and so, whether it's me, my mum or a qualified medic, he must travel with someone who knows how to give him his regular medication and injections. As I said in the house, if I were to pay privately for a chauffeur and a nurse for four journeys a day it would cost me more than £1,000, but that's not the price that the local authority pay to transport Harvey.

In exactly the same way that Katie judged the parents of obese children, she couldn't wait to have a dig at me for using taxpayers' money to fund Harvey's school taxi. I bit my lip but I felt so upset by her words: *With the amount you earn, I'd find that tricky as you could afford it yourself . . . I've always held dear that if you can afford to pay for something, you should, and you shouldn't rely on the government. I think that's wrong.*

Again, as a mother of three herself, I find it incredible that Katie has so little imagination that she couldn't put herself in the shoes of a parent with a severely disabled child. Firstly, I do earn a lot but I am also a taxpayer and, believe me, I pay a lot in tax! Secondly, I have never claimed state benefits, but I believe I should be able to access a universal, non-means-tested benefit for my son in the same way as any other parent with a disabled child. Seriously, I'd rather a local council use their money on helping disabled children access decent education than spending thousands on a fireworks display! Thirdly, had Dorton House School not closed and had our proposal to create our own school not been rejected, or had the local council been able to provide a school for Harvey closer to home, I wouldn't be in this position. Rant over? I haven't even got started . . .

What shocked me the most about Katie's argument was how she completely failed to think of Harvey in all of this. As his mother, I am fully aware of how unstable my career is. I don't know how long my present income will last. If I got run over by a bus tomorrow, how would Harvey manage? How will Harvey manage for the rest of his life? What people don't seem to get is that Harvey being able to access state help is not about ME, it's about HIM. I do not get free travel, Harvey does. And it's an entitlement that is given to every disabled child in the country without question. And rightly so.

As my brother said on my Twitter feed while I was in the Big Brother house, it needed no justification. And my mum also put it perfectly when she was interviewed by the *Sun* three days after the episode aired: Katie Hopkins would never know how difficult having a disabled child can be. No one can unless they have lived it. Thanks, Mum. I couldn't have put it better myself! I would love Katie to spend a week in my shoes and then see what she says about Harvey's travel. I can't imagine she'd last a day.

But, surprise, surprise, for all those people who applauded Katie Hopkins's ignorance, I received so many amazing messages of support, many from parents with special needs children. Even Liberal Democrat leader Nick Clegg gave me his backing on LBC, saying he would be 'reluctant to throw out the idea of universally treating all children with disabilities with the same kind of compassion and support everywhere we can'. If, God forbid, one of Katie Hopkins's children needed emergency help, I'm sure she wouldn't be stopping paramedics saying, 'I'm sorry, please don't rush my child to hospital. I can afford to pay for treatment.' Did anyone say to David Cameron that he shouldn't take his disabled son Ivan to an NHS hospital? I don't think so. There are some things that are sacred in this country and the NHS and disability benefits are two of them.

I was also very touched to have the support of the panel at *Loose Women*, who discussed Harvey's travel arrangements on the show that same week. Of course, at the time I had no idea that this was going on, but Jamelia said it was 'ridiculous' that I couldn't access a service that I helped to fund. Janet Street-Porter confessed that she was moved almost to tears because I had tried to set up a school closer to home, not only for Harvey but for other disabled children, and she thought that no disabled child should be forced to travel three hours a day to go to school. However, as much as I respect guest panellist Deborah Meaden as a businesswoman, I disagree with her view that I should pay even though Harvey is entitled to state help. She described the argument between myself and Katie Hopkins as a 'missed opportunity' and thought that I should have used my public profile to say, 'I could access state help but I've taken the decision to pay for Harvey privately.' In fact, I think the opposite. I want to use my celebrity status to highlight how critical it is for ALL parents with disabled children to have equal access to help, and for other people to know how important these benefits are.

And as for those estimates of how much I'm worth . . . Ha! First of all, it's no one's business how much money I have but I can safely say the outrageous sums I've seen bandied around are wrong. Mistakenly, too, people seem to think that throwing money at Harvey will make everything okay. Yes, perhaps unlike other families I *am* fortunate that I can pay a nanny to help care for him if I need to work. And, yes, I *can* make his life that bit more comfortable. But no amount of cash in the world could stop Harvey having to go through everything he endures every single day. Why can't people see that?

Phew! Rant officially over . . . take a breath, Kate . . . back to Harvey's new school.

From early on he responded brilliantly to his new teachers. He has one main teacher who takes the class of nine and another who works with Harvey on a one-to-one basis. Every morning his timetable is explained to him. He does maths, English and even French, just like other children, but his favourite lessons are definitely music and drawing. If Harvey could draw frogs all day he'd be in heaven. He's obsessed! And his artwork never ceases to amaze me. He knows exactly which colours go together and his use of perspective is unbelievable! Not long ago he drew a train speeding through a tunnel with the whole family waving as it whizzed past. I had a lump in my throat looking at it.

The school has such an energetic feel about it and is kitted out with so many great facilities that Harvey feels physically challenged too, which is really important because of his weight. He adores trampolining and playing football. They even take him rock climbing and to an artificial ski slope. But because Harvey's stubborn and wants to drive everything himself, the staff have to be very strict with him. They'll say things like, 'Okay, Harvey, if you want to go trampolining you have to do your French,' or, 'If you want to go rock climbing, you must finish your maths.' It's all about explaining consequences to Harvey. But I can't talk. It's a hard lesson for everyone to learn – if you want to do the fun things in life, the hard work always has to be done first!

I am hoping too that as his reading progresses he'll be able to communicate better with us. Harvey is partially sighted and so while he copes in a familiar environment, he always needs help in strange places. And, as he has no sense of danger whatsoever, he can't really be on his own for one moment. He manages to read in large type (48-point) but many of Harvey's frustrations stem from the fact that a lot of the time he can't tell us how he is feeling or what he wants. At school he's taught Makaton, a form of sign language, and that does help him talk to us. It calms him down too. 'Good boy, you're using your Makaton,' I tell him. Or, if I can see he's on the verge of a tantrum, I'll encourage him, 'Harvey use his Makaton.' He could have a sore tummy or be feeling sad, but once Harvey can begin to sign his problem the words seem to follow. It's as though working through his thoughts triggers his speech.

Recently to alleviate Harvey's extreme feelings of anxiety, which he suffers from all the time, he's begun picking the skin on his legs. It's really upsetting and is becoming a serious issue. He suffered horrific burns on his legs in 2006 when he climbed into a bath full of scalding hot water. The accident happened on New Year's Eve during a party. Although the house was completely baby-proofed, a guest must have left a gate open, leaving Harvey able to sneak upstairs to my bathroom and turn the taps on himself. I wasn't there when the accident happened but when I arrived he was thrashing around in agony on my bed and we had to rush him to the specialist burns unit at the Chelsea and Westminster Hospital.

Thankfully, he made a full recovery but the scars on his legs remain and where the skin is thin he picks great big holes in it, particularly when he experiences a build-up of stress. And the wounds never have a chance to heal because he's always picking, picking, picking. Even if the doctor wraps bandages around his legs Harvey manages to poke his fingers down the side. To try and stop him, I've had to resort to all sorts of blackmail. Harvey lives for swimming but because his legs are so bloodied, it's a health hazard to take him in the pool. 'If Harvey picks his legs, he won't go swimming,' I remind him. Disappointingly, it hasn't had any effect so far but I am praying it's only a phase he's going through. His doctors are also constantly looking at how they can adjust his medication so he doesn't feel so anxious all the time.

At school, Harvey's super-quick at picking things up, but like any little boy he's lazy too, and needs to be pushed. We are constantly thinking of ways to make learning fun for him. For Christmas my mum bought him the CDs of Roald Dahl's and David Walliams's children's books and he's also getting into the *Horrid Henry* series. As he listens to the CD he follows the story in his book. He's also started the Oxford Reading Tree, which teaches children to read through the use of phonics, a method where they learn the sounds of words and their corresponding spelling patterns.

I'm hoping too that as Harvey grows up he'll have friends who visit him at home regularly. It's the one disadvantage of his school being in Wimbledon. If you ask Harvey who his friends are, he'll reel off a list of his classmates, but during the holidays they live too far away to play with him. Of course, he's got Junior and Princess and Jett and Bunny, but Harvey will never be able to phone anyone himself and invite them over, so his social life has to be arranged for him. This year we've been working with social services to try and find activities for him outside term-time, so he can make friends nearer home. So far, we've found a tailor-made centre for disabled people in the South Downs set in thirty-two acres of beautiful woodland. There he can take part in all sorts of activities from mountain biking and archery to climbing and orienteering.

But while Harvey is making great strides at home and at school, his health has to be constantly monitored. In the past two years he's been put on three new drugs to help with his ADHD and ODD. Harvey already takes medication five times daily and a hormone injection before he goes to bed. We always have to prepare him carefully for having an injection, but he really copes with it amazingly well.

He's under the care of four different hospitals: our local hospital, Great Ormond Street for his septo-optic dysplasia, Moorfields Eye Hospital for his blindness, and The Maudsley in South London for his mental health. That means a lot of appointments and a lot of information to co-ordinate, and again I have to thank my mum for helping me with that. Harvey's doctors are brilliant too. If he is placed on a new drug, we get a phone call every couple of weeks monitoring his response. Because of Harvey's weight, there's extra pressure placed on his heart and so he also needs to be admitted for regular blood tests and ECG tests. When I think of all the prodding and poking and being wired up to machines and needles and tests and meetings that Harvey has to go through every time he visits a hospital, I feel so much pride in him. He's an incredibly brave boy.

I think everybody could see for themselves what an amazing child Harvey is when my mum and I were invited to bring him on to the *This Morning* couch on Mother's Day earlier in the year. Harvey was incredibly excited about appearing, but he's impatient at the best of times. While Ruth and Eamonn were introducing the show, all you could hear was Harvey in the background, shouting, 'I'm bored with this!' Well, I had forewarned the production crew they needed to be patient! During the interview, I asked him, 'You do play up for Mummy sometimes, don't you, Harvey?' 'Yeah, babe!' he replied cheekily. He's never called me 'babe' before, but it was absolutely hilarious. When Eamonn told him how clever he was, Harvey said, 'That's awesome!' He has such a brilliant sense of humour and I had so many lovely messages of support after the show.

Although it was the first time Harvey had appeared on live TV for seven years, and it's nerve-wracking having him there because he can be unpredictable, I have no intention of hiding him away from the world. I want everyone to see that disability doesn't have to mean a life lived within limits. There are things Harvey can now do, like reading, that we once believed would never be possible. In fact, when he was born, the experts were doubtful he'd even be able to speak, cuddle me, or do half of the things that he now does. But with the right encouragement and help he's developed into a gorgeous, funny, smart, mischievous and incredibly courageous little boy who plays a central and positive role in our family.

CHAPTER 17

KIERAN'S NEW BIRDS

When it comes to thinking about great love affairs, I'm always tempted to burst into a rendition of the song 'It Started With a Kiss'. But Kieran's and my romance with the countryside didn't start like that at all. It started with four chickens. I know! Doesn't have quite the same ring, does it? But just like the Hot Chocolate classic says, 'I never thought it would come to this!'

As our own little family has grown, so have the numbers of our birds and animals. Four chickens have multiplied into forty-two chicks, ninety chickens, nineteen ducks, five geese, three turkeys, one peacock, three pigs, two goats, four dogs, four horses . . . and by the time this book's published, God knows what numbers we'll have reached.

Anyone who knows me knows how much I love the

outdoors. I always have done. While everyone else was swotting up for their exams at school, I was bunking off to go horse riding. If you ask me what the capital of China is, I haven't got a clue, but I know every second of a dressage routine off by heart. Intelligence comes in many forms, I like to think.

It's always been my dream to have a big house with acres of land so I can look out of the window and see my horses. I was lucky enough to have that in my last house, and my new one has land too. Since we moved there, our assortment of animals has steadily grown. I've been thinking about becoming self-sufficient too, and with Kieran's help that dream is gradually turning into reality. Despite everything that's happened, I'm convinced we're made for each other. What with Kieran's granddad having been a farmer and Kieran himself spending his boyhood outdoors, we have so much in common we make the perfect team. We're like Tom and Barbara out of *The Good Life* – but without the posh accents. Kieran's got the know-how and I've got the business brain. Hopefully, in time, our growing farm will become profitable. We're not at that stage yet, but we have plans. So many plans!

We have pens and stables in the grounds of our new home and, until my horses are transferred from a nearby livery yard, where they've been for far too long, our birds and livestock have a temporary home there.

In the beginning, I did have a man come to the house every day to feed and muck out the animals but as

Kieran wasn't working it seemed stupid to carry on paying someone to do a job he could easily get on with. I jokingly call Kieran 'Farmer Giles' and, with him sporting his new beard, I don't think I'm that far off.

Kieran might be largely self-taught when it comes to keeping livestock but he has great instincts, and taking responsibility for our little farm has been the perfect way for him to spend quality time with the kids too. Sometimes they can all be outside for hours. I won't have a clue what they're up to and then, all of a sudden, Princess or Junior will charge through the back door yelling that a chick's hatched or they've been hand-feeding the goats.

So now we have a morning routine that involves children and animals!

Each day we take it in turns to get the kids ready. Either Kieran showers and gets Harvey ready for when his driver comes to take him to school, or I do. Whichever way, whoever isn't sorting out Harvey is sorting out Princess and Junior's breakfast and driving them to school. We try not to make too much noise near Jett's and Bunny's rooms because we want them to sleep for as long as possible while the other kids are running around. Once one lot have left the house, the person left occasionally gets to crawl back into bed for a snooze before the routine begins all over again with the youngest two. More often than not, though, it's full-on from the time Harvey gets up.

Then, any time between 8 and 10 a.m., depending

on when Jett and Bunny stir, Kieran's outside routine begins.

First of all we let the dogs out. There's our Labrador Kevin, a French Bulldog called Derek, and two Dogue de Bordeaux mastiffs called Trevor and Vera. It's lucky we're living in a building site at the moment because Kevin can't stop shitting on my dining-room rug and Kieran is constantly bringing in pig poo on the bottom of his wellies. All the smells roll into one after a while, and I'm 24/7 armed with a bottle of carpet cleaner and my Jo Malone candles to mask the stench.

Each day, the pigs are the first to be fed. We have three Large Whites called Patsy, Priscilla and Peggy. Kieran has reared them from eight-week-old piglets. At the moment they're housed in one stable and, make no mistake, they are absolutely filthy. They say pigs are very clever animals but I haven't seen much evidence of it yet. To me, they just stink! Kieran cleans them out every two days and gives them new straw and water. And they are seriously thirsty animals. They drink up to ten litres of water every single day.

Junior and Princess adore them. Surprisingly, they are incredibly friendly and the kids spend ages hand-feeding them pig nuts. Princess even rides on their backs. She looks tiny up against these heavy moving beasts but they've never thrown her off or turned on her once.

It's so hard not to get attached to them. Princess, Junior and even Kieran can't bear the thought of them becoming bacon but Kieran reckons he'll sell their offspring for slaughter later this year because more pigs mean more work for him. One pig is heavily pregnant as I write so I'll have to report back on whether he can bear to let them go. My bet is he'll chicken out at the last moment. Imagine parting with a twelve-week-old piglet? He's far too much of a softie.

After the pigs, the goats are next. They're pygmy goats and we bought them as birthday presents for Junior and Princess, although Jett also spends loads of time with them. Once again, Kieran has reared them from babies – we got them when they were three months old. Junior's is called Benjamin and Princess's is called Angel. It was so cute watching them being bottle fed and then seeing Kieran wean them on to proper food when they were around six months old. They're so affectionate too. When they were babies Kieran taught them how to jump up on his back to take their bottle and they still do it now. And although they're pets and definitely not for eating, Angel's babies will eventually be used to produce milk.

With those kinds of animals you can actually have them indoors and house-train them. But Kieran doesn't have the time, and I don't think the dogs would be pleased. Even though Benjamin and Angel have never head-butted or charged at the kids, I don't think Trevor, Vera, Derek or Kevin would enjoy having two pairs of goat's horns permanently up their backsides.

So that's our four-legged livestock but our collection

of two-legged animals is even more impressive. There are seven pens outside and two sheds packed full of chickens. In the smaller pens, we keep around six chickens and the larger ones hold around fifteen. Each pen holds a different breed and every morning Kieran feeds them and changes their water. There's bog standard chickens and a variety of rare breeds like Bantams and Silkies, which have the most gorgeous white plumage that feels like the softest feather boa.

During the winter the birds don't lay at all, but this spring we had so many eggs we didn't know what to do with them. Luckily, I'm a sucker for fried egg sandwiches. Depending on the breed, you get a different colour of egg. There's green, blue, white and brown, and they all taste delicious.

During breeding season the chickens produce around thirty to forty eggs a day in total, which we want to start selling when we have our farm shop up and running. We try and give them a good organic diet too because we eat the eggs and someday we'll be eating the chickens. They say if you can't dispatch, don't hatch, so we know we're going to have to get used to treating them as a going concern rather than a growing collection of birds!

Kieran cleans them out once a week and replaces their bedding, and in one of the pens he's even created a nursery by installing an incubator. And that's where all of our chicks are hatched. Obviously the eggs have to be fertilised, but this year we had no problems in that department. The minute we put a cock in with the hens they were at it like nobody's business. All day, every day. It made us tired listening to it!

After twenty-one days under a hot lamp the chicken eggs hatch, although it's a few days longer for the turkey and duck eggs. As for our geese, Kieran's not successfully hatched a single egg yet. Apparently geese are a lot more difficult to breed, but he'll keep going.

That's not the story with the ducks, though. Last year we kept six and this year they've more than tripled to a whopping nineteen. If ever one of them is sick we bring it indoors. And if it was up to Kieran he'd have them in the bath splashing around with the kids. They're so friendly, but I have to put my foot down on that idea for hygiene reasons.

Having said that, the kids really do get their hands dirty and I don't mind at all. Naturally, the first thing they have to do is wash their hands if they've been out playing with the animals but Kieran and I both believe that kids shouldn't be wrapped in cotton wool. It's good for them to be exposed to different kinds of bacteria because it builds up their immune system. Too much cleanliness and disinfectant around the house can actually give them allergies whereas being exposed to dirt and the outside world is far better for them, so long as they're careful.

In fact we let them have as much contact with the animals as possible. Whether it's touching them, feeding them, or rolling around in the straw with them, it's fine by us. Princess loves watching the chicks too and whenever they have friends playing at the house the first thing they do is take them out to the sheds, show them around and check on what chicks have hatched or how big the babies have grown.

Already we are looking towards Christmas because I want a plump home-reared turkey sizzling away in my Aga. I can't wait. It'll be like having our own Tesco, only it's outside the back door. At the moment we've got three turkeys, which we jokingly call Roast, Dinner and Sunday Lunch, but they're not the ones we're planning on eating. As soon as they have babies we'll rear up the poults for 25 December.

If all goes well we'll have our own veg on the plates too. Kieran's bought a polytunnel to replace the battered old greenhouse. As soon as it's up, the seeds we're currently growing on the kitchen windowsill will be transferred into it. So far we've got cucumbers, cabbages, lettuces, rocket, herbs, peppers, aubergines, courgettes, chillies and strawberries, but I'm sure we'll branch out into potatoes and carrots and loads more too. And if Kieran and I ever fall out, I've told him that the polytunnel will make his perfect second home!

We've got twelve acres of land to play with so the plan is that my horses will eventually occupy the field at the back of the house. But there's so much room, the sky's the limit.

Since we've moved and I've not been able to bring my horses home, I miss them so much. I can't wait till the day when I can look out and see them grazing outside. Being pregnant with both Jett and Bunny has meant I've not done half as much riding as I would have liked to either, so I'm raring to get back in the saddle. The best thing is that I don't have to explain my passion for horses to Kieran. He gets it. And for someone who'd never ridden before he met me, he's really progressed and loves riding too, which is brilliant. Junior and Princess have both got their own horses and I'm also hoping to get Harvey on a pony soon, as he keeps asking. I never thought my love of horses would become a family affair, but it's wonderful it's turned out that way.

And last but not least there is our peacock. She's also very tame and the kids bring her into the kitchen if she's poorly. Someday we'll get a male so they can mate, but she loves sleeping in with the pigs. Each to their own, I say.

My dream was also to have two emus out the front so that they would be the first thing to greet people coming to the house. They'd look amazing strutting around, but Kieran's told me I have to be practical. Apparently, they're very unpredictable birds and can be dangerous too. Probably not the best idea with five children running around. And neither I nor Kieran fancy wrestling one to the ground if they ever get out of hand, so for now that dream is on hold.

One idea that I think we could make a go of, though, is to host small private children's parties during the summer. If we created a petting zoo, our animals would fit perfectly into it, and, like I said, they are all so tame. The children enjoy the animals so much and I'd love it if we could share all that fun with others.

I'm always thinking up new ideas for what we can do with our land and our animals and now Kieran's decorated the study on the top floor of the house, I have a control room from which to plan our farm shop and our petting-zoo empire. He's also got his smallholder's licence, which means we can transport livestock and sell eggs at the local market, as well as being registered with the authorities if there's an outbreak of something like avian flu or foot and mouth disease in the area. There's so much to learn and, like all my other businesses, once I put my mind to it, I know I can make it succeed.

CHAPTER 18

MY SEVENTH BOOB JOB

Before I became pregnant with Jett in early 2013 I had my best boob job ever. It was my sixth. On recommendation, I'd flown to the Be Clinic in Belgium to have the procedure done there. My surgeon did a wonderful job and, trust me, I know what a good boob job looks and feels like.

Of course the shape you choose is a matter of personal preference. Some women love the teardrop look with an implant that slopes downwards with the natural curve of the breast but that's never been the shape for me. I adore that round, uniform, all-American stuck-on look. Always have done, always will.

Even though new boobs normally take between three and six months to settle into the body, I could tell straight away that these were perfect: perfect size, perfect shape, perfect look, and the surgeon had done a perfect job.

When I developed an infection in my left boob and had to go back for follow-up treatment, the scar eventually healed so neatly that I couldn't even tell he'd made an incision. And the infection wasn't the result of poor surgery. The problem was that my body simply took a longer time than expected to heal.

So there I was with boobs I loved . . . and bang! I met Kieran, fell in love and got pregnant. I wouldn't change most of that for the world, but bad timing or what? There's nothing worse than a new baby to mess up your mammaries, fake or otherwise. Pregnancy automatically changes the shape of your boobs and they usually enlarge. So, when I fell pregnant with Bunny I knew it was a foregone conclusion that I'd have to go under the knife again.

I don't know whether it was because I'd gotten so big with Jett but, this time around, I'd thought about going smaller. Sometimes when you've got big boobs you can appear larger than you actually are and I'd had enough of looking fat and feeling uncomfortable in all of my clothes.

If anyone read that the reason I wanted a breast reduction was to 'be taken more seriously', I can hand on heart say that wasn't true. I am who I am. I can be serious and I can be funny. I've had large boobs for twenty years and they've never stopped me from doing anything I've wanted to do. I've never had a boob job for work or any reason other than it was my choice to do so.

The advice I always give people who are thinking

about having any kind of cosmetic surgery is, 'Do it for you and no one else.' If you're not sure why you're doing it, don't go ahead until you've thought it through. Like any major operation, it should be taken very seriously. It's not a game, you should always choose a surgeon by reputation. Be warned. There are a lot of charlatans out there.

I said as much when I was asked by the *Independent* newspaper before the 2015 general election what changes I would bring in if I were prime minister – and no, I wasn't planning on running! It may surprise many people, but I always say I would increase the legal age for cosmetic surgery from eighteen to twenty-one. As I see it, there's lot of external pressure on young girls growing up, which is resulting in them turning to surgery. I'm not convinced that the reason they're doing it is to please themselves and I wonder whether it's to please other people. I feel the same about young girls who desperately want to be thin. My advice is to be fit and healthy before you're thin. Besides, who wants to look like a walking coat hanger?

Anyway, once we'd got Bunny settled in at home, I booked in my seventh boob job, again with the same surgeon in Belgium. He could fit me in at the end of November. That was enough time for me to arrange the shoot for my annual calendar, which I always bring out before Christmas.

Obviously I wanted my new boobs on show for that and, as for the location, I'd imagined going back to Cape

Verde. Yes, yes, I know it was the place where I found
Kieran and Jane kissing but there was method in my
madness. I always think it's better to take a deep breath
and face your demons than to run from the past. Ever
the optimist, me! If I could combine that with working
on a beautiful, tropical beach in the sunshine then
why not?

On the afternoon I flew to Brussels, I admit, I was
nervous. When I was nineteen and had my first boob job
I was so headstrong that I didn't care. Now I'm older
and wiser, I do consider the risks more – especially
because I've got five kids. Nevertheless, these boobs had
to go so there was also part of me that couldn't wait to
get on with it.

Again, I wasn't disappointed with the results. Implants
are measured in cubic centimetres. I've been as big as
1095cc in the past, which in surgery-speak means XL.
During this operation I wanted them reduced to around
925cc, which is a nice C cup, and that's exactly what I
got.

Frustratingly, for the second time running, my recovery
didn't go smoothly at all. The same infection that I'd
developed under my left boob after my last surgery
appeared in precisely the same place where I'd been
stitched.

As I had work booked in the week after my operation
I kept my dressings on, hoping the infection would heal
naturally and, after a few days, it did look like I might
recover. What a wake-up call I got later that week

though . . . On the morning I was due to do a shoot and an interview for the *Sun*'s *Fabulous* magazine, I woke up in agony.

The last thing I wanted to do was cancel as this was my first big interview since Kieran and I had decided to make a go of things. I wanted to say, 'I'm Katie Price! I've had the year from hell, but I'm back! I'm stronger, fitter, and up for any challenge!' But that wasn't how I was feeling at all. Underneath I was thinking, I'm Katie Price . . . I can't lift my arms above my shoulders . . . I'm having difficulty holding my own baby, and quite frankly I feel like a pile of shit!

There was a moment before we started when I didn't think I could carry on. My brother Dan, my manager, and my publicist Lauren watched me slump down on a chair outside the studio. 'I can't go in yet,' I admitted to my manager.

'Are you kidding? Is it that bad?' he asked, sounding concerned. He'd not realised I'd been putting on a brave face, but my boob felt like it was being fired at with a nail gun. Rat-tat-tat-tat-tat . . . Thank God everyone knows me well at the venue, The Worx, because I was forced to sit in the corridor, undo my bra and cup my boob in my hand to help ease the pain. It had swelled like an angry toad.

Normally, I would have loved that shoot. The stylist had picked out a beautiful black beaded Egyptian-style headdress for me to wear and a gorgeous black lace leotard. The whole set had a classy but 'don't mess with me' feel about it. The photographer Mark had wanted to take some really arty shots of me slightly hunched over, which was just as well because it was one of the only positions I could manage! I'm sure people thought I looked so serious in the photographs because of my marital problems, but that couldn't have been further from the truth. I was in so much pain, I had to dig deep just to get through it.

Then the following day I had a press call for my new perfume Kissable Fierce. Instead of wearing the giant inflatable red lips that I'd pulled on when I launched Kissable back in 2013, I'd had a smaller pair made that strapped around my front with a large cerise ribbon tied around my body. The prop covered my new boobs nicely, but if the lips had been any heavier I think I would have collapsed.

The studio crew had also rigged up a ring of fire for me to pose behind. I'd never worked with live flames before. I loved it! The atmosphere was edgy and dramatic but as the cameras click, click, clicked away not only did my boob feel like it was on fire, my tight black latex catsuit came dangerously close to igniting too. Katie Price really does suffer for her art!

Fortunately, I've been doing shoots for so long that I know how to pose my body in a way that minimises any pain. But when I look back at those pictures now, I can see how tired and lacklustre I look. Directly afterwards I rang my surgeon, who coincidentally was flying into London the next day, and booked an appointment to see him in his Harley Street clinic. Meanwhile all the arrangements had been finalised for Cape Verde so my fingers were firmly crossed he would give me the all-clear to fly out on 4 December.

Unfortunately that wasn't to be. 'You're not going anywhere, Kate,' he said the minute he looked at my boob.

'You need to be operated on straight away.' Obviously that was disappointing for me and the crew accompanying me although, to be fair, everyone had told me I was mad to want to go back to the same beach in Sal. I was more pissed off that I lost money as everything had already been booked.

After my stitches had been taken out, my surgeon drained and cleaned the wound and then sewed it back up again. And when I say drained, I mean drained. I had what's called a seroma – and this bit's not for the faint-hearted among you. It's when fluid gathers in the chest – the same yellowy liquid that fills blisters. My swelling was so full that I was packed off on the plane with a tube inserted into the side of my boob connected to a bottle to catch the fluid.

The next morning I woke in a panic. 'Where the hell's my drain gone?' I quizzed Kieran, as I began frantically snatching away the duvet. Although I'd been forced to sleep in a sitting position, propped up on pillows, I must have knocked the tube out in the night. All I could feel underneath me was a wet, sticky bed sheet. No amount of painkillers or antibiotics could have perked me up that day. I felt so low and, of course, had to fly back to Belgium to be checked out and have the drain reinserted.

It was becoming obvious that, however much I rested, the skin around my scar wasn't going to heal. So to give myself the best chance, I opted to have smaller implants put in that would hopefully take the pressure off the wound. In the end, that turned out to be nothing more than wishful thinking too . . .

In the meantime, I couldn't put off my calendar shoot any longer. It had already been delayed, plus I'd been promising a new offering on my website for ages and I won't let my fans down. With bi-weekly flights to Brussels, shooting the photographs anywhere abroad was completely out of the question. So I booked a studio in London and managed to get the whole lot in the can in four hours. Considering the circumstances, I was pleased with the results but that shoot felt like the longest four hours of my life!

There's nothing like constant throbbing pain to make you feel utterly deflated, although when I'm working I try my best not to be grumpy and take my frustrations out on the people around me. At the end of the day, I'm not ill. I'm not asking for sympathy. My numerous boob jobs are wholly self-inflicted and you'd think I'd have learned my lesson by now. It's the reason I always warn people to think carefully before they opt for surgery because you never know what's around the corner . . .

As Christmas approached, I thought, I'm living in the

middle of a building site. I can't work properly. I can't look after my kids properly. Please can I have my life back? Thank God for Kieran, that's all I can say, because during December he did absolutely everything around the house – washing, childcare, cooking. You name it, he was on duty. On top of that he was trying to plaster the walls upstairs and install our new kitchen as well as tending to the animals. That month, I couldn't thank him enough but the worst thing was I couldn't even hug him! It was just too painful. Though I hope taking up the domestic slack did give him an appreciation of how exhausting it is bringing up five kids . . .

*　*　*

In between bouts of bed rest I wanted to keep working as much as I could. In November, I'd started appearing as a guest with the Australian TV network Channel 7. *The Morning Show* had invited me to do a weekly ten-minute slot, to talk about anything from fashion to hair and make-up, and even do a spot on being an entrepreneur called *The Price is Right*, where I let people in on the secret of my success. And the biggest secret is . . . there is no secret! It all comes down to hard work, determination, being able to spot a good business opportunity, being realistic about achieving your goals and being smart with your money. For example, when I started out, many of my industry friends were wasting their money on buying designer clothes, but I invested my money in a house the minute I was old enough to buy one. So that was the kind of advice I wanted to share on *The Morning Show*. Doing it was so much fun but because of the time difference I had to arrive at the studio in London every Tuesday and be camera-ready by 9 p.m. to connect to Melbourne via a live satellite link-up. By the time I got home it was the early hours of Wednesday morning, but again I'm such a trouper that I didn't want to let anyone down.

On one Wednesday morning journey home Kieran and I were so hungry that we grabbed a chicken sandwich from a petrol station. What a disaster that turned out to be! I'm sure it's because Kieran had been cooking us all such healthy meals at home that we were both struck down with food poisoning. Sickness, diarrhoea, and a dodgy boob. A fabulous combination! Sadly, that meant I couldn't take the kids for a night of festive fun at Winter Wonderland in Hyde Park, which had been in the diary for ages. It was very disappointing.

Actually, Christmas was turning out to be a bit of a wash-out. That was tough for me because it was a year when I had all the kids on Christmas Day and I really wanted it to be special. As I've mentioned before, Pete and I take it in turns to have the kids for Christmas and New Year.

Normally, I'd have decorated the outside of the house and the trees in the driveway with multicoloured lights and flashing Santa sleighs, but last Christmas that would have been ridiculous. For starters, our front yard looked like a building site, and even if I'd wanted to, I wouldn't have been able to find the decorations in all of our unopened boxes piled up in various rooms. We did put up a lovely tree indoors, though, and Kieran and I took the kids outside on Christmas Eve to see if they could spot Santa and his reindeers crossing the moon. Princess is still a believer, I think, but Junior is definitely catching on that it's Mummy who's the real Santa Claus.

Also, another problem was that Kieran had been so preoccupied with looking after the children that it was becoming clear that only part of our kitchen was going to be up and running by Christmas Day.

The week before, he ended up rushing out to buy a plug-in electric hob just so we could cook our veggies. The roasties and turkey could sizzle away in the Aga which, thankfully, remained in action. With fifteen guests coming, we were forced to use the utility kitchen and had to ferry everything back and forth to the dining room. Again a big thank you goes to my mum for keeping a clear head in all of the chaos! And for preparing the turkey the night before. In fact we slow cooked it all night . . . delicious!

As much as I tried to take things easy, I had to face facts. My boob wasn't getting any better. The infection would improve for a day or so and then it would swell up all over again especially if my period was due. I spent Christmas Day walking around holding it and I think everyone could tell I wasn't my bubbly self. Plus I also think they were getting totally bored of my epic boob saga so I didn't want to keep banging on about it.

Shut up and take the pain, Kate, I thought, but that was almost impossible.

Initially, we'd planned to renew our vows at New Year but we'd shelved that idea in mid-December and decided to postpone the ceremony until I was well enough. I think it was the *Mirror* who reported that I'd wanted a *Frozen*-themed extravaganza with Idina Menzel's 'Let it Go' power ballad belting out as I walked down the aisle. *Please!* That was never on the cards, and besides, anyone who knows me will tell you I much prefer being warm. Why on earth would I want to look frozen?

But I did feel like such a failure. I couldn't even organise a New Year's party! Deep down, though, I wasn't sure that I wanted one. Me and Kieran had agreed on a fresh start, we wanted to renew our vows, but it was early days and I still felt haunted by the image of Kieran and Jane having sex at my onesie party the previous year. I couldn't get it out of my brain!

In the end we hooked up with my friend Melodie, her partner and a few other friends in London and went out for a Japanese meal followed by cocktails in the Sanctum Hotel and a dance at DSTRKT nightclub. Both of us loved being out with mates but, let me just say, I think my days of clubbing at New Year are done. I would never have said that a few years ago. But now? Oh, how I wanted to be home with my slippers on. As the countdown to 2015 began I didn't suddenly think, Wow! A new year, a new us, a new life. Neither did I want to look back. I didn't need reminding what a shit year I'd had. I'd lost two friends; I'd almost lost a husband; my body was hanging together by a stitch ... Instead, I kissed Kieran and quietly wondered, Is it too early to book a taxi? Dancing was excruciating too as I could barely move. So I probably looked ridiculous and the whole thing felt incredibly impersonal.

New Year's Day was the first time that Kieran and I had had sex in ages but even that bright idea descended into utter disaster: me on all fours, holding the underneath of my boob and yelping in agony. Sex goddess Jordan I was not! It's a disturbing vision, I know, but as soon as we made it back to Sussex I stood in front of the mirror and slowly unpeeled my dressing. 'Fuck! What's this?' I shouted. All I could see was a gaping black hole. Some of the stitches underneath my boob had actually unravelled and my implant was hanging out from the skin!

The next day I was due to travel to Birmingham to see my very good friend Tania. We'd not caught up in a long time and because she was pregnant I didn't want suddenly to change plans. Fortunately I know Tania's doctor as he's accompanied me to Belgium before, so we set off and on arrival I had him check me out. I also sent pictures of the black hole to my surgeon in Brussels.

Unsurprisingly, less than twenty-four hours later I was taking another trip across the Channel. I'd had so many general anaesthetics since November that in January they had to use gas to knock me out because they couldn't find the veins in my arm. And the drip needed to be inserted through a vein in my ankle. Admittedly, it's a weird pleasure, but I normally love the feeling of going under. I like that sensation of gradually feeling more woozy, but I was beginning to hate it too. Too many anaesthetics are not good for a person. And for weeks after all my complications began I couldn't even have Botox. The thought of more needles, more clinics and more pain sent shivers down my spine. I'd had enough.

'Would I heal better if I took both implants out?' I asked my surgeon. He said I would, even though it was the last thing I wanted. It would be the first time I'd had natural boobs since I was a teenager. Weird! Maybe I'd give the implants one last go . . . I agreed to try again with another smaller pair.

Waiting for me on the dining-room table when I got home was a beautiful bouquet of flowers from Kieran: white lilies and baby pink roses. As soon as I saw them I felt this warm glow. And no, it wasn't the anaesthetic wearing off! Despite my ongoing boob drama, I could see that he was making such an effort and there were moments now when I felt so in love with him. He'd come through his therapy and I was proud of him. What a difference a few months had made!

Most of that week I spent curled up under my duvet. The only thing I lifted a toe out of bed for was *Celebrity Big Brother*. I'm an avid watcher of the show and this year I knew some of the characters in the house, which

So cute! Bunny and Princess's outfits for mine and Kieran's vow renewal.

Nothing like a makeover to hide the nerves.

A final cuddle with the kids before I said 'I do' again…

My handsome guys.

Love – I need to spell it out to
Kieran!

My re-worked diamond ring
was made in record time.

After what he'd put me through, Kieran didn't have a leg to stand on.

A fresh start together.

Junior entertains our wedding guests – a born performer!

All my dreams come true – duet with my music legend Alexander O'Neal.

Sister Sophie and my stepdad Paul.

The last photo before it was time for bed.

Harvey is my best man in the world.

Double trouble and best friends too.

(L–R) My stepdad, Mum, Kieran, Me, Mark (Kieran's mum's partner) and Kieran's mum Wendy – all looking amazing!

Let the fun begin!

So many guests helped us celebrate.

This time around it feels like we are a proper family.

Falling in love all over again.

Our summer in our new house.

It's amazing to be a happy family again.

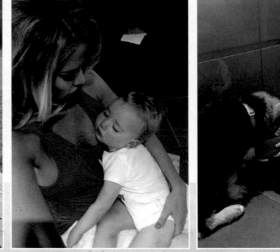

always makes watching it more fun. I'd met Perez years ago and I'd always liked him. I also knew Calum Best from way back and even vaguely remember snogging him in nightclub called Jet Black sometime in the nineties! Nadia I knew from my appearances on *Loose Women* and I'd always considered her a genuinely sound person.

I'd often been asked whether I would take part but for one reason or another it had never happened. The timing hadn't been right for me on this occasion either. Kieran and I were getting back on track and with my ongoing health problems it wasn't an experience I thought I'd enjoy. I had said I'd do the summer series, even though Kieran wasn't keen. One shared house, summer sunshine, me half-dressed among a bunch of charged up bikini chasers . . . what could possibly go wrong? But who was he to talk? I kept teasing him that now he'd shagged Jane and Chrissy I should be allowed two free passes of my own. I don't know why, but he didn't look that impressed . . .

Anyway, by the looks of things the house didn't need summer sunshine for passions to run high. The minute the show started, I breathed a huge sigh of relief that I hadn't gone in. OMFG! The housemates' honeymoon period lasted two days tops! By day three Perez and Katie Hopkins were rowing. Two days later, *Baywatch* star Jeremy Jackson had turned into a drunken sex pest and was evicted for trying to look at model Chloe Goodman's boob.

The following day, former *Coronation Street* actor Ken Morley was booted out for being a sexist, racist pig, and then all hell broke loose between Katie and Perez. Jesus! Compulsive viewing or what?

One night when it was all kicking off I said to Kieran, 'Thank God I'm not in that house.' Believe it or not, I don't like confrontation although if someone starts on me, I'll be sure to have the last word.

* * *

It was 11 January before I could even contemplate taking on any work again. I felt so depressed and found it difficult to have a proper conversation with anyone other than Kieran and the kids. Even my poor accountant Ally had to come to the house and meet with me dosed up on painkillers and propped up in bed with the duvet up to my neck. And it was halfway through our meeting that my phone rang . . .

'What are you doing, Kate?' It was my manager calling.

'What do you think I'm doing? I'm on bloody bed rest again!' I replied, more than a little pissed off.

'Are you still that bad?' he asked, hesitantly.

'Yup!'

'Ah . . . you won't be able to do the job that's come in then,' he went on. Of course, it was *Celebrity Big Brother*. Since Ken's departure they needed another contestant and they wanted someone super-quick to fill his place. In precisely two days' time! Fuck!

'I can't,' I said, highly disappointed. 'I'm due back in Belgium tomorrow for another check-up. I've got no clothes packed, no hair done, no nails done. I feel like someone's crapped on my head and I'm the pastiest shade of white . . .'

As soon as I clicked off I regretted that decision. Ally must have seen the expression on my face because he said, 'You know, Kate . . . you could just do it.' That's a dangerous thing to say to me at the best of times! I thought about it for . . . ooh . . . around five seconds, and rang my manager back, telling him I'd changed my mind. But I stressed that it was on proviso I got the all-clear from my surgeon and the *Big Brother* production team had to be made fully aware of my situation.

The thought of doing *CBB* was actually pretty daunting but the curious side of me was itching to go in there. 'How hard can it be?' I kept asking Kieran. If I was at home I'd be recuperating anyway so I may as well do it in the Big Brother house and get paid for it! I was talking myself into it, so deep down I knew I wanted to go in. Kieran agreed he'd be fine looking after the kids and getting on with plans for the ceremony to renew our vows, which we'd rebooked for 21 February.

Louisa accompanied me to Brussels the next day, where I was brought down to earth with a bump. The prospect of me being in the house for three weeks did not please my surgeon one little bit. I explained to him that I would be allowed medical help once inside the house, but he said my scar hadn't healed enough for me even to consider it. He unstitched and cleaned the wound one more time and by the afternoon I was homeward bound.

At the airport I rang my manager. I'd been mulling over the whole proposal in the taxi and I'd come to the conclusion that it wasn't the most sensible decision. 'There's absolutely no way I can do this,' I told him apologetically. 'I can't be on my way back from Belgium, then have everything ready, then have all my pre-show photographs done et cetera, all before tomorrow night. And I'm in pain! I'd have to be super-human to cope with it all, and that I am not.'

Then, just at the moment we were about to board the plane, Louisa tapped me on the shoulder. 'Kate, you could always ask whether they'd postpone your entry from Tuesday until Friday night . . .'

Hmmm . . . Not a bad idea. If they really wanted me, they'd wait. Several phone calls later and we had a deal on our hands. Shit! What had I let myself in for?

CHAPTER 19

22 DAYS IN THE BIG BROTHER HOUSE

If anyone ever asks if I'm a superstitious person I say 'no', but sometimes coincidences happen in life that can't be explained away. Take the number twenty-two, for example. My birthday is on the twenty-second, Kieran's birthday is too. When I appeared on *Deal or No Deal* in 2012 I picked box number twenty-two and came away with £16,000 for charity. And this year, my lucky number hit the jackpot one more time. In January I lived in the Big Brother house for twenty-two days. I know . . . freaky!

Before I entered the house I would never have dreamed that I'd last that long, let alone win. I'd never won anything in my life! In fact if you'd told me that I'd last more than a few days, I would have said 'pull the other one'. Only one thing was certain – the week leading up to going in was absolutely crazy!

For starters the press speculation was insane. My mobile rang non-stop but I'd been sworn to secrecy so I was terrified of picking up in case I let something slip. Only a handful of close friends and family were in on it. Even my mum didn't know until two days before! Plus I had so much to sort out . . .

Perhaps it was a good thing that I had so little time. All the other housemates had had months to prepare, but I know what I'm like. I'd be overanalysing everything and making myself more and more anxious. Though I'd be lying if I said I wasn't shitting myself!

There I was, in pain and about to leave Kieran and the kids for three weeks. People asked me how I could even contemplate leaving him alone after what he'd done. But the bottom line is, if I hadn't trusted Kieran there's no way I would have agreed to go. And anyway, I can't monitor him all of his life. That's not a relationship, that's a prison sentence! Still, we did have to get used to the idea because we'd spent every waking moment together since Kieran's intensive therapy had ended and now we were going to be separated.

Also at the back of my mind was my last big stint on a reality game show. In 2009 I'd returned to the jungle to take part in *I'm a Celebrity* . . . but far from being fun, it turned out to be a complete disaster . . .

I'd first appeared on *I'm a Celebrity* . . . in 2004. Before then, I think people saw me as a trashy, blonde bimbo who got pissed and fell out of nightclubs, but after the show they changed their opinion. Not only did they see that I was a woman capable of falling deeply in love, as Pete and I did in the jungle, but I wasn't afraid to throw myself into the Bushtucker trials either.

At heart I'm a team player even though it meant I had to do some vile things. More than ten years later, I've never forgotten the trauma of having to eat a kangaroo's arsehole! But my task was to win luxuries for the team, so I took a deep breath and got on with it.

Six years later I was in a completely different place. Pete and I had just split and the tabloids had turned against me. I was branded 'desperate' for wanting to go back to the place where we'd met and there was this tired line they kept trotting out about me secretly wanting to rekindle the relationship. It was nonsense. By then I was in love with Alex Reid, although we'd kept our feelings for each other secret from the press.

Even so, it was emotionally very tough. I missed my kids like crazy and, at times, the memories of what Pete and I had had together did flood back, so I suppose the experience brought me closure. But what made things worse was that the public wanted to punish me. It was like they'd swallowed all those stories about me being a complete bitch.

They voted me into every Bushtucker trial going. And by day nine I'd had enough. I didn't care about the money or winning, I just wanted to see my family and I quit the show.

When I was offered *Big Brother* I did question whether I'd be able to handle it given the events of the past year.

The idea of being cooped up with people I don't know sends me into a panic at the best of times. Perhaps the public would not believe I'm like that but I can be shy and insecure without someone I know around to hold my hand. I'm a big baby really! Plus I had my medical problems to consider too.

I also remembered when Alex Reid took part in *Celebrity Big Brother* in 2010. He had entered the house in the month before we were married to boos and hisses. He came out victorious to whoops and cheers. I'm smart enough to know it's panto but to face a baying crowd like that you do have to feel mentally prepared. I knew I could back out if the pressure got too much but, I promise, that's not what I would have wanted. I'm a fighter, not a quitter!

* * *

On the day I arrived back from Belgium it was all hands on deck. My friend Lara, who runs an online boutique, was roped in to sort out enough tracksuits, evening wear and nightwear to fill the three suitcases I'd been allocated. Next up was an eyebrow and eyelash tint so I didn't look a complete mess when the photographer arrived to do my pre-entry pictures.

Then on Thursday I left Lara at home packing while Kieran and I flew back to Belgium for one final check-up.

As all the tabloids were now reporting that I was going in, I couldn't resist posting a picture of me and

Kieran as we boarded the flight, just to fool everyone. It worked . . . according to the next day's headlines I'd snubbed *Big Brother* and was jetting off on holiday with my man. If only! In truth, we flew to Brussels then two hours later I was stretched out on a trolley having the dressing removed from my boob and forty-five minutes after that we were en route home. It really was a flying visit!

Before I'd left for the clinic I'd made the decision that if my boob hadn't healed, I did want both implants taken out. There was no point in me entering the house in agony and not being able to join in the fun. Fortunately I didn't have that decision to wrestle with. Although my surgeon still wasn't happy about me doing the show, he reported that I had healed a little and that was a good sign, so we agreed to carry on as planned.

Kieran and I didn't even have chance to think about our wedding anniversary on 16 January, which was the Friday I eventually entered the house. Instead, we stayed in London the night before. I spoke to the kids, I had a few extensions put in my hair, had my nails done, and tossed and turned all night thinking about my adventure.

I won't lie. In just twelve hours I'd gone from being excited to absolutely bricking myself. It suddenly hit me that there were people in the house who would probably want to be vile to me. Let's face it, the *Sun* had already billed my entrance as the ultimate bitch-off between me and Katie Hopkins even though they should have known from my time in the jungle that I'm not like that at all.

Thankfully, Kieran, my brother Danny and my sister Sophie all accompanied me from the hotel to Elstree Studios. It turned out to be an emotional journey. 'Shit! I'm not going to see you, Kieran. I'm not going to see the kids!' I kept saying. How mad was that? Only four days ago I'd been on bed rest . . .

My sister, who's halfway through a history degree, was also off to study in Belgium the next morning and I knew she wouldn't be there when I came out either. 'Pull yourself together, Kate,' I kept telling myself but, God, I was a blubbering wreck. Rules are rules and I'd been told that Kieran could only be with me until 3 p.m. and I'd have to surrender my mobile phone too. I don't know how, but somehow we wangled it that he stayed with me almost up until the last minute. I think the crew felt sorry for me. And I think they were astonished by how upset I was. To be fair, so was I. I hadn't expected to feel like that at all! Various people kept saying to me, 'Have a glass of wine, Kate, to steady your nerves,' but I refused. Not only was I on antibiotics but I had so much adrenalin running through me that I really didn't need one!

When I spoke to my mum by phone just minutes before I was due live on stage she could barely make out what I was saying through my tears. All these emotions were churning around inside me – fear, dread, sadness – and I'd almost forgotten that feeling of knowing that everything I did from now on was going to be watched and judged – not that I'd ever play to the camera just to win votes!

By the time I was being interviewed by Emma Willis I couldn't stop shaking. It didn't help that I was standing in sub-zero temperatures dressed as a princess in a paper-thin gold ball gown. All these months later and I've still not watched that moment, but Kieran assures me there was no embarrassing celebrity fripple action, probably because my boobs were strapped down with surgical dressings! All I could see were camera bulbs flashing. And around me the sound of the crowd was deafening, which was amazing but I was almost hyperventilating. What the fuck am I doing? I wondered.

Beforehand, everybody wanted to know whether I had a 'game plan', but I honestly didn't. I just wanted to be myself. Most people have such preconceived ideas about me that I think they're surprised when they realise how down to earth I am. One thing I had decided was that I wasn't going to judge other people either because I've had that done to me enough times and know how unfair it is. I think one of the best lessons I've learned in life is not to have an opinion unless you truly know something. For me, that was especially the case with people like Katie Hopkins and Alicia Douvall. I had history with Alicia.

Years ago, before Harvey was born, Alicia had claimed that she, Dwight Yorke and I had had a threesome. The papers were full of it and I was gutted because it was complete bullshit. Alicia and I had never even met, but apparently she'd been Dwight's girlfriend, although I never did know the full story. Likewise, Katie Hopkins had said some pretty hurtful things about me but we'd also never met. I wanted to enter the house with an open mind. Weird, I know, but more than anything, I wanted to like them both.

* * *

All too quickly, Emma placed a gold wand in my hand and ushered me up the stairs. Within seconds I could hear the house doors close behind me. 'Fuck. Shit. Fuck,' I kept repeating because when I'm nervous I've got a mouth like a sewer. I can't help it! I thought, You don't have to do this, Kate . . . but I am doing it! I know I was still swearing when I reached the bottom of the stairs because then I could feel all my fellow contestants' eyes on me: Alexander O' Neal; Alicia Douvall; Calum Best; Cami Li; Chloe Goodman; Katie Hopkins; Kavana; Keith Chegwin; Michelle Visage; Nadia Sawalha; Patsy Kensit and Perez Hilton were standing in the living room, frozen to the spot.

For a moment I completely forgot that I was live on TV. That was until Big Brother spoke directly to the house. Up until that point housemates had been enjoying a ball and, unbeknown to them, it was in my honour. Now, this booming voice said I must use the wand to banish three people to a gilded cage for the rest of the evening. I'd been warned seconds before I got on stage that that would be my first task, but now I was really panicking . . . I didn't know half of them! Here we go again, I thought, I'm being made out to be the villain!

I reminded myself that it was only a game and I needed to throw myself into it. But without the chance to catch my breath, I launched into a speech about how I wanted to spend time getting to know everyone and I asked people not to judge me . . . blah, blah, blah. Hang on. Where the hell did that come from? I'd been struck by a bout of verbal diarrhoea!

Thankfully, Big Brother cut me off mid-flow, urging me to hurry up with my decision. Arrrghhh! Who to choose? Under pressure, I banished Perez because I thought the house needed a break from all the arguments. I put American model Cami Li in the cage too, even though we'd never met. From what I'd seen she and Perez had been at each other's throats and I reckoned they needed to sort out their differences. Lastly, I banished Nadia. She's a strong mother figure and I knew she'd be tough enough to cope.

After that entrance I no idea whether the housemates were going to love me or loathe me and for the next few days I did feel like an outsider. Everybody was very welcoming, but it was tough going in late because friendships had already been made and broken. On the first night there wasn't even a bed for me. All the single beds had been taken and there were a couple of spaces in the doubles. There was no way I was going to share a bed with a straight man so Calum's bed was off limits.

I ended up snuggling in with Cami Li, which was fine by me. Though I did go to bed thinking it all felt remarkably like a first day at school when you suss out your classmates and wonder who your friends are going to be.

From the off I also knew I was going to have to ask the girls if they minded helping me with simple stuff like washing my hair because I couldn't get my dressings wet. Although I expected people to be kind it automatically made me feel more vulnerable.

My surgeon had also insisted that I couldn't do anything that required me to lift my arms above my shoulders.

So, written into my contract was a request to have my hair blow-dried and styled by a hairdresser every few days. Actually, that was my only rider. But when I saw what some of the others had negotiated I kicked myself for not bargaining harder. Not mentioning any names, but I could have had full-body spray tans – the lot!

If people thought I was going in all guns blazing they definitely pinned their hopes on the wrong person. I had no intention of causing trouble just for the sake of it. One, I don't argue at home so why would I want to argue in the Big Brother house? And two, these days I'm more like a champagne cork. I bubble, bubble, bubble. Then . . . I pop.

My mum, Kieran, everyone had warned me: 'For God's sake, don't bang on about Jane and Chrissy.' But what could I do? It was one of the first things the housemates asked about, so I wasn't going to be rude and not reply. I probably shouldn't have been surprised but Kieran told me that was one of the first sequences broadcast. Anyway, my description of them both as 'mingers' was spot on.

Apparently he had his mates round to watch and got straight on the phone to my mum afterwards to complain, 'Is she ever going to let me live this down?' Well, I have one answer to that. 'Hubby – if you can't do the time, don't do the crime!'

Back in the house, Alexander O' Neal said my entrance had calmed the atmosphere down. Thank God for that! Out of all the housemates, I was most excited about spending time with him. He's one of my musical idols. I remember dancing to all his hits: 'Fake', 'Criticise', 'Saturday Love'. I think the secret's out that I'm no Whitney Houston but I was desperate to chirp out a tune with him. I even invited him to sing at our vows ceremony. Well, if you don't ask, you don't get and it turned out to be a great ice-breaker. He's a lovely man.

I felt so disappointed that all hopes of us doing a duet live in the house were dashed when, on my second day, he stormed out of the house following a clash with Perez. Big Brother's announcement that he'd left voluntarily was a bolt from the blue for me. Okay, I'd watched them wind each other up from the comfort of my own sofa but I hadn't realised how bad it was until I actually became a housemate. That day Alexander accused Perez of having a 'silly-ass faggot' look on his face, but I knew that Alexander wasn't homophobic. I also knew Perez wasn't the maniac he was making himself out to be. Whatever viewers saw at home, in my opinion Perez was bullied and I think the only way he could handle it was to throw it back in people's faces. Trust me, that place can do really strange things to a person . . .

As a late entrant I didn't want to jump to conclusions about anyone which I'm sure riled the others, especially Katie Hopkins who was on a mission to isolate Perez. But I stuck to my guns. From the minute I got in there I sensed Katie was angling to draw me into her 'camp', which rivalled Nadia's, Patsy's and Perez's 'camp'. Maybe people watching thought I'd be more easily swayed, but Katie shouldn't have underestimated me. I'm quite capable of making up my own mind, thank you very much!

I think I showed that with Alicia Douvall. I could have ignored Alicia or laid into her about lying over the threesome but instead I opted to bury the hatchet. After all, Dwight's a pin dot of insignificance in my life. It's funny though because I always used to tell my mum that I was sure he was two-timing me. I'd find scrunchies in his shower and I noticed that my shampoo had always been used. Until *Celebrity Big Brother* I had no idea that other person was Alicia. 'No way!' I exclaimed when she told me she'd been living with him and he would bundle her out of the flat every time I was due over. When I fell pregnant with Harvey they split but she blamed me for stealing Dwight from her, hence the story. The truth was I didn't know anything about her until the allegation appeared!

However, I'm glad Alicia and I got the chance to air our differences because I found her very sweet – not what I would have predicted at all. I make no apologies to viewers who would rather have seen a love-rival slanging match. That was never on the cards. It shows that when you make the effort to befriend someone, it's amazing what can happen.

* * *

Unlike being in the jungle where I felt like I was on the go a lot of the time, the *CBB* house was brain-dead boring! There was nothing to read, fuck-all to do, yet nowhere to hide. In truth, there was no stimulus whatsoever other than a few tasks and the company of the housemates. And there's only so much talking you can do! Still, there were some surprises. The house was much bigger than I'd expected but it was also very quiet, which you don't get a sense of at home. There were even times when I was lying on my bed and I could hear the camera operators behind the mirrors coughing. And it was so obvious where all the cameras were located – you could see some of them through the glass – though I'm so used to being filmed I hardly registered that they were on.

The diary room was another mystery to me. For the same reason that I'd not demanded extras in my contract,

I didn't want to be a pain in the arse and moan to Big Brother all the time. But I noticed other housemates practically camped out in there. What they had to talk about I have no idea. I can only assume that they were using it as an opportunity for more positive airtime. I thought, No way. Viewers can take me as I am! Call me lazy, but I couldn't even be bothered climbing the stairs to get there!

But I'd always planned to stick it out as long as I could even though, I swear, from the minute I got in there, I couldn't wait to be evicted. Every waking moment I thought about the kids and Kieran and how the boredom was killing me. I'd brought with me pictures drawn by Harvey, Princess and Junior, a heart-charm bracelet brought from India by my mum after she did some charity work out there, and a necklace from my friend Lara. I'd even made Kieran spray his aftershave on my clothes to remind me of his smell. I talked non-stop about him and the kids. I even kept apologising to Calum for boring the arse off him, though I understand very little of that was broadcast. Instead, the editors showed all my conversations about my ex-sex: the bits about Alex liking weird and wonderful objects up his bum and how Leo was so well hung he gave me nothing but cystitis the whole time I was seeing him. What can I say? I always tell people, 'I'm a very upfront person.' Ask me an honest question and I'll give an honest answer!

I did feel sorry for Kieran. He said afterwards that

for the first few days of me being in the house it felt as though there had been a death. He thought about me all the time. The kids asked about me all the time. To focus on the days ahead, he'd even blown up eight photos of us and had taped them to the walls. They were absolutely massive!

I'd got a nanny in to help out, but in between looking after the kids and taking care of the animals he spent the rest of his time in therapy with Gaylin. So few of my conversations about him were broadcast that he assumed I'd fallen out of love with him. He got it into his head that I was going to finish with him the moment I left the house. After everything we'd salvaged from our relationship he should have known me better than that!

*   *   *

Within four days of being in the *CBB* house the novelty had definitely worn thin and time began to drag seriously. It felt like the days were an endless cycle of waking, eating, sleeping, with some chatting in between. I was probably the first person to go to bed because I was knackered and I was counting down the sleeps until I got out. Sad but true, when I was given a secret mission by Big Brother it was the highlight of my day, even though it was a horrible mission. The next evening I had to save the housemate I found the most entertaining from the nominees up for eviction that Friday, and elect the housemate I found least entertaining to take their place.

'Hi, Mum! Hi, kids! Hi, Kieran!' I said nervously as I sat in the diary room to deliver my names. Thinking on my feet, I saved Katie Hopkins because it was still early days and I admit that I found her fun and witty at first. I even thought she was a bit like me, only I'm a nicer version!

However, the second nomination was a nightmare. Under pressure, I picked Calum. It wasn't because I thought he was boring. I was trying to be clever by nominating someone I thought would be safe from the public vote. Let's face it, he was the only eye candy in that house.

Sure, that got me the reputation of being someone who sits on the fence and doesn't like to upset anyone but I couldn't give a shit! I'd gone in there to make friends, which I know people found odd, but why not? With two friends who fucked my husband, all I wanted was to meet loyal people. What's wrong with that? And who says you can't meet people on a reality show anyway? I met my first husband on one. Two of my children wouldn't have been born without *I'm a Celebrity* . . . !

Next up was the housemates' debate, and I swear on my life that the questions were directed straight at me! The first topic under discussion was whether celebrities set a bad example by having plastic surgery. Kate, I thought, put forward your view and be honest. So I talked about how I wanted the legal age limit for cosmetic surgery to be raised, but I did feel I was being judged while I spoke, especially by Katie Hopkins. The next question was, 'Should people stay neutral?' Oh, here we go again, I thought. Clearly alongside Keith everybody thought I was Switzerland or something!

The next two days were probably the hardest for me. I'd tried not to think about the possibility of Kieran being unfaithful while I was in the house. We'd come so far. But Alicia, Perez, Nadia and I were talking in the kitchen on day when paranoia got the better of me.

Alicia reckoned Kieran didn't have a problem even though I'd explained all about his sex addiction diagnosis and how it was really about him being hooked on adrenalin. She'd pointed out that he could get the same buzz from a ride at Thorpe Park. Maybe she had a point. I couldn't help it but the whole conversation wormed its way into my mind. When they kept going on about how I couldn't be sure what Kieran was doing in my absence, all the insecurity and doubt rose up inside me again.

Later when Big Brother called me to the diary room I burst into tears which is so unlike me. What's wrong with me? I thought. I know Kieran loves me. I know he's not fucking around. But it's so easy to feel like that in there because everybody's emotions are so heightened. Thankfully, by the next morning the feeling had passed but it was destroying me not being with him!

To make matters worse, Katie Hopkins decided to have a pop over Harvey's transport to school, which I regretted even mentioning to her. As I've said before, I believe that regardless of my status, Harvey has every right to access state-funded transport. I'd watched as Katie stirred the pot with other contestants, so I realised what her game was. Nonetheless, I had to bite my lip. If there's one thing I won't tolerate it's comments made about my kids. One more jibe like that, I thought, and you and I will go head to head. Funny, though, because for the rest of the time she was mostly fine with me. The only thing was, she kept chuntering on about wanting to see more of 'The Pricey'. Underneath I thought, What the fuck are you on about? I'm the same person!

One evening she even washed my hair for me in the shower and, let me say, she was gagging to get in there with me so that she could get some extra air time. My impression was that she was desperate to show me her softer side. But from the moment we got out of the house, that opinion changed. Katie was such a bad loser and so vicious about me afterwards that I'm now convinced she helped me purely as a tactic. She was demonstrating to the voting public, 'I'm not a bitch! Look, I can even be nice to Katie Price!' Well, if people were undecided about her before, I think they can't be in any doubt now . . . she is a complete bitch.

Can you believe, she even sat with me in the bedroom one night and asked me which of my parents I'd like to die first? I didn't have an answer because I'd never thought about it! What kind of person would even think to ask that unless they were dark and twisted and fuelled by hatred? It summed her up completely.

Most of the time I found myself hanging out with Keith because he was such good company and a genuinely nice man. He was a real team player and we had loads to bond over too because his wife keeps horses and he knew about dressage. When I came out, I joked that I followed Keith around like a lost sheep, but it was true! The arguments between Katie and Perez and Calum and Perez were so extreme they became laughable towards the end. As they raged around me I automatically made a beeline for Keith and we'd sit in a corner and natter together for ages. Or if I was ever bored, which was most of the time, I'd say, 'Where's Keith? What's he up to?' Then I'd go off to find him.

Either that or I'd get my fake tan out. The bathroom was chock-full of all sorts of cosmetics and goodies so it filled some time to tan myself and everyone else. I thought, I may as well play to my strengths! I think the more stressed out I got, the more fake tan I applied. My brother said I looked like a mahogany leather sofa on some days. Oops!

As the days wore on I was amazed that I was still there. I was so boring and I knew it! I had the British public to thank for my survival – oh, and my family who I'm sure were hogging the voting lines on the few occasions I was up for eviction. I kept daydreaming about how Kieran was managing, having to put the finishing touches to our vows ceremony on his own. Then I'd think about the kids. I hoped that Kieran was letting them watch some of me on TV, just to remind them that I was still alive, but obviously not any of the rude bits!

Big Brother kept asking me how my boob was and whether I was in pain. I was, but I didn't see any point in moaning about it. It didn't want to keep requesting medical attention but I was holding it every time I walked, which must have looked bloody odd on-screen. When Katie Hopkins said it smelled like a dead person, I thought, You can talk! Her breath stank! At first I thought she had food stuck in her teeth but when I got closer I realised it was actually a rotting crown. Eeewww!

And on my second to last day in the house, she really showed her true colours. By then I was in agony and was granted special dispensation to leave and see the doctor. I don't know why it was made such a big deal of because loads of the housemates had been going in and out for toothaches or whatever, but that hadn't been shown. And it's not like I advertised it either. I didn't want people to say I was drawing attention to myself or playing for sympathy because I wasn't. I was genuinely in pain!

'I'm worried that the doctor won't let me come back in,' I said to Keith in the bedroom, knowing by now that my scar had not healed and I may need immediate surgery.

'Why would you come back? You haven't been here since the start so you don't need to stay until the end,' Katie interrupted us.

OMG! You bitch! I thought. I even said later that if by

a complete miracle I did win, I'd never hear the end of me being boring; me not being in the house from the start . . . snore! Not that I thought I could win. I hadn't been firing on all cylinders. I was realistic enough to know that the public hadn't had their money's worth but at least I was honest about it!

In truth, I was convinced I would leave on the second to last day when Eamonn Holmes came in to do a mock-up news programme and grilled us on our time in the house. Maybe people thought I was the most animated during that discussion – I even told Katie Hopkins to fuck off! – but my mind was somewhere else. I kept imagining Kieran outside, dressed up and waiting for me in the crowd. Not seeing him was driving me mad. I was like a prisoner marking down each day in chalk on my cell wall. Never in a million years did I think I'd make it to the final . . .

That day the doctor said I did need urgent treatment. The wound was so infected I was in danger of getting septicaemia 'I've lasted this far,' I said. 'One more day's not going to make a difference!' I think he realised I wasn't taking no for an answer and allowed me to go back in. I fully expected to go that evening anyway. But no . . . Kavana was evicted on Day Twenty-nine. Holy shit! How? I couldn't understand it.

The next day when I saw the psychologist for a pre-exit debrief he told me, 'You've come across fine, Katie. We'd thought you'd be the biggest diva of them all, but you've been brilliant!'

'Really?' I replied disbelievingly. Phew! I thought, because when you're in the thick of it you've no idea. That made me feel so much better. Nevertheless, I was crossing toes, fingers, everything. I wanted to be out of there so badly it hurt! Those last few hours of getting ready and sitting around felt like torture . . .

First went Michelle . . . then Keith . . . I was gutted about that because I thought he deserved to win. Every time we linked up live to the outside world we could hear the crowd and the atmosphere was so charged. What's going on? I thought. It *must* be me next. Then Calum's name was called. Now I was absolutely convinced that leaving me and Katie till last was one big set up. For me, it was a forgone conclusion that she'd come out victorious. I told her as much as we anxiously waited on the sofa. Get on with it! I thought, as Emma strung out the final announcement. And the winner of *Celebrity Big Brother* 2015 is . . . drum roll . . . Katie Price!

'What the fuck?' I was gobsmacked. 'How? What the fuck's going on?'

I didn't know whether to laugh or cry, so I just cried! Katie didn't even say goodbye. She turned and ran up the stairs. If that had been me, I would have said 'Well done!' at least. It just showed what a bad loser she was.

As I made my way up the stairs all I could hear were chants of 'Price-y, Price-y!' It was bonkers! Kieran, my mum, brother and friends were all waiting on my left-hand side when I finally walked through the doors. My heart leaped when I saw them. All I remember is mouthing to Kieran 'Why have I won?' which, if I recall, is all I kept saying to Emma in my post-win interview. I didn't understand! My boob was killing me and I had to hold it all the way down the stairs but I didn't care. Then I remembered the picture on the living-room wall of the Big Brother house. It was of a princess with dark hair and green eyes, next to the words, 'Who is the fairest of them all?' Well, I'd gone in a princess with dark hair and green eyes and I'd come out a winner. Bloody hell! Fairytale endings really do come when you least expect them!

CHAPTER 20

I DO . . . AGAIN!

As soon as I got out of the house I focused on the ceremony to renew our vows. I'd thought I was cutting it fine with only two months to organise our wedding blessing back in 2013, but third celebration around I surprised myself. A ceremony for more than 200 guests to arrange in two weeks? Easy! That's the thing about being involved in a Pricey do — you have to work well under pressure!

This time around I hadn't wanted wedding planners or even my management company to help. I'd wanted to do it by myself although because of *Celebrity Big Brother*, Kieran had had to step in. I knew there wasn't time to pull off a themed do like my Willy Wonka wedding but I didn't want one either. I wanted close to home, simple and stylish, and Kieran was totally up for that too. We'd done all the big spectacle stuff and this was 100 per cent about the re-commitment we were making to one another . . . or should I say the re-commitment Kieran was making to me? Though I didn't scale down my outfit . . . or my diamond ring.

I know people will be reading this and thinking I've lost the plot. How many weddings can one couple want? But if Kieran and I are going to grow old together, it was important to me that we should start afresh. What's more, all the official photographs of my Bahamas wedding and my wedding blessing have Jane in them and there's no way I want them framed and on our walls. All memories of her are slowly being erased from our lives.

'Oh, god, Kate, it's not going to be a weepy one, is it?' my mum kept asking, when I first told her and Paul that I wanted to renew my vows. They even said, 'Really? Do you have to?' But me being me, I need to do things my way. I put my foot down. 'I'm starting over again and so I'm doing it again.'

They even tried to make me promise not to play any Whitney Houston! Apparently her ballads are too depressing but I happen to think 'The Greatest Love' is one of the best love songs of all time and I'd already thought I might like to walk down the aisle to it.

One thing I did accept was that Paul and my brother didn't want to make any speeches. Over the years they've had a fair few to do between them and Dan says he's exhausted all his good material. As we weren't planning on a sit-down meal, I was fine with that, although Dan's speeches did always crack me up.

Initially we'd thought about hiring a hotel, but nothing seemed to fit. I also considered waiting for the summer and having a marquee in the garden but we didn't want to delay it for that long. Anyhow, with our house still looking like a building site we wouldn't have been able to accommodate any guests. With only weeks to go, a friend recommended Long Furlong Barn, a Grade II-listed venue right in the heart of the South Downs, which sounded promising . . .

When we went to look around it was perfect: close to home; we could have the hog roast we wanted; it had an outbuilding for me to get ready in, and lots of car-parking space. And because it was a self-contained venue I didn't have to worry about fighting my way through the paps as I've had to do at all my other weddings. When I married Alex Reid, I thought they were going to tip over the eighties-style A-Team van I arrived in just to get their shots. It was absolutely terrifying!

The barn was perfect too. Guests would be greeted in the Cart Shed where our ceremony would take place and where food would be served later. Then they would be ushered through to the main barn where the bar and entertainment would be set up. We didn't want the barn dressed formally but we did want to add some glitz and glamour to proceedings and I just had time to choose the cream-covered chairs and drapes before I entered the Big Brother house . . .

Luckily I'd also thought about my ring too. Well, it's hardly something I'd forget and I'd asked my favourite jeweller Bill Foreman to sketch out a design for me. Kieran had a new ring made too but I wanted some of the diamonds from my last wedding ring set into the new one. I had a vision of a diamond-encrusted three-row band set with a large teardrop centre stone. Poor Bill! Over the years he's gotten used to making rings quickly for me but this time he pulled off an amazing feat. In between me flying back and forth to Belgium then preparing for *Celebrity Big Brother* he had two weeks to finish two rings. Normally the rings have to go through a six-step process of shaping and moulding and polishing. Bill never holds back on telling me a job like this should normally take ten weeks but, respect is due, he's never once let me down and nor did he on this occasion.

Meanwhile in the Big Brother house I'd been dreaming of the dress I would wear for the ceremony. Because it was an evening wedding I didn't want a big meringue number. Anyhow, it wasn't an actual wedding, it was a renewal of vows. I did want to stick to white though and I'd seen a dress online that I wanted it to be modelled on: a dramatic backless style with a short front and a long ruffled train . . . perfect! No sooner had I come out of the house than I warned my dress designer Adrian I wanted it to be beautiful and magical . . . and made in record time. But first things first. I couldn't even have a fitting because the day after I won I had to fly to Belgium to get my boobs sorted out!

This time I asked my surgeon to take the implants out completely. I was so fed up of feeling depressed and in pain and I didn't want my boobs to spoil my big day. 'I want my life back!' I told him, and we agreed that it was best to let the wound heal before I considered another boob job. People have asked me whether I even want another one now because I've had so many problems but the answer is, 'Of course!' There's no way I'm living with these small, saggy excuses for boobs. I will go under the knife again but I do want to make sure I'm fully recovered before I do.

Once back from Belgium the clock was ticking . . . fourteen days . . . ten days . . . We didn't even have time for formal invitations! Instead we had to send texts and emails. Because I'd won *CBB*, I also had loads of requests for photoshoots and interviews, only some of which I could fulfil because of my medical problems. As it turned out, Katie Hopkins did most of my press for me anyway! She went on talk show after talk show telling everyone I wasn't a deserving winner, that it was all a big con . . . Jesus! Why couldn't she lose graciously? To me, she came across as very bitter. But I had neither the time nor the inclination to get into a fight with her. As I said on my Twitter feed: *A fire requires oxygen to stay alight and be angry, take away its oxygen, it'll eventually quieten down and disappear.* I think she got the message.

With a few days to go until the ceremony Kieran talked me through everything he'd arranged. Usually you can't trust a man to choose anything but, bless him, he'd done a brilliant job. The white chair covers would be wrapped with taffeta ivory sashes and secured with round diamante buckles; storm lanterns would hang off the beams; white drapes would surround the barn. Near to where we renewed our vows there would be two floor-standing candelabra and large illuminated letters spelling out the word LOVE. In the entertainment room we had K&K in the same bulb lettering. Kieran had also a picked a single standing bouquet of pink roses, cream roses, white hydrangeas, lisianthus and freesias, interlaced with drop crystals, and a beautiful heart arrangement for the wedding room. See, he does know me better than anyone!

With the venue taking shape I wanted to concentrate on the vows. While I knew that most people would understand the reason why we were there, I felt it was important to recap on the past year's events just in case they'd missed any of the detail. Some people may have found that uncomfortable listening but, there you go, that's me all over.

I planned to have a projector screen at the foot of the barn showing photos of Kieran and me and the kids. And we each pre-recorded a speech that would play before I walked down the aisle. Kieran had wanted to say his words facing the guests but I said that would be too weird! I wasn't going to stand there talking people through my year of hell, but I did want everybody to know how I'd been betrayed by my husband and my so-called friends, how my heart had been broken and how Kieran and I had come through it.

If the speeches played before the ceremony then we need never say Jane's and Chrissy's names again . . .

However, it did mean that Kieran had to sit in front of everyone and take it like a man. But that wasn't such a bad thing, was it? If it hadn't been for him, we wouldn't have been there! I wrote and recorded my speech two days before but, typical Kieran, he left his to the last night. What are men like? Then my friend Melodie's sister quickly edited the words and pictures so we were ready to roll.

When it came to the bridesmaids I'd had my fill of inviting friends, especially as Jane had been my bridesmaid three times. No, I just wanted my family. Junior and Harvey would walk first, followed by Jett (he had a nasty bout of conjunctivitis and had to be carried by our nanny in the end). Princess couldn't lift Bunny so I'd suggested she push her in my vintage Silver Cross pram. When that turned out to be too wide for the aisle our florist mentioned she had a white version from when she was a baby and we decorated that in netting and roses and placed Bunny on top.

On the morning of the wedding I had enough time to apply my fake tan, but until the big day I hadn't even tried on my dress. Poor Adrian had come to meet me in London two nights before for a final fitting but we'd missed each other. I'd been appearing in Naomi Campbell's Fashion for Relief Show at Somerset House to raise money for Ebola victims. It ended up going on late and I needed to jump straight into a cab afterwards because my jeweller

Bill was waiting for me at home with our rings. He wanted final sign off but it was past 10 p.m. when I made it back to see him. Arrgggh . . . stress!

The rings were beautiful and the dress fitted perfectly too, even though I didn't have boobs any more! So what? Hand on heart, I didn't care. This ceremony was all about me and Kieran. I think most of our guests understood that, but one – I don't know who – did end up leaking a story to the *Mirror* afterwards, complaining about how low-budget the whole event was. Low-budget? There was a free bar all night, free food and free top-class entertainment. It was more than most people spend on their actual wedding! I thought, Fuck you, whoever you are! The whole point was that we didn't want a showy or overly expensive celebration. Clearly it was someone who was used to celebrity parties that are all style and no substance. How disappointing it must have been that ours was homely and full of love! And if they thought they were having a pop at me, they got that wrong too because it was Kieran who arranged the lot. Anyway, nothing would spoil our fun.

As the sun set on the South Downs and I was still having my hair and make-up done I could hear all our guests assembling in the barn. There was a packed crowd and we'd probably overdone the numbers because a few people did have to stand at the back. But I'd got word that the room looked so romantic, decked out in the white drapes and hanging lights.

Then, as planned, there was silence, the photo-montage began playing and my voice was heard loud and clear over the VT:

Hi, everyone,

Thank you for joining Kieran and me at our vows today. We have decided to do our speeches this way so after the ceremony we can party Pricey style . . . oh, and Hayler style (which won't be as fun as mine).

Some of you are probably thinking why are we doing our vows two years on, and some of you already know.

Here's the long story shortened. Yes, Kieran, this is probably when you'll want to do the walk of shame and wish the ground would swallow you up. But this is where you have to listen like a man and realise that this is not what a man should have done. You shattered my heart into so many pieces. I can't find a number to define this, so here we go . . .

When Kieran and I met, it was such a whirlwind. We both fell in love and after five weeks we were married and I was pregnant. Crazy, I know. But you only live once.

Everything seemed so perfect, and why shouldn't it have been? I really thought Kieran was the man I wanted to spend the rest of my life with. He seemed so perfect and made me feel complete. But I never expected what was around the corner.

To my disbelief, Kieran started texting my best friends three months after our wedding in England. Then, shortly after that, he started a ten-month sexual affair with my best friend. And to make matters worse, as a double blow he started seeing another best friend of mine. Both these women were friends of mine for almost 20 years.

So the whole time I was pregnant with Jett, until I was five months pregnant with Bunny, he was having an affair. I caught Kieran on the beach then, kissing my best friend, and interrupted their sex session. I stood and watched them for thirty seconds before I pulled her, and punched her, and knocked her tooth out, which I have never done in my whole life, as it's not my nature.

Of course, they denied it. At this point, when my life flashed in front of me, it was like I was about to die – my heart was shattered. My confidence instantly broke down.

I felt ugly and fat, even though I was pregnant. My self-esteem hit rock-bottom. Not only did I lose my husband, he was my love, my best friend, my soulmate.

I also lost two best friends. When we got back off holiday that was when Kieran admitted to another sexual affair after a lie detector test. And it was revealed it was with another best friend of mine.

Never underestimate the Pricey. I believe in karma. I know their life is hell at the moment and long may that last. Everyone who knows me, knows I'm a strong, ballsy woman, but hand on heart, this was the saddest and most heartbreaking moment of my life.

My marriage was in tatters, my life too, and I didn't know if I had the strength to face the future. If it wasn't for me being pregnant with Bunny, I don't know if Kieran and I would have made it. On the plus side, at least he will still want me when I'm fifty and haggard . . .

There's more I could say, but I've said enough. I'm sure you understand the situation I was in.

Through nine months of intense therapy that we have gone through together and that Kieran will continue, he has turned from a boy to a man, a family man. The family man we both needed. The true gentleman he had in him.

But what I will say is this. Our relationship has always been the same: loving and full on, which is why I will never understand why he did what he did . . .

Well, actually I do know what it is . . . it's addiction. He's not the groomed, dirty stripper I met, he's now a hairy farmer, and the centre of my universe and my children's.

The reason for renewing our vows today, is so that we can recommit to each other and he can stick to the vows he says today and not break them like before.

And now I pass you over to . . . Mr Kieran Hayler.

Believe me, that speech must have felt like a lifetime to Kieran but he looked surprisingly composed when I finally entered the barn and he took my hand to lead me down the aisle. In the end, I had Sam Smith's version of the Whitney Houston song 'How Will I Know?' playing in the background. That was my idea too. Well, it seemed very apt!

I was overcome with unexpected emotion but I fought back the tears because I could see my photographer Andrew snapping away and he was poised for my dramatic entrance shot. As I walked, I did have time to take note of how gorgeous Kieran looked in his cream linen suit. So did my kids, who all had matching outfits. They were all so brilliant and had patiently waited for me! Was I late? Ooh . . . only forty-five minutes, I'd say, which is nothing when it's third time round!

Then humanist celebrant Croianna Bradshaw took us through our vows. After two powerful speeches, it was time to lighten the mood. As we repeated her words Kieran even promised to sit by me as I had my hair, nails and eyelashes done. And he promised to care for our growing family, animal and human.

When it came to repeating my vows I cheekily promised to be faithful to Kieran, adding, 'Like I always have been!' at the end.

With the formal part of the ceremony over, we wanted to kick off our shoes and have fun. I didn't need asking twice, even though Kieran had bought me the most gorgeous gold-studded Louboutin stilettos to wear. I managed our first dance in them but the fur-lined Uggs put in an appearance not long after that. There's nothing I like more than to feel comfortable, especially at my own party!

After a few glasses of bubbly I had enough Dutch courage to get up on stage and try my hand at a duet with the star performer of the evening, Alexander O'Neal, who, since his exit from the house, had agreed to sing for us. Under a canopy of white fairy lights and next to tables adorned with more flowers, glitter globes and diamante tea lights, we belted out the Cherrelle hit 'Saturday Love'. As if I hadn't had enough to prepare, I'd learned all the words. Singing with Alexander had been one of my all-time ambitions so I wasn't going to waste the chance, even if some of my high-notes were a bit off!

My friend Sam Bailey, who I met while recording *All Star Family Fortunes* in 2014, kindly agreed to do a few numbers too even though I hadn't formally booked her. It was just one of those great impromptu moments when she took to the stage to sing several songs including Oleta Adams's 'Get Here'.

Even Junior, who I swear is going to end up on *X Factor* one day, got up to sing Beyoncé's 'Listen' with my friend Andrew Derbyshire, who starred in *Britain's Got Talent*. Junior also took to the stage with Kavana later on to sing 'End of the Road' by Boyz II Men. He truly blew me away. He's so talented!

By now the food had been served and it looked delicious: a whole pig that had been roasting away outside while our service was underway. It must have been a monster to carve, but it was served with coleslaw, a puy lentil salad, and an assortment of bread, potatoes and dips. Simple, wholesome food, just how we like it. And, no, we didn't use one of our own pigs!

At around 10 p.m. covers band Ultra 90s took to the stage. Kieran and I had booked them previously for our wedding in Rookery Manor and they were brilliant the first time around. Our guests hit the dance floor and even I threw a few shapes. I think the noise was a bit much for Harvey, though, as he ended up whacking Princess on the dance floor, but by then I think all the kids were tired and overexcited. It had been a very long day!

We jumped into a waiting taxi and made it home by around 1 a.m., shattered but very, very happy. In the car I told Kieran that this felt like our proper fresh start. We could now put the past behind us and move on with our lives. He agreed. That night we felt stronger than ever, like we'd come through a force-ten gale but were still standing. As soon as we got home we fell into bed exhausted. With my boob still healing we couldn't even give each other a proper cuddle once we'd put the lights out, but it wasn't a problem. We both knew there was plenty of time. For that moment, it was enough to know we would have years ahead of us as Mr and Mrs Hayler. What's the saying? Third time lucky. I certainly felt like the luckiest woman in the world that evening. I had Kieran back and we were falling in love with each other all over again. It just goes to show, the dreams that you dare to dream really do come true.

CHAPTER 21

WE'RE ALL GOOD

Oh my God! If someone had told me two years ago that I'd still be here, I'd still be married to Kieran and that I'd be loving life again, I would have laughed in their face – seriously.

Don't get me wrong, it's not been easy. It's taken all our strength to overcome the past. But it's been totally worth it.

Anyone who follows my posts on Instagram will know that I'm a big fan of words of wisdom – you know, those little sayings that help you focus on the future when life goes wrong, or if you're having a difficult time. The one that I really believe in is: 'One small positive thought can change your whole day.'

Thinking positively is something I tried to do a lot in the weeks and months after mine and Kieran's vow renewal. I think we both did. It sounds mad, but I knew in my heart that Kieran was a good guy and, each day, I spent a moment imagining what a happy future with him and the kids would be like. Likewise, he says that gradually his therapy has helped him discover the real man he was all along. Talk about growing pains. Before all this stress began, I'd only ever imagined going through pains with my kids!

Looking at it now, the only way that I can describe how we both feel is like we were trapped in this dark hole for two years and slowly chinks of light started to shine in. Then, at last, we were able to climb out. They say what doesn't kill you makes you stronger, right? Trust me, I'm living proof!

The funny thing is that as soon as I started feeling more confident about my life, and about us, lots of great opportunities started to come my way. It was like I'd become this magnet for good stuff. Being preggers almost constantly for two years meant that much of my career had frustratingly been on hold. All that time, I desperately wanted to get back to being the businesswoman and mum I've always been – and show people what I'm really good at.

A few weeks after our vow renewal the *Evening Standard* magazine approached me for an interview and a photo shoot. We talked about how I should be styled and someone – I can't remember who – suggested a really stripped-back me: my hair pulled back, hardly any make-up on and a beautiful but very understated black lace dress. It wasn't going to be anything like my usual shoots, but I'm always up for trying something fresh. So we worked on that idea, and even I was taken aback by the results! The day the cover hit the newsstands, lots of people messaged me saying, 'Jesus! Is that really you, Kate?'

I guess the public have always seen me as this larger-than-life character – and, at times, I have been larger than life – well, the plastic parts of me, anyway! But I loved this shoot because it was so, so simple. It was like I was saying: *Throw your worst at me! This is who I am and nothing can touch me!* Flicking through those photographs now, I look powerful, even though I recall feeling anything but. Although I do remember being very determined.

If there's one thing that the past few years have taught me it's that there's strength in showing others your vulnerability. To be honest, I don't think people had ever seen that side to me. They'd only ever seen the ballsy, brash, confrontational Kate, but the vulnerability's always been there. Maybe all the drama with Kieran just exposed it to the world. And that makes me think of another one of those sayings I love: 'Don't be ashamed of your story, it will inspire others.' It's sad, but many women who have gone through what I've been through end up feeling completely crap about themselves. Even though Gaylin kept telling me that I'd done nothing wrong, it was impossible for me to truly believe that. But it shouldn't be that way! Unbelievable, I know, but I spent months blaming myself for Kieran's sordid, dirty affairs!

Now, I reckon that if I can come out the other side, feeling proud of myself for being the mum and career woman that I am, why shouldn't I share my story? Let's face it, all the shit I've been through has to count for something. Do I care that my heartbreak happened in public? Not at all. I've said before I'm not the 'perfect' celebrity. And if my story can make others feel less alone in their problems, then that can only be a good thing.

Even now, my friends and family are surprised I've stuck with Kieran because my marriage has been far from 'normal', whatever that is. In fact, I still tell Kieran that our relationship is like a crumpled bit of paper. No amount of ironing will smooth out the creases, but it's what we have and we have to make the best of it.

Believe me, though, there have been many moments when I've tried to talk myself out of being with Kieran, telling myself it would never work, and always looking for clues that he's cheating again. But then I also had this gut instinct, this little voice inside telling me that what I was doing was right for me and the kids. And I always say, Kate, it doesn't matter what your head is saying, trust your gut. Somehow, I knew that by getting to rock-bottom we could start rebuilding our lives until we had a rock-solid marriage. That's a decision I've not regretted, but it has taken a lot of me keeping that faith in Kieran, and a lot of hard work from him in sticking to his therapy and turning himself around. Now he calls me his 'guardian angel'. Too bloody right! My halo should be glowing.

It's actually really weird now when I think of how much we've moved on. Not long after we renewed our vows, I even had the chance to drop everything and jet across the world to spend a few months in Melbourne, to take part in Australia's version of *Strictly Come Dancing* called *Dancing with the Stars*. When I first got the call I was super-excited about the opportunity. Taking part in the show is something I've always wanted to do, although I'd be the first to admit I have two left feet. Still, it's the joining in that counts!

We even had someone check out apartments for us, along with schools because we were planning to go en masse with the kids. But, as the time drew nearer, we realised it wasn't going to work. Not only would it have been unfair on Junior and Princess, as they spend half their time with Pete, but Kieran and I were just getting back on track. That summer was our first in our new home, which Kieran is still helping to renovate. And I knew he wasn't keen, although he wouldn't have stopped me if it's what I'd really wanted. Instead, we talked about it, and came to the conclusion that we didn't want to turn our backs on all the positive steps we'd been making. Plus I hate spending any time away from the kids. Hate it. Moving the family, albeit temporarily, would have been a major undertaking and we would probably have had to leave Princess and

Junior behind with 10,000 miles between us. I would have died!

Naturally, the production company were disappointed and even came back to ask me if I'd take part again in the 2016 season, but the obstacles would have been just the same. No matter how I planned it, I just couldn't upend everyone not knowing how long we'd be out there. Plus our summer months are the winter months in Oz, so it's not as if we could even have enjoyed the outdoors either: sea, sand, sun and barbies!

But, I always say third time lucky. So maybe, just maybe, if *Dancing with the Stars* knock on my door again I'll be in a position to say yes. I'd love to physically push myself learning the tango or the rumba, and because I'm not precious, I reckon I'd throw myself into it just like I did with *I'm a Celebrity* . . . and I'd get to wear those amazing dresses! Bring it on! For the time being, though, I'm sticking to working closer to home.

What did happen, again not long after our vow renewal, was that another production company approached me about doing a show based around being in therapy, to be aired on Channel 5. Some of the tabloids reported that Kieran and I would take part in it together and that we'd both be working through our marriage problems with a therapist on-screen, but that was never on the cards.

In fact, the initial idea for the show wasn't even going to be about my marriage. Originally, I was approached with the idea of filming a series about how I might be addicted to plastic surgery – or at least that's what we talked about. But it became clear to the therapist that I wasn't. I may have had eight boob jobs but it's not like I'm in and out of a clinic having surgery all the time. It's no secret that I think a bit of Botox and filler here and there never did anyone any harm, but I'd never do anything too extreme! Some celebrities' faces look like they'd melt at the whiff of a naked flame, but I'll never go that far.

Having said that, plastic surgery would have been a good focus for a show, because in the end I wasn't too sure what the theme was. I visited Dr Claudia Bernat in her clinic over a couple of months. She's a top psychologist who works at the Priory. We did around four filmed sessions, but I came out of each one thinking, 'What the hell was that all about?'

Claudia was a really nice lady, but she asked me all sorts of difficult questions about myself and my marriage and my family. I kept stopping the crew and asking them what they wanted me to say. They replied I should tell Claudia whatever I felt but, believe it or not, sitting with a camera in your face, talking about yourself for a long time is hard. I'm not a person who keeps bleating on about the past. It's done. Over. Move on. Also, I didn't understand half of the questions – it was as if everyone else had this agenda but I was the last one to know. Maybe I was just being paranoid but it didn't feel comfortable at all!

Then Claudia concluded by saying that maybe I revealed too much about myself and perhaps I shouldn't talk about my private life so much. But I was in therapy! On TV! Isn't that what you're supposed to do? Anyway, I'm just me. What you see is what you get. I'm so open anyway. What I couldn't fathom is what else the programme makers needed from me that they didn't know already. Then Claudia said I needed to love myself a bit more. But I could have told her that. It's not like I don't know. So, while it was an interesting programme to do, I didn't feel it changed anything.

Embarrassingly, I ended up crapping on about how I thought me and Pete would have been together forever, which is *really* weird because both of us are remarried and we're both happy. I'm with Kieran, who I love, and Pete's with Emily. She's so much better suited to him because she's really feminine and posh and not gobby like me at all. Plus I actually like it that Princess and Junior are around someone who's a proper lady. If Emily were anything like me, I'd be thinking, *Oh my God!* It'd be totally nuts.

What I don't regret saying, though, is that I wished Jane had died in a car crash or contracted a terrible illness or something. It sounded utterly cruel, I know, and of course it's the one line all the newspapers picked up on, probably to make me out as a callous bitch. Well, I reckon that if you ask any woman who's been in my position, most of them would say that they are so hurt and angry that all they want is revenge. It's completely natural to feel like that.

The funny thing is that now, I couldn't care less if

I never saw Jane again. And I don't give a moment's thought to what I'd say to her. I'm sure we will meet because we live close to one another, and Kieran has seen her already, although they didn't speak.

It was one day last year and I'd known something was up because when I watched him from the kitchen window pull up in his 4x4, he looked really stressed and angry. He'd only gone to get petrol, but apparently he'd seen Jane on the forecourt while he was filling up. As far as he knew, she didn't see him but, according to Kieran, she looked terrible. Her hair was straggly and she'd put all her weight back on. And she was chain-smoking in her car. Secretly, that made me feel pleased. She should be suffering! All that time I was fat and pregnant and she was shagging my husband. It's about time the tables got turned!

It's weird too that Kieran said he felt really angry with her, even though I know he was as much to blame. As soon as he clocked her, he said he hid from view because he didn't want to speak to her. The good thing was that as soon as he got inside the front door, he blurted out the story to me. His whole body was shaking. I have to believe that Kieran and I have made progress and, to me, that proved it. He doesn't keep secrets from me any more. He doesn't tell lies. He's grown from this immature boy into a man who loves his wife, loves his family, and we love our life together. At last it feels like we're the team that I've always wanted.

He even hates anyone talking about Jane, he's so

disgusted with himself. The really odd part is that whenever I'm reminded of the Kieran of two years ago, it's like I'm looking at an ex-boyfriend. It's like I was in a relationship with some other man, not the person who's my husband now. He's changed physically and mentally. I suppose we both have. Now, my friends totally rip the piss out of him if we both go out. He's not the pristine Adonis he once was. He's so comfortable with himself that he wears any old clothes and my friends always say to him, 'What the hell are you wearing, Kieran? It's so old, like dad-wear!'

Not dissimilar to Kieran seeing Jane, there was another awkward situation at my friend Melodie's engagement party. I had an inkling that Derrick would be there. Inside I was dreading it, thinking, *Fucking hell, what's this going to be like?* Although in lots of ways it was nice to see him.

I had thought that I'd like to have lunch with Derrick and maybe talk over what had gone down between us all. Life had been so busy, though, that I'd not got round to it. Then the time for that just passed. But our relationship had gone from being full-on friends to zilch in the space of a few months. And that was mad because I didn't blame Derrick at all.

Not long after we arrived at the party, Derrick walked over to me. 'Hi, Kate,' he said, but I was shocked at how tired and depressed he looked. He was still in that 'moment' – still in that place we were all in two years ago. 'Let's talk about things,' he kept saying, but it's not what I wanted at all – especially at a party! 'We've moved on now, Derrick. There's nothing to talk about,' I kept dismissing him. 'But don't you still feel hurt?' he continued. Deep down, I felt sorry for him because Jane had put everyone through so much, but he was also really starting to get on my nerves. 'There's nothing to talk about, Derrick. We don't even talk about the past any more. Jane's a slag and always will be and we've moved on,' I said.

In the end, I had to leave him standing on his own and I went to join Kieran, talking to all the other guests. We were there to celebrate my mate's engagement and I wanted it to be a happy, positive party. The last thing I wanted was to be huddled in a corner digging up the past. I'm sure Derrick and I will meet again, but I hope he'll have moved on by then and we can start afresh. I can't forget, and I'll never forgive, but time is helping repair my heart and I hope that Derrick can find a place in time when he is happy too.

Like I say, positive thoughts do change what comes your way and the brilliant thing is I've truly been able to kick-start my career again. It's been a relief not feeling like a sack of spuds day-in, day-out, and being able to say yes to so many opportunities.

Take the advert I was asked to do for the National Lottery, for example. Such a laugh! We filmed it over two days and, I won't lie, it was hard work and I was nervous, but the script completely matched my dry sense of humour. The main theme was that anyone has a chance of winning the lottery, and if more people buy a ticket it might stop me from winning and funding my own non-stop TV Channel called KTV. The 'Please, don't let it be her' storyline was such a hoot and I had to act out all these shows where I played the lead part. I was a cop in a crime drama; a judge in court; a stand-up comic; a cowgirl and more. So many outfits and such a lot of filming for just two minutes of advert! But I really got into it, and I'd love to play more roles that show my fun side in the future.

Then, in the run-up to Christmas, I was approached by the New Victoria Theatre in Woking to play the part of the Wicked Fairy in *Sleeping Beauty*. Believe me, I get asked to do panto every year and I usually turn it down, but the stars were aligned, and the price was right, so I thought, why not? I'm not sure who was more excited – me or the kids – and I was worried about what they'd think, seeing me up on stage being so evil! I'm not like that at home at all!

I was to appear for a two-week run and we had two weeks' rehearsal time too. I mentioned earlier that I'd appeared in panto all that time ago with the Gladiator Mark 'Rhino' Smith. As I remember, I only had one line to say. This, on the other hand, was a proper part and one I could get my teeth into. Honest to God, at first I was shitting myself! All those parents with kids in the audience! I'd die if I forgot my lines, so I spent ages rehearsing them beforehand. I'm a real believer that if you are going to do something, you should do it well, and I'm sure the director and the rest of the cast were really surprised when I turned up to the first rehearsal knowing all of my words off pat. Better to be professional, I figured. See . . . not just a pretty face!

The show worked brilliantly with juggling the kids, too. I was still able to help Kieran in the morning with Harvey and get Princess and Junior off to school, and then sort out Jett and Bunny. All that before arriving at my dressing room to begin getting ready for a morning and afternoon performance. My hairdresser Mikey and make-up guy Buster set to work and then it was time for costume – a sparkly leotard with the most amazing feather ruff. All pink, of course! And, a red and gold embroidered number with a gorgeous red fur coat. The best part was I got to wear two amazing headdresses, both with huge gold horns. When Princess tried them on they almost covered her whole head! After each performance, other than a couple of late nights, I was home by 7 p.m. so I could still help with the kids' baths and bedtime routines.

Over the duration of the run I got into a real rhythm. I even had time for a quick sunbed some days before I got on the train home. Or I'd squeeze in a sunbed in my lunch hour and then pop to the noodle bar next door for a bite to eat. I had it all worked out! Although, when I returned to my dressing room, the guys always had to put my slap back on because I'd either suntanned my face or managed to get grease up my cheeks!

People kept asking me how I had the energy to do all

that and then perform to an audience, but what people have to remember is that when I'm doing a job, I have no kids, no animals to feed, and nobody pulling me in all directions. And, because it was Christmas time, I was even able to go out, do a bit of shopping and wrap presents in my breaks. Mikey and Buster, who were with me most days, both said that I should have been exhausted, because they were knackered, but I was telling anyone who'd listen, 'I'm loving life again!'

I'd like to say there were no fuck-ups on stage, but I'd be lying. There was one performance where I forgot a whole scene. *Oh shit, Kate, what are you doing?* I was panicking. On the spot, I made the decision to brazen it out and just carry on. The mad thing is that I don't reckon anyone in the audience even noticed. We all had a laugh afterwards because Mikey and Buster were in the wings and obviously, being there every night, they knew the script backwards. Buster said he froze thinking, 'What the *hell* is Kate doing?' Relief, though, that I got through it without too many red faces!

In fact, the whole experience set me up for more live TV, because at the beginning of the year I was offered a permanent slot on the ITV series *Loose Women* – see, I told you I'd become a magnet for good stuff!

After being on the show as a guest now and again, I was so excited to be contracted as a panellist. Again, I was seriously nervous. I am when I do anything new. Then I get the hang of it and seem to hit my stride. Sometimes I'm sure people want me to fail, though. And, okay, hands up, I did balls up the name of the actor Eddie Redmayne when I called him Eddie Redmar in my debut appearance. What the audience didn't understand is that I'd rehearsed my words in my head and then, two minutes before we were due to film, I was asked to read from an autocue. I'm rubbish at reading from those things under pressure, so I knew I'd get all tongue-tied. But it's not as if I didn't know who Eddie Redmayne was or that the public didn't know who I meant! The papers made such a big deal out of it. Anyway, if that's all that people can moan about then I'm pretty flattered. And ITV still want me to appear on the show, so I can't be that bad!

Unlike panto, it's a really early start. I'm picked up at 6 a.m. and the team have their first meeting at 8.30 a.m. That's when we run through the topics we'll discuss on that day's show and mull over what we might say. Then we'll prepare for the guests that are coming on. At first, I was reading, reading, reading all the instructions on the cue card in case I got my words mixed up again, but now I feel at home just turning up and pitching in like all the other panellists do. I'm sure the director is terrified I'll say something really controversial or dirty and, I admit, I do have to stop myself and remind myself I'm on live TV! But so far, so good!

However much they might take the piss out of me, I challenge anyone to get up there and do it themselves.

I know for sure that the director expected that it would definitely be me putting my foot in it, and not

Harvey. But, of course, that's what happened when he came on with me to talk about cyber bullying. I'd brought up the topic on the show before because, as I've said previously, I'm disgusted with people who think it's okay to abuse a disabled boy online. I even asked publicly that those responsible be named and shamed.

Having Harvey on the programme in May was intended to highlight how upsetting it is for him – which, as he gets older, is a problem. But Harvey is unpredictable at the best of times and he doesn't know what you can and can't say on TV, however much you tell him. I'm always so nervous if he appears live, although I didn't want to have this show pre-recorded because I wanted people to see the real Harvey. He's such an adorable boy.

On this occasion I had asked him backstage not to swear. 'Harvey, no swearing,'" I warned him, and his reply was, 'Yes, Mummy.'

But on set, when I asked him what his message would be to people who are horrible to Harvey he replied, 'Hello, you c**t.' Oh my God! There was no time to censor the word and it went out live on air.

Okay, you might say, it was exactly the right word to use for that kind of scum, and I got loads of tweets afterwards saying, '*Well done, Harvey!*' As a mother, though, I was completely torn. I felt angry yet protective towards him, and at the same time apologetic that he'd dropped the C-bomb live on a lunchtime show! I couldn't believe it! The stupid thing is that Harvey doesn't usually understand that kind of question. Normally, he'll respond by saying something like, 'Can I have a blueberry muffin?' or another phrase that's completely unconnected. I can only think he'd planned it in his head.

Oh well, he did it and it's too late to change it, but judging from all the supportive messages I've received, the public were less appalled and more sympathetic than I could have imagined. I know some people out there hate me, but to hate my son is below the belt. And anyway, if people hate you it's usually for one of three reasons: they see you as a threat, they hate themselves or they really want to be you. Whichever way, I couldn't give a monkey's because having Harvey in my life makes me the luckiest mum in the world, although maybe next time we'll pre-record.

Sometimes, though, I do get the feeling that I'm being used as a punchbag. It's like the press or the Twitterati are just waiting and thinking, 'Oh, what's Kate going to do next?' Or, they're desperate to say I'm an awful mother or cruel to my animals or any other crap that's been thrown at me. At least on *Loose Women* I get to say my piece.

Take the whole drama at the beginning of the year about Princess putting make-up on and me taking a photo of her and posting it online. I mean? What? Crazy! What eight-year-old girl doesn't get dressed up or ask to have make-up put on, or put it on herself with her friends? Just because I post a lot on social media, I'm the one who's labelled a bad mother. But girls in every household around the country are doing exactly the same!

On *Loose Women*, I was given a really hard time about it, and I said that I was sorry that I'd posted the picture on my account. Honestly, I said that for an easy ride. I won't stop Princess from putting on make-up and I won't stop taking pictures of her. Just because I'm in the public eye, people think they can constantly judge me and my kids. Get a life! The good thing was that Princess came on the programme a few weeks later and confirmed that it was she who had asked me if she could wear eyeshadow and lipstick. I didn't force it on her. But all the furore it created? It was as if I'd signed her up as an eight-year-old glamour model! What Princess chooses to do when she's older is her decision and I will support her, but anyone who is in any doubt about my mothering skills should come to my house. There, they'll see a happy family, with happy kids and happy animals and they'll hear laughter all the time.

They might even hear a few other noises too because recently I had to bring in an exorcist because Kieran and I were convinced that the house was haunted.

As soon as we'd moved in, we started hearing noises at night, and it's an old house – built in the 1930s. Although we've had all the beams covered and made it look really modern, it still has an old feel about it.

Kieran swore there was someone moving about as

soon as we'd gone to bed and, sometimes, I could hear this weird breathing noise. Then, I'd wake up at around 3 a.m. to clattering and strange sounds, like there was a party in the kitchen. And occasionally Kieran could smell these weird smells like pipe smoke. I was convinced. It's got to be a ghost, I told Kieran, because neither of us smoke!

At first, I thought I'd never be able to live happily with a ghost, so I called a woman in to cleanse the house. In the end I had to go to Belgium to have my boobs seen to when she arrived but, apparently, she walked around the house for an hour dangling crystals in all the rooms. She claimed she'd cleared it of all spirits and that she'd discovered extreme depression at one end of the house – I knew that was bullshit because my house is a happy house! To be honest, I didn't believe a word she said, and to this day we are still hearing noises. Now Kieran says it always happens when I'm away, which is bizarre. I guess we're just going to have to live peacefully alongside our unusual guests.

We clearly didn't succeed with the spirits, but in so many ways this year has been about laying the past to rest. Not only did Kieran and I move on, but Pete and I also settled a long-running court dispute. What a relief that we can all now focus on what's important – our lives and the kids' lives. For the first time in a long time I feel at peace with Pete and I hope our relationship will flourish so we can be brilliant parents to Princess and Junior. Even the kids say they are happy with me and

Kieran being together, and with Pete and Emily. And if they're happy, I'm happy.

As well as all our plans for the animals and hosting private parties on our animal farm, we're also looking into converting the annex in our house to a business hub. I'd take the upstairs and run my own beauty salon, and Kieran would take the downstairs and develop the gym, run his own classes and privately train people. All in good time! At the moment, with the house being an ongoing project, we need to have as much renovated as possible before we make that leap.

What is exciting, though, is that there's been some jumping of a different kind going on. Finally, I've been able to get back in the saddle, and the kids and Kieran have been joining me horse riding. In fact, just as this book comes out, so will my latest TV series, *Katie Price's Pony Club*.

I can't even begin to describe how excited I was when that idea was first discussed. Not only will it be my first reality TV show in four years but I get to indulge my ultimate passion for horse riding and share it with my kids and four of their friends. If I can inspire a future generation of horse lovers then that's good enough for me! But the filming? Oh my God! As I write, we are filming two nights every week with the kids after school and every weekend for nine weeks. I'd forgotten just how much upheaval making a six-part reality show involves – but I'm enjoying every minute of it.

The whole idea is to teach kids horse-riding skills,

from absolute beginners right up to their competing in a polo game at one of the poshest riding events. There'll be lots of pink, lots of noise and loads of chaos, because I'm definitely not one of those posh mums! However, I know exactly how elitist the world of horse riding can be. In 2009, Cartier refused me entry to the Guards Polo Club and called me 'too chavvy' or something ridiculous. Ha! Pure snobbery! What people don't realise is that it takes an enormous amount of skill and guts to ride a pony at a competitive match, but it should be open to everyone to enjoy a brilliant day, not just the super-rich! And if me and Camilla Parker Bowles can rub shoulders in a cheeky snap, like we did last year at Ladies Day at Cheltenham, then the world's your oyster!

What's also brilliant is that the public have never really seen that side to me – the devoted mum, the career woman and the horse lover all rolled into one. I know my fans will be glued! I shouldn't have been surprised, but as my series was announced, I got the usual crap from the press. I'd shaved hearts and diamonds into my horses' bums – they looked fantastic! Princess, especially, loved the diamonds on the rear end of her horse, Sandie. Of course, some woman from some animal rights charity branded it as cruel. What absolute horseshit! Clipping a horse doesn't hurt it – it happens all the time, which is why I plastered up loads of pictures on my Instagram account of the most amazing designs by horse body-clippers. When we did the photo call for the show it was exactly the same – just because I posed with a horse dyed pink I got loads of complaints. *Boring!* Again, not cruel at all. It's a water-based dye so no chemicals go anywhere near the horse's skin. And it was done by professionals who work with horses and know exactly what they are doing.

Encouragingly, I got loads of tweets from people who ride saying that they supported me. If people want to believe I would ever be cruel to my horses then more fool them. Anyone who knows me knows that I adore my ponies as much as I adore my kids and I'd do nothing whatsoever to hurt them.

A little bit of gentle humiliation, on the other hand, never did anyone any harm. Poor Kieran agreed to be dressed up as a unicorn for the launch press call. According to several newspapers I 'forced' him. Again, utter crap. He agreed to pose in the sparkly blue hooves and white pantaloons. He wouldn't do anything he didn't want to do and I would never make him. The whole day was such a laugh and it's not like I didn't join in looking like a prize idiot too! I was also dressed as a unicorn. Having all the kids there, kitted out in mini versions of the horse costumes, was the icing on the cake.

Sometimes I have to pinch myself. It feels as if the fresh start I wanted has really happened. So, watch this space ... the Pricey may have been to hell and back over the past two years, but I've picked myself up, dusted myself down and got on with loving life. I'm back, and feeling better, bolder, brasher and happier than ever . . .

* * *

But I would like you all to know that it doesn't end here. Unfortunately there's a certain word count in a book and there's a few chapters I was going to put in that I couldn't fit in here. But I think maybe that's a good thing. You know: will I be Elizabeth Taylor and marry more men or not?

I'll leave you to find out in the next book.